HTML5 Game Development by Example Beginner's Guide
Second Edition

Make the most of HTML5 techniques to create
exciting games from scratch

Makzan

open source *
community experience distilled

PACKT
PUBLISHING

BIRMINGHAM - MUMBAI

HTML5 Game Development by Example Beginner's Guide
Second Edition

First published: August 2011

Second edition: June 2015

Production reference: 2250615

Published by Packt Publishing Ltd.
Livery Place
35 Livery Street
Birmingham B3 2PB, UK.

ISBN 978-1-78528-777-0

www.packtpub.com

Credits

Author

Makzan

Reviewers

Lauri Hosio

Dan Nagle

Matt Palmerlee

Leonardo Risuleo

Commissioning Editor

Dipika Gaonkar

Acquisition Editors

Vivek Anantharaman

Sam Wood

Content Development Editor

Arwa Manasawala

Technical Editor

Menza Mathew

Copy Editors

Ameesha Green

Jasmine Nadar

Project Coordinator

Shweta H Birwatkar

Proofreader

Safis Editing

Indexer

Tejal Daruwale Soni

Production Coordinator

Manu Joseph

Cover Work

Manu Joseph

About the Author

Makzan focuses on the fields of web development and game design. He has over 14 years of experience in building digital products. He has worked on real-time multiplayer interaction games, iOS applications, and rich interactive websites.

He has written three books, on building a Flash virtual world, and creating games with HTML5 and the latest web standards and developed a video course as well. He currently teaches courses in Hong Kong and Macao SAR. He writes tutorials and shares his know-how on `makzan.net`.

I wish to thank my wife, Candy, for her patience and understanding. I would also like to thank the entire team at Packt Publishing. The book would not have been possible without their help. I thank all the reviewers for providing useful comments from which I have learned a lot.

About the Reviewers

Lauri Hosio has been making games since he discovered QBASIC with his friends in elementary school. Professionally, he's worked with web and mobile games for over 7 years.

Previously, he worked at Rovio as the acting lead game programmer on Angry Birds Friends. At other companies, he has also worked on web-based MMO games and general web development.

Before HTML5, he made independent web games with Flash that were played by millions of players. Some of his games have been published by AddictingGames and ArmorGames. Lauri currently works in Kansas City, Missouri, on mobile games and full-stack web development.

Dan Nagle has, since graduating as a valedictorian in computer engineering from the Mississippi State University in 2003, written and published apps for Android, Windows, Mac, Linux, iOS, numerous web apps, network servers, and pure embedded C. He is the author of the book, *HTML5 Game Engines: App Development and Distribution*, which was published by CRC Press. He has also written articles and spoken at conferences about developing websites and HTML5-based games.

For about 4 years, he owned and operated a web company that focused on website hosting and custom game development. Before that, he was an electrical engineer who developed embedded systems.

Currently, he is a senior software engineer who writes control software, web interfaces, and mobile apps for network devices that distribute HD video. He can be reached through his website at http://DanNagle.com/.

Matt Palmerlee has been developing software professionally since 2001 and has a passion for JavaScript and HTML5 game development. He built Astriarch, an open source multiplayer space strategy game, using HTML5 and Node.js. Matt has developed other HTML5 games, which were published by Mastered Software, his software development consulting company.

Matt occasionally blogs about interesting aspects of software development and HTML5 games on his personal website at http://mattpalmerlee.com/.

Leonardo Risuleo is the owner and creative director of Small Screen Design. He is a designer and developer with several years of experience in mobile, new media, and user experience. Leonardo is a highly dedicated professional, and he's passionate about what he does. He started his career in 2003, and in the last few years, he has worked on a variety of different mobile and embedded platforms for a number of well-known brands and studios. Leonardo designs, prototypes, and develops mobile applications, games, widgets, and websites.

From 2008 to 2010, he had the honor of being the Nokia Developer Champion, a recognition and reward program for top mobile developers worldwide. In 2008, Leonardo formally founded Small Screen Design (https://www.smallscreendesign.com), a design and development studio focused on mobile design and user experience. In 2015, he became Digital Champion—an ambassador for the Digital Agenda—for Squillace, to help every European become digital.

www.PacktPub.com

Support files, eBooks, discount offers, and more

For support files and downloads related to your book, please visit www.PacktPub.com.

Did you know that Packt offers eBook versions of every book published, with PDF and ePub files available? You can upgrade to the eBook version at www.PacktPub.com and as a print book customer, you are entitled to a discount on the eBook copy. Get in touch with us at service@packtpub.com for more details.

At www.PacktPub.com, you can also read a collection of free technical articles, sign up for a range of free newsletters and receive exclusive discounts and offers on Packt books and eBooks.

https://www2.packtpub.com/books/subscription/packtlib

Do you need instant solutions to your IT questions? PacktLib is Packt's online digital book library. Here, you can search, access, and read Packt's entire library of books.

Why subscribe?

- Fully searchable across every book published by Packt
- Copy and paste, print, and bookmark content
- On demand and accessible via a web browser

Free access for Packt account holders

If you have an account with Packt at www.PacktPub.com, you can use this to access PacktLib today and view nine entirely free books. Simply use your login credentials for immediate access.

Table of Contents

Preface

HTML5 promises to be the hot new platform for online games. HTML5 games work on computers, smartphones, tablets, iPhones, and iPads. Be one of the first developers to build HTML5 games today and be ready for tomorrow!

This book will show you how to use the latest HTML5 and CSS3 web standards to build card games, drawing games, physics games, and even multiplayer games over the network. With this book, you will build six example games with clear systematic tutorials.

HTML5, CSS3, and the related JavaScript API are the latest hot topic in the Web. These standards bring us the new game market of HTML5 games. With the new power from them, we can design games with HTML5 elements, CSS3 properties, and JavaScript to play in browsers.

The book is divided into 10 chapters with each one focusing on one topic. While building the six games in the book, you will learn how to draw game objects, animate them, add audio, connect players, and build physics game with the Box2D physics engine.

What this book covers

Chapter 1, *Introducing HTML5 Games*, introduces the new features of HTML5, CSS3, and the related JavaScript API. It demonstrates what games we can make with these features and their benefits.

Chapter 2, *Getting Started with DOM-based Game Development*, kickstarts the game development journey by creating a traditional Ping Pong game in DOM and jQuery.

Chapter 3, *Building a Card-matching Game in CSS3*, walks you through the new features of CSS3 and discusses how we can create a memory card-matching game in DOM and CSS3.

Chapter 4, Building the Untangle Game with Canvas and the Drawing API, introduces a new way to draw things and interact with them in a web page with the new canvas element. This also demonstrates how to handle dragging on touch devices.

Chapter 5, Building a Canvas Game's Masterclass, extends the Untangle game to show how we can draw gradients and images in the Canvas. It also discusses sprite sheet animations and multilayer management.

Chapter 6, Adding Sound Effects to Your Games, adds sound effects and background music to the game by using the Audio element. It discusses the audio format capability among web browsers and creates a keyboard-driven music game by the end of the chapter.

Chapter 7, Saving the Game's Progress, extends the CSS3 memory-matching game to demonstrate how we can use the Local Storage API to store and resume game progress and records the best scores.

Chapter 8, Building a Multiplayer Draw-and-Guess Game with WebSockets, discusses the WebSockets API that allows browsers to establish persistent connection with the socket server. This allows multiple players to play the game together in real time. A draw-and-guess game is created at the end of the chapter.

Chapter 9, Building a Physics Car Game with Box2D and Canvas, teaches you how to integrate a famous physics engine, Box2D, into our canvas games. It discusses how to create physics bodies, apply force, connect them together, associate graphics with the physics, and finally create a platform car game.

Chapter 10, Deploying HTML5 Games, shares the different ways in which we can publish our games. It discusses wrapping the web into a native app for Apple's App Store.

Appendix, Pop Quiz Answers, gives the answers to the pop quiz questions in each of the chapters.

What you need for this book

You need the latest modern web browsers, a good text editor, and a basic knowledge of HTML, CSS, and JavaScript. In *Chapter 8, Building a Multiplayer Draw-and-Guess Game with WebSockets*, we need the Node.js server, which we will help you to install in that chapter.

Who this book is for

This book is for web designers who have a basic knowledge of HTML, CSS, and JavaScript and want to create Canvas or DOM-based games that run on browsers.

Sections

In this book, you will find several headings that appear frequently (Time for action, What just happened?, Pop quiz, and Have a go hero).

To give clear instructions on how to complete a procedure or task, we use these sections as follows:

Time for action – heading

1. Action 1
2. Action 2
3. Action 3

Instructions often need some extra explanation to ensure they make sense, so they are followed with these sections:

What just happened?

This section explains the working of the tasks or instructions that you have just completed.

You will also find some other learning aids in the book, for example:

Pop quiz – heading

These are short multiple-choice questions intended to help you test your own understanding.

Have a go hero – heading

These are practical challenges that give you ideas to experiment with what you have learned.

Conventions

You will also find a number of text styles that distinguish between different kinds of information. Here are some examples of these styles and an explanation of their meaning.

Code words in text, database table names, folder names, filenames, file extensions, pathnames, dummy URLs, user input, and Twitter handles are shown as follows: "Open the `index.html` file in the code editor."

A block of code is set as follows:

```
var matchingGame = {};
matchingGame.deck = [
  'cardAK', 'cardAK',
  'cardAQ', 'cardAQ',
  'cardAJ', 'cardAJ',
  'cardBK', 'cardBK',
  'cardBQ', 'cardBQ',
  'cardBJ', 'cardBJ',
];
```

When we wish to draw your attention to a particular part of a code block, the relevant lines or items are set in bold:

```
$(function(){
  matchingGame.deck.sort(shuffle);

  for(var i=0;i<11;i++){
    $(".card:first-child").clone().appendTo("#cards");
  }
```

New terms and **important words** are shown in bold. Words that you see on the screen, in menus or dialog boxes for example, appear in the text like this: "In MAC, click on the **Get the code** tab and you will see the following screenshot; this shows a guide on how to embed this font into our web page."

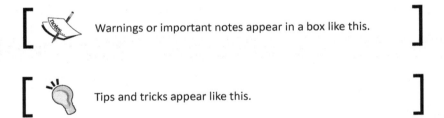

Warnings or important notes appear in a box like this.

Tips and tricks appear like this.

Reader feedback

Feedback from our readers is always welcome. Let us know what you think about this book—what you liked or disliked. Reader feedback is important for us as it helps us develop titles that you will really get the most out of.

To send us general feedback, simply e-mail feedback@packtpub.com, and mention the book's title in the subject of your message.

If there is a topic that you have expertise in and you are interested in either writing or contributing to a book, see our author guide at www.packtpub.com/authors.

Customer support

Now that you are the proud owner of a Packt book, we have a number of things to help you to get the most from your purchase.

Downloading the example code

You can download the example code files from your account at http://www.packtpub.com for all the Packt Publishing books you have purchased. If you purchased this book elsewhere, you can visit http://www.packtpub.com/support and register to have the files e-mailed directly to you.

Downloading the color images of this book

We also provide you with a PDF file that has color images of the screenshots/diagrams used in this book. The color images will help you better understand the changes in the output. You can download this file from https://www.packtpub.com/sites/default/files/downloads/7770OS_ColoredImages.pdf.

Errata

Although we have taken every care to ensure the accuracy of our content, mistakes do happen. If you find a mistake in one of our books—maybe a mistake in the text or the code—we would be grateful if you could report this to us. By doing so, you can save other readers from frustration and help us improve subsequent versions of this book. If you find any errata, please report them by visiting http://www.packtpub.com/submit-errata, selecting your book, clicking on the **Errata Submission Form** link, and entering the details of your errata. Once your errata are verified, your submission will be accepted and the errata will be uploaded to our website or added to any list of existing errata under the Errata section of that title.

To view the previously submitted errata, go to https://www.packtpub.com/books/content/support and enter the name of the book in the search field. The required information will appear under the **Errata** section.

Piracy

Piracy of copyrighted material on the Internet is an ongoing problem across all media. At Packt, we take the protection of our copyright and licenses very seriously. If you come across any illegal copies of our works in any form on the Internet, please provide us with the location address or website name immediately so that we can pursue a remedy.

Please contact us at copyright@packtpub.com with a link to the suspected pirated material.

We appreciate your help in protecting our authors and our ability to bring you valuable content.

Questions

If you have a problem with any aspect of this book, you can contact us at questions@packtpub.com, and we will do our best to

1
Introducing HTML5 Games

Hypertext Markup Language, HTML, has been shaping the Internet in the last few decades. It defines how content is structured in the Web and the linkage between related pages. HTML has kept evolving from version 2 to HTML 4, and later to XHTML 1.1. Thanks to the web applications and social networking applications, it the era of HTML5 now.

Cascading Style Sheet (CSS) *defines how web pages are presented visually. It styles all HTML elements and the styles of their states, such as hover and active.*

JavaScript is the logic controller of a web page. It makes the web page dynamic and provides client-side interaction between the page and users. It accesses the HTML through **Document Object Model** *(***DOM***). It controls the new HTML features via their APIs.*

There are modern web browsers in most desktop and mobile devices. These latest web techniques bring us the new game market—the HTML5 games. With the new power from these techniques, we can design games with HTML5 elements, CSS3 properties, and JavaScript to play in most browsers and mobile devices.

In this chapter, we will cover the following topics:

- ◆ Discovering new features in HTML5
- ◆ Discussing what makes us so excited around HTML5 and CSS3
- ◆ Previewing what games we are going to build in later chapters
- ◆ Preparing the development environment

So, let's get started.

Discovering new features in HTML5

There are many new things introduced in HTML5 and CSS3. Before getting our hands dirty by creating the games, let's take an overview of the new features and see how we can use them to create games.

Canvas

Canvas is an HTML5 element that provides drawing shapes and bitmap manipulation functions in low levels. We can imagine the Canvas element as a dynamic image tag. The traditional `<img>` tag shows a static image. This image is usually static after it's loaded. We can change the `<img>` tag to another image source or apply styles to the image, but we cannot modify the image's bitmap context itself.

On the other hand, Canvas is like a client-side dynamic `<img>` tag. We can load images inside it, draw shapes there, and interact with it using JavaScript.

Canvas plays an important role in HTML5 game development. It is one of our main focus areas in this book.

Audio

Background music and sound effects are essential elements in game design. HTML5 comes with native audio support from the `audio` tag. Thanks to this feature, we do not require the proprietary Flash Player to play sound effects in our HTML5 games. However, there have been some restrictions on using Web Audio on the Web. We will discuss the usage of the `audio` tag in *Chapter 6, Adding Sound Effects to Your Games*.

Touch Events

Besides the traditional keyboard and mouse events, there are touch events that we can use to handle single and multi-touch events. We can design a game that works on mobile devices with touches. We can also handle gestures by observing the touch patterns.

GeoLocation

GeoLocation lets the web page retrieve the latitude and longitude of the user's computer. For example, Google's Ingress game makes use of GeoLocation to let players play the game in their real city. This feature may not have been so useful years ago when everyone was using the Internet with their desktop. There are not many things for which we need the accurate location of the road of the user. We can get the rough location by analyzing the IP address.

These days, more and more users are going on the Internet with their powerful smartphones. Webkit and other modern mobile browsers are in everyone's pocket. GeoLocation lets us design mobile applications and games to play with the inputs of a location.

WebGL

WebGL extends the Canvas element by providing a set of 3D graphics APIs in the web browser. The APIs follow the standard of OpenGL ES 2.0. WebGL provides a powerful GPG-accelerated, 3D rendering API for HTML5 games. Some 3D game engines support the export of WebGL, including the popular Unity engine. We can expect to see more HTML5 3D games waiting to be released using WebGL.

The techniques used to create games with WebGL are quite different than using Canvas. Creating games in WebGL requires handing the 3D models and using an API similar to OpenGL. Therefore, we will not discuss WebGL game development in this book.

WebGL has a better performance than 2D Canvas because of the GPU-rendering support. Some libraries allow a game to use Canvas 2D drawing API, and the tools render the canvas by drawing on WebGL to gain performance. Pixi.js (`http://www.pixijs.com`), EaselJS (`http://blog.createjs.com/webgl-support-easeljs/`) and WebGL-2D (`https://github.com/corbanbrook/webgl-2d`) are several such tools among them.

WebSocket

WebSocket is part of the HTML5 spec to connect the web page to a socket server. It provides us with a persistent connection between the browser and server. This means that the client does not need to poll the server for new data within short periods. The server will push updates to the browsers whenever there is any data to update. One benefit of this feature is that game players can interact with each other in almost real time. When one player does something and sends data to the server, we can send the individual player the update to create one-on-one real-time page play, or we can iterate all the connections in the server to send an event to every other connected browser to acknowledge what the player just did. This creates the possibility of building multiplayer HTML5 games.

Local storage

HTML5 provides a persistent data storage solution to web browsers.

Local Storage stores key-value pair data persistently. The data is still there after the browser terminates. Moreover, the data is not limited to be accessible only to the browsers that created it. It is available to all browser instances with the same domain. Thanks to Local Storage, we can easily save a game's status, such as progress and earned achievements, locally in web browsers.

Another database on web browser is IndexedDB. It's key-value pair too, but it allows storing objects and querying data with condition.

Offline applications

Normally, we need an Internet connection to browse web pages. Sometimes, we can browse cached offline web pages. These cached offline web pages usually expire quickly. With the next offline application introduced by HTML5, we can declare our cache manifest. This is a list of files that will be stored for later access when there is no Internet connection.

With the cache manifest, we can store all the game graphics, game control JavaScript files, CSS stylesheets, and the HTML files locally. We can also pack our HTML5 games as offline games on the desktop or mobile devices. Players can play the games even in the airplane mode. The following screenshot from the Pie Guy game (http://mrgan.com/pieguy) shows an HTML5 game being played on an iPhone without an Internet connection; note the little airplane symbol indicating the offline status:

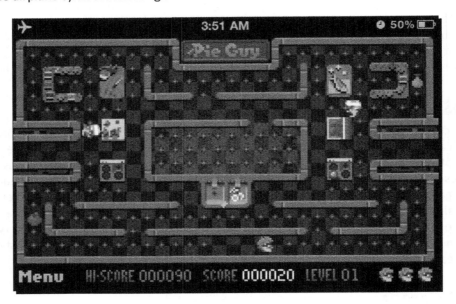

Discovering new features in CSS3

CSS is the presentation layer and HTML is the content layer. It defines how the HTML looks. We cannot miss CSS when we create games with HTML5, especially DOM-based games. We may purely use JavaScript to create and style the games with a Canvas element. However, we need CSS when we create DOM-based HTML5 games. Therefore, let's take a look at what is new in CSS3 and how we can use the new properties to create games.

Instead of directly drawing and interacting on Canvas' drawing board, new CSS3 properties let us animate the DOM in different ways. This makes it possible to make more complicated DOM-based browser games.

CSS3 transition

Traditionally, the style changes immediately when we apply a new style to an element. CSS3 transition renders in-between styles during the style changes of the target elements over duration. For example, here, we have a blue box and want to change it to dark blue when we do a mouseover. We can do this by using the following code snippets:

HTML:

```
<a href="#" class="box"></a>
```

CSS:

```
a.box {
  display: block;
  width: 100px;
  height: 100px;
  background: blue;
}
a.box:hover {
  background: darkblue;
}
```

The box changes to dark blue immediately when we do a mouseover. With CSS3 transition applied, we can tween the styles for a specific duration and easing value:

```
a.box {
  transition: all 0.5s ease-out;
}
```

Downloading the example code

For all the Packt Publishing books you have purchased, you can download the example code files from your account at http://www.packtpub.com. If you purchased this book elsewhere, you can visit http://www.packtpub.com/support and register to have the files e-mailed directly to you.

In the past, we needed JavaScript to calculate and render the in-between styles; this is much slower than using CSS3 transition because the browser natively makes the effects happen.

Since some CSS3 specifications are still in the draft stage and not yet fixed, implementation from different browser vendors may have some minor differences to the W3C spec. Therefore, browser vendors tend to implement their CSS3 properties with a vendor prefix to prevent conflict.

Safari uses the `-webkit-` prefix. Opera uses the `-o-` prefix. Firefox uses the `-moz-` prefix and IE uses the `-ms-` prefix. Chrome used to use `-webkit-`, but now it doesn't use any prefix after switching its engine to Blink. It is a little complex now to declare a CSS3 property, such as flex, with several lines of the same rule for several browsers. We can expect the prefix to be dropped after the property spec is fixed.

In order to make the code cleaner in this book, I will use non-vendor prefix for all the properties in this book. I recommend you to use JavaScript-based libraries to automatically add the required vendor prefix for different web browsers. The prefix-free library (`http://leaverou.github.io/prefixfree/`) is one of them.

Alternatively, if you are using preprocessors, the compilation process may also add the necessary vendor prefix for you.

CSS3 transform

CSS3 transform lets us scale the elements, rotate them, and translate their position. CSS3 transform is divided into 2D and 3D. By combining the transform origin and 3D rotation and translation, we can animate 2D graphics in a 3D space.

CSS3 animation

CSS3 transition is one type of animation. It declares the tweening animation between two styles of the elements.

CSS3 animation is one step further in animation. We can define key frames of an animation. Each key frame contains a set of properties that should change at any particular moment. It is like a set of CSS3 transitions that are applied in sequence to the target element.

The AT-AT Walker (`http://anthonycalzadilla.com/css3-ATAT/index-bones.html`) shows a nice demo on creating a skeleton bone animation with CSS3 animation key frames, transform, and transition. This is shown in the following diagram:

The benefit of creating HTML5 games

We have explored several new key features from HTML5 and CSS3. With these features, we can create HTML5 games on browsers. But why do we need to do that? What is the benefit of creating HTML5 games?

Free and open standards

The web standards are open and free for use. In contrast, third-party tools are usually proprietary and they cost money. With proprietary technologies, the support from them may drop because of changes to the company's focus. The standardization and openness of HTML5 ensures that we will have browsers that support it.

Support for multiple platforms

With the built-in support of all the HTML5 features in modern browsers, we do not require the users to preinstall any third-party plugin in order to play any file. These plugins are not standard. They usually require an extra plugin installation that you may not be able to install. For instance, millions of Apple iOS devices around the world do not support third-party plugins, such as Flash Player, in their mobile Safari. Despite whatever the reason might be, Apple does not allow Flash Player to run on their Mobile Safaris, instead, HTML5 and the related web standard are what they get in their browsers. We can reach this user base by creating HTML5 games that are optimized for mobiles.

Native app-rendering performance in particular scenarios

When we code the game in a Canvas, there are some rendering engines that can translate our Canvas drawing code into OpenGL, thus rendering in native mobile device. This means that while we are still coding the game for a web browser, our game can gain benefits in mobile devices by the native app OpenGL rendering. **Ejecta** (http://impactjs.com/ejecta) and **CocoonJS** (http://ludei.com/cocoonjs) are two such engines.

Breaking the boundary of usual browser games

In traditional game designing, we build games within a boundary box. We play video games on a television. We play Flash games in web browsers with a rectangle boundary.

Using creativity, we are not bound in a rectangle game stage any more. We can have fun with all the page elements.

Twitch (http://reas.com/twitch/) is a game from Chrome Experiments. It is a collection of mini games where the player has to carry the ball from the starting point to the end point. The fun part is that each mini game is a small browser window. When the ball reaches the destination point of that mini game, it is transferred into the newly created mini game browser to continue the journey. The following screenshot shows the whole map of Twitch with the individual web browsers:

Building HTML5 games

Thanks to the new features of HTML5 and CSS3, we can now create an entire game in the browser. We can control every element in the DOM. We can animate each document object with CSS3. We have Canvas to dynamically draw things and interact with them. We have an audio element to handle the background music and sound effects. We also have Local Storage to save game data, and WebSocket to create a real-time multiplayer game. Most modern browsers are already supporting these features. It is now time to build HTML5 games.

What others are playing with HTML5

This is a good opportunity to study how different HTML5 games perform by watching other HTML5 games that are made with different techniques.

Coca-Cola's Ahh campaign

Coca-Cola had run a campaign known as **Ahh** (`http://ahh.com`) with lots of interactive mini games. The interactions combined several techniques that included canvas and device rotation. Most of them work well in both desktop and mobile devices.

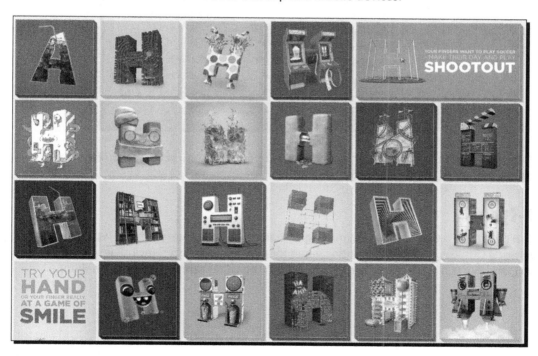

Asteroid-styled bookmarklet

Erik, a web designer from Sweden, created an interesting bookmarklet. This is an asteroid-styled game for any web page. Yes, any web page! It shows an abnormal way to interact with any web page. It creates a plane on the website you are reading from. You can then fly the plane using arrow keys and fire bullets using the space bar. The fun part is that the bullets will destroy the HTML elements on the page. Your goal is to destroy all the things on the web page that you choose. This bookmarklet is another example of breaking the boundary of usual browser games. It tells us that we can think outside the box while designing HTML5 games.

The following screenshot shows the plane destroying the contents on the web page:

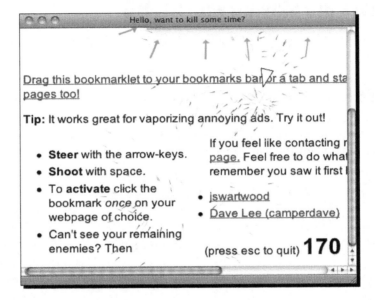

The bookmarklet is available for installation at `http://kickassapp.com`. You can even design the space ship that you control.

X-Type

The creator of a Canvas-based game engine named Impact, created this X-Type (`http://phoboslab.org/xtype/`) shooting game for different platforms, including web browsers, iOS, and Wii U. The following screenshot shows the game running smoothly in iPhone.

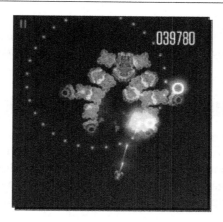

Cursors.io

Cursors.io (`http://cursors.io`) demonstrates a nicely designed real-time multiplayer game. Every user controls an anonymous mouse cursor and takes a journey through the levels of the game by moving the cursor to the green exit. The fun part of the game is that players must help the others to advance to the level. There are toggles that some cursors click on them to unlock the doors. The anonymous players must take up the role to help the others. Someone will take your role so that you can advance to the next level. The more players that help you, the higher your chance is to succeed in the game. In case only a few players are playing and you can't experience the game, I have recorded my playing screen in 12 x speed (at `http://vimeo.com/109414542`) to let you have a glimpse of how this multiplayer game works. This has been captured in the following screenshot:

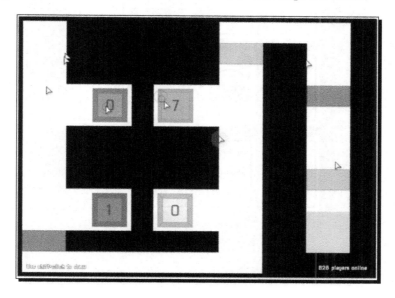

We will discuss building a multiplayer game in *Chapter 8, Building a Multiplayer Draw-and-Guess Game with WebSockets*.

What we are going to create in this book

In the following chapters, we are going to build six games. We are going to first create a DOM-based Ping Pong game that can be played by two players in the same machine. Then, we will create a memory matching game with CSS3 animation. Next, we will use Canvas to create an Untangle puzzle game. Later, we will build a music game with audio elements. Then, we will create a multiplayer draw and guess game with WebSocket. Lastly, we will use the Box2D JavaScript port to create a prototype of a physics car game. The following screenshot shows the memory matching game that we will build in *Chapter 3, Building a Card-matching Game in CSS3*. You can play the game at `http://makzan.net/html5-games/card-matching/`.

Preparing the development environment

The environment for developing HTML5 games is similar to designing websites. We need web browsers and a good text editor. Which text editor is good is a never-ending debate. Each text editor comes with its own strengths, so just pick your favorite one. I personally recommend text editors with multiple cursors, for instance, Sublime Text or Brackets. For the browser, we will need modern browsers that support the latest HTML5 and CSS3 specs and provide us with handy tools for debugging.

There are several modern browser choices on the Internet now. They are Apple Safari (`http://apple.com/safari/`), **Google Chrome** (`http://www.google.com/chrome/`), Mozilla Firefox (`http://mozilla.com/firefox/`), **and Opera** (`http://opera.com`). These browsers support most of the features that we will discuss in the examples in the whole book. I personally use Chrome because it has great built-in developer tools. The powerful developer tools make it popular with web and game developers.

We will also need Android phones and an iPad/iPhone to test the games in mobile devices. Simulators may also work, but testing with real devices gives closer results to real-world usage.

Summary

In this chapter, we've learned a lot about the basic information of HTML5 games.

Specifically, we covered new features of HTML5 and CSS3. We gave you a glimpse of what techniques we will use to create our games in later chapters—Canvas, audio, CSS animation, and more new features were introduced. We will have many new features to play with. We discussed why we want to create HTML5 games—we want to meet the web standard, meet mobile devices, and break the boundary of a game. We took a look at several existing HTML5 games that were created with different techniques, which we will also use. You can test these games before we create our own. We also previewed the games that we are going to build in the book. At last, we prepared our development environments.

Now that we've some background information on HTML5 games, we're ready to create our first DOM-based, JavaScript-driven game in the next chapter.

2

Getting Started with DOM-based Game Development

We've got an idea about what we are going to learn in the whole book in Chapter 1, Introducing HTML5 Games. From this chapter onwards, we will go through a lot of learning-by-doing sections, and we will focus on one topic in each section. Before digging deeply into the cutting-edge CSS3 animations and HTML5 Canvas game, let's start with traditional DOM-based game development. We will warm up with some basic techniques in this chapter.

In this chapter, we will be:

- ◆ Setting up our first game—Ping Pong
- ◆ Learning basic positioning with the jQuery JavaScript library
- ◆ Getting mouse inputs
- ◆ Creating the Ping Pong game that displays the scores
- ◆ Learning to separate data and view rendering logic

We will create a Ping Pong game that a player plays against the computer via mouse input. You can try the game at `http://makzan.net/html5-games/pingpong/`.

The following screenshot shows the look of the game at the end of this chapter:

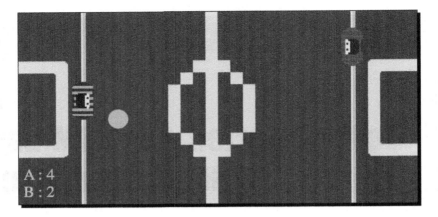

So, let's get on with making our Ping Pong game.

 At the time of writing the book, the jQuery version is 2.1.3. The jQuery functions that we used in the examples are basic functions that should work in future versions too.

Preparing the HTML documents for a DOM-based game

Every website, web page, and HTML5 game starts with a default HTML document. Moreover, the document starts with a basic HTML code. We will start our HTML5 game development journey with index.html.

Time for action – installing the jQuery library

We will create our HTML5 Ping Pong game from scratch. It may sound as if we are going to be preparing all the things ourselves. Luckily, we can use a JavaScript library to help us. **jQuery** is the **JavaScript library** that is designed to navigate the DOM elements easily, manipulate them, handle events, and create an asynchronous remote call. We will be using this library in the book to manipulate DOM elements. It will help us to simplify our JavaScript logic:

1. Create a new folder named pingpong as our project directory.

2. Inside the pingpong folder, we will create the following file structure, with three folders—js, css, and images—and an index.html file:

   ```
   index.html
   js/
   ```

```
  js/pingpong.js
css/
  css/pingpong.css
images/
```

3. Now, it's time to download the jQuery library. Go to `http://jquery.com/`.

4. Select **Download jQuery** and click on **Download the compressed, production jQuery 2.1.3**.

5. Save `jquery-2.1.3.min.js` within the `js` folder that we created in step 2.

6. Open `index.html` in text editor and insert an empty HTML template:

```html
<!DOCTYPE html>
<html lang="en">
<head>
  <meta charset="utf-8">
  <title>Ping Pong</title>
  <link rel="stylesheet" href="css/pingpong.css">
</head>
<body>
  <header>
    <h1>Ping Pong</h1>
  </header>
  <div id="game">
    <!-- game elements to be here -->
  </div>
  <footer>
    This is an example of creating a Ping Pong Game.
  </footer>
  <script src="js/jquery-2.1.3.min.js"></script>
  <script src="js/pingpong.js"></script></body>
</html>
```

7. Finally, we have to ensure that jQuery is loaded successfully. To do this, place the following code into the `js/pingpong.js` file:

```javascript
(function($){
  $(function(){
    // alert a message
    alert("Welcome to the Ping Pong battle.");
  });
})(jQuery);
```

8. Save the `index.html` file and open it in the browser. You should see the following alert window showing our text. This means that our jQuery is correctly set up:

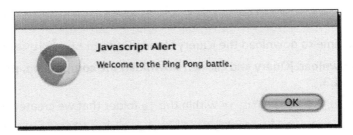

What just happened?

We just created a basic HTML5 page with jQuery and ensured that the jQuery is loaded correctly.

New HTML5 doctype

The `DOCTYPE` and `meta` tags are simplified in HTML5.

In HTML 4.01, we declare doctype using the following code:

```
<!DOCTYPE HTML PUBLIC "-//W3C//DTD HTML 4.01//EN"
    "http://www.w3.org/TR/html4/strict.dtd">
```

This is a long line of code, right? While in HTML5, the doctype declaration couldn't have been more simpler:

```
<!DOCTYPE html>
```

We do not even have the HTML version in the declaration. This is because HTML5 is now a living standard without a version number.

Header and footer

HTML5 comes with many new features and improvements, and one of them is semantics. HTML5 adds new elements to improve **semantics**. We just used two of the elements: `header` and `footer`. **Header** gives an introduction to the section or the entire page. Therefore, we put the `h1` title inside the header. **Footer**, like the name suggests, contains the footer information of the section or the page.

 A semantic HTML means that the markup itself provides meaningful information to the content instead of only defining the visual outlook.

The best practice to place the JavaScript code

We put the JavaScript code right before the closing `</body>` tag and after all the content in the page. There is a reason for putting the code there instead of putting it inside the `<head></head>` section.

Normally, browsers load content and render them from top to bottom. If the JavaScript code is put in the `head` section, then the content of the document will not be loaded until all the JavaScript code is loaded. Actually, all rendering and loading will be paused if the browsers load a JavaScript code in the middle of the page. This is the reason why we want to put the JavaScript code at the bottom, when possible. In this way, we can deliver the HTML content to our readers faster.

At the time of writing this book, the latest jQuery version is 2.1.3. This is why the jQuery file in our code examples is named `jquery-2.1.3.min.js`. The version number in the filename ensures that web developers don't get confused with different versions of the same filename in different projects. This version number will be different, but the usage should be the same, unless there is a big change in jQuery without backward compatibility.

> Please note that a few JavaScript libraries have to put the `<head>` tag before loading any HTML elements. When you're using third-party libraries, please check whether they have such a requirement.

Choosing the jQuery file

For the jQuery library, there are currently two major versions; they are **1.x** and **2.x**. The 1.x version keeps backward compatibility to older browsers, mainly for IE versions 6, 7, and 8. Since our HTML5 games target modern browsers, we chose the 2.x version that has dropped support to IE 8 or the older versions.

There are two common ways to include the jQuery library. We can either download a **hosted** version or use the **CDN** version. Hosted version means that we download the file, and we host the file ourselves. CDN stands for Content Delivery Network. The jQuery files are hosted in several central servers to improve the file downloading time. For the CDN version, we can find the URL at `http://code.jquery.com`. We can directly include the file with the `<script>` tag in HTML as: `<script src="http://code.jquery.com/jquery.min.js"></script>`.

Otherwise, we can specify the version number in the filename as: `<script src="http://code.jquery.com/jquery-2.1.3.min.js"></script>`.

Running jQuery inside a scope

We need to ensure that the page is ready before our JavaScript code is executed. Otherwise, we may get an error when we try to access an element that is not yet loaded. jQuery provides us with a way to execute the code after the page is ready by using the following code:

```
jQuery(document).ready(function(){
  // code here.
});
```

Most of the time, we uses a $ sign to represent jQuery. This is a shortcut that makes calling our jQuery functions much easier. So essentially, we use the following code:

```
$(function(){
  // code here.
});
```

When we call $(something), we are actually calling jQuery(something).

There may be conflicts on the $ variables if we use multiple JavaScript libraries in one project. For best practice, we use an **anonymous function** to pass the jQuery object into the function scope where it becomes a $ sign:

```
(function($){
  // jQuery code here with $.
})(jQuery);
```

An anonymous function is a function definition that has no name. That's why it's called anonymous. Since we cannot refer to this function anymore, the anonymous function always executes itself. JavaScript's variable scope is bound to the function scope. We often use anonymous function to control certain variables' availability. For instance, we passed the jQuery into the function as the $ variable in our example.

Running our code after the page is ready

$(function_callback) is another shortcut for the DOM elements' ready event. The reason we need jQuery ready function is to prevent the execution of JavaScript logic before the HTML DOM elements are loaded. Our function that is defined in the jQuery ready function is executed after all the HTML elements are loaded.

It is identical to the following line of code:

```
$(document).ready(function_callback);
```

 Note that the jQuery `ready` event fires after the HTML structure (DOM tree) is loaded. However, this does not mean that the content, such as the actual image content, is loaded. The browser's `onload` event, on the other hands, fires after all the content including the images are loaded.

Pop quiz

Q1. Which is the best place to put JavaScript code?

1. Before the `<head>` tag
2. Inside the `<head></head>` elements
3. Right after the `<body>` tag
4. Right before the `</body>` tag

Downloading the image assets

We need some graphic files in this step. You can download the graphic files in the code bundle or from `http://mak.la/book-assets/`.

In the assets bundle, you will find image files for `Chapter 2`. After downloading them, put the files in the `images` folder. There should be four files, as shown in the following screenshot:

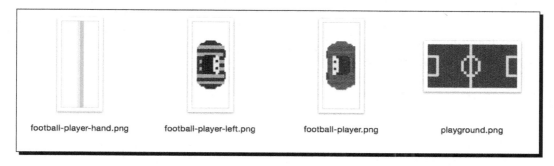

football-player-hand.png   football-player-left.png   football-player.png   playground.png

Setting up the Ping Pong game elements

We have made the preparations, and now it's time to set up the Ping Pong game. The following graph shows how we place the game elements. The game element contains our playground and later the scoreboard. Inside the playground, we place two decorative elements, namely **paddle hand**, which acts as the handle of the soccer machine. Then, we have two **paddle** elements—one on the left and one on the right.

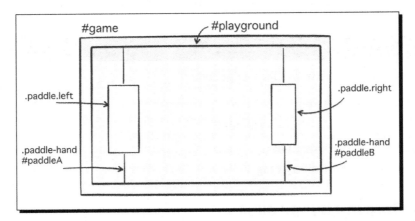

Time for action – placing Ping Pong game elements in the DOM

1. We will continue from our jQuery installation example, and open the `index.html` file in a text editor.

2. Then, we will create the following playground and `game` objects with DIV nodes in the body. There are two paddles and one ball inside the playground, and the playground is placed inside the game:

```
<div id="game">
  <div id="playground">
    <div class="paddle-hand right"></div>
    <div class="paddle-hand left"></div>
    <div id="paddleA" class="paddle"></div>
    <div id="paddleB" class="paddle"></div>
    <div id="ball"></div>
  </div>
</div>
```

3. We now have the structure of the `game` object ready, and it is time to apply styles to them. We will add the following styles to the `pingpong.css` file:

```
#game {
  position: relative;
```

```
    width: 400px;
    height: 200px;
  }
#playground{
  background: url(../images/playground.png);
  background-size: contain;
  width: 100%;
  height: 100%;
  position: absolute;
  top: 0;
  left: 0;
  overflow: hidden;
  cursor: pointer;
}
#ball {
  background: #fbb;
  position: absolute;
  width: 20px;
  height: 20px;
  left: 150px;
  top: 100px;
  border-radius: 10px;
}
```

4. Then, we will define the dimensions and positions of the two paddles by appending the following code inside the `pingpong.css` file:

```
.paddle {
  background-size: contain;
  top: 70px;
  position: absolute;
  width: 30px;
  height: 70px;
}

#paddleA {
  left: 50px;
  background-image: url(../images/football-player-left.png);
}
#paddleB {
  right: 50px;
  background-image: url(../images/football-player.png);
}
```

5. We will continue with the styles in the `pingpong.css` file and define `paddle-hands`, which is the decoration for the paddles:

```
.paddle-hand {
  background: url(../images/football-player-hand.png) 50% 0
repeat-y;
  background-size: contain;
  width: 30px;
  height: 100%;
  position: absolute;
  top: 0;
}
.left.paddle-hand {
  left: 50px;
}
.right.paddle-hand {
  right: 50px;
}
```

6. Now that we are done with the CSS styles, let's move to the `js/pingpong.js` file for JavaScript's logic. We need a function to update the DOM elements of the paddles based on the position data. To do this, we will replace the current code with the following one:

```
(function($){
  // data definition
  var pingpong = {
    paddleA: {
      x: 50,
      y: 100,
      width: 20,
      height: 70
    },
    paddleB: {
      x: 320,
      y: 100,
      width: 20,
      height: 70
    },
  };

  // view rendering
  function renderPaddles() {
    $("#paddleB").css("top", pingpong.paddleB.y);
    $("#paddleA").css("top", pingpong.paddleA.y);
```

```
    }

    renderPaddles();

})(jQuery);
```

7. Now, we will test the setup in a browser. Open the index.html file in a browser; we should see a screen similar to the one shown in the following screenshot:

What just happened?

Let's take a look at the HTML code that we just used. The HTML page contains header, footer information, and a DIV element with the ID, game. The game node contains a child named playground, which in turn contains three children—two paddles and the ball.

We often start the HTML5 game development by preparing a well-structured HTML hierarchy. The HTML hierarchy helps us to group similar game objects (which are some DIV elements) together. It is a little like grouping assets into a movie clip in Adobe Flash, if you have ever made animations with it. We may also consider it as layers of game objects for us to select and style them easily.

Using jQuery

The jQuery command often contains two major parts: **selection** and **modification**. Selection uses CSS selector syntax to select all matched elements in the web page. Modification actions modify the selected elements, such as adding or removing children or style. Using jQuery often means chaining selection and modification actions together.

For example, the following code selects all elements with the box class and sets the CSS properties:

```
$(".box").css({"top":"100px","left":"200px"});
```

Understanding basic jQuery selectors

jQuery is about selecting elements and performing actions on them. We need a method to select our required elements in the entire DOM tree. jQuery borrows the selectors from CSS. The selector provides a set of patterns to match elements. The following table lists the most common and useful selectors that we will use in this book:

Selector pattern	Meaning	Examples
`$("Element")`	Selects all elements with the given tag name	`$("p")` selects all the p tags. `$("body")` selects the body tag.

`$("#id")`	Selects the element with the given ID of the attribute	Consider the following code:
		
		 `<div id="box1"></div>`
		 `<div id="box2"></div>`
		
		 `$("#box1")` selects the highlighted element.

`$(".className")`	Selects all elements with the given class attribute	Consider the following code:
		
		 `<div class="apple"></div>`
		 `<div class="apple"></div>`
		 `<div class="orange"></div>`
		 `<div class="banana"></div>`
		
		 `$(".apple")` selects the highlighted elements with class set to apple.

`$("selector1, selector2, selectorN")`	Selects all elements that match the given selector	Consider the following code:
		
		 `<div class="apple"></div>`
		 `<div class="apple"></div>`
		 `<div class="orange"></div>`
		 `<div class="banana"></div>`
		
		 `$(".apple, .orange")` selects the highlighted elements that class is set to, either apple or orange.

Understanding the jQuery CSS function

The jQuery `css` function works to get and set the CSS properties of the selected elements. This is known as getting and setting pattern where many jQuery functions follow.

Here is a general definition of how to use the `css` function:

```
.css(propertyName)
.css(propertyName, value)
```

The `css` function accepts several types of arguments as listed in the following table:

Function type	Arguments definitions	Discussion
`.css(propertyName)`	`propertyName` is a CSS property	The function returns the value of the given CSS property of the selected element.
		For example, the following code returns the value of the `background-color` property of the `body` element:
		`$("body").css("background-color")`
		It will only read the value and not modify the property value.
`css(propertyName, value)`	`propertyName` is a CSS property, and `value` is a value to set for the property.	The function modifies the given CSS property to the given value.
		For example, the following code sets the background color of all elements with the `box` class to red:
		`$(".box").css("background-color","#ff0000")`

Manipulating game elements in DOM with jQuery

We initialized the paddles' game elements with jQuery. We will do an experiment on how we should use jQuery to place the game elements.

Understanding the behavior of absolute position

When a DOM node is set to be at the `absolute` position, the left and top properties can be treated as a **coordinate**. We can treat the left/top properties into X/Y coordinates with Y positive pointing down. The following graphs show the relationship. The left side is the actual CSS value, and the right side is the coordinate system in our mind when programming the game:

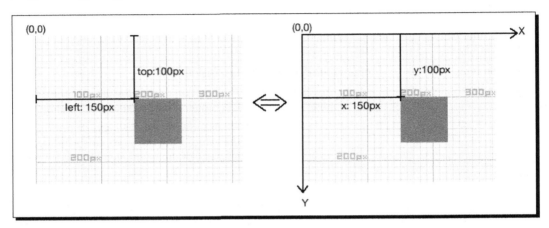

By default, the left and top properties refer to the top-left edge of the web page. This reference point is different when any parent of this DOM node has a `position` style set explicitly to `relative` or `absolute`. The reference point of the left and top properties becomes the top-left edge of that parent.

This is why we need to set the game with a relative position and all game elements inside it with an absolute position. The following code snippet from our example shows the position values of the elements:

```
#game{
  position: relative;
}
#playground,
#ball,
#paddle {
  position: absolute;
}
```

Declaring global variables in a better way

Global variables are variables that can be accessed globally in the entire document. Any variable that is declared outside any function is a global variable. For instance, in the following example code snippet, a and b are global variables, while c is a **local variable** that only exists inside the function:

```
var a = 0;
var b = "xyz";
function something(){
  var c = 1;
}
```

Since global variables are available in the entire document, they may increase the chance of variable name conflicts if we integrate different JavaScript libraries into the same web page. As good practice, we should minimize the use of global variables.

In the preceding *Time for action* section, we have an object to store the game data. Instead of just putting this object in the global scope, we created an object named pingpong and put the data inside it.

Moreover, when we put all our logic into a self-executing function, as we discussed in the last section, we make the game's data object locally inside the function scope.

 Declaring variables without var puts the variables in the global scope even when they are defined inside a function scope. So, we always declare variables with var.

Pop quiz

Q1. Which jQuery selector is to be used if you want to select all header elements?

1. `$("#header")`
2. `$(".header")`
3. `$("header")`
4. `$(header)`

Getting mouse input

You learned how to display game objects with CSS and jQuery in the previous sections. The next thing we need to create in the game is a way to get input from the players. We will discuss about the mouse input in this section.

Time for action – moving DOM objects by mouse input

We are going to create a traditional Ping Pong game. There is a paddle on both the left and right sides of the playground. A ball is placed in the middle of the playground. Players can control the right paddle and move it up and down by using the mouse. We will focus on the mouse input and leave the ball movement for a later section:

1. Let's continue with our `pingpong` directory.

2. Next, add a `playground` object inside the `pingpong` data object in the `js/pingpong.js` file. This stores variables that are related to `playground`:

```
// data definition
var pingpong = {
  paddleA: {
    x: 50,
    y: 100,
    width: 20,
    height: 70
  },
  paddleB: {
    x: 320,
    y: 100,
    width: 20,
    height: 70
  },
  playground: {
    offsetTop: $("#playground").offset().top,
  }
};
```

3. Then, create the following function that handles the mouse's enter, move, and leave events, and place it inside the `js/pingpong.js` file:

```
function handleMouseInputs() {
  // run the game when mouse moves in the playground.
  $('#playground').mouseenter(function(){
    pingpong.isPaused = false;
  });

  // pause the game when mouse moves out the playground.
  $('#playground').mouseleave(function(){
    pingpong.isPaused = true;
  });

  // calculate the paddle position by using the mouse position.
```

```
$('#playground').mousemove(function(e){
  pingpong.paddleB.y = e.pageY -
    pingpong.playground.offsetTop;
});
}
```

4. We had the `renderPaddles` function in the previous section. In this section, we are defining a `render` function and calling the paddles rendering logic. We then call the `render` function on the next browser redraw via the `requestAnimationFrame` function.

```
function render() {
  renderPaddles();
  window.requestAnimationFrame(render);
}
```

5. Finally, we create an `init` function to execute the initial logic.

```
function init() {
  // view rendering
  window.requestAnimationFrame(render);

  // inputs
  handleMouseInputs();
}
```

6. Finally, you need to call the `init` function that starts our game logic:

```
(function($){
  // All our existing code

  // Execute the starting point
  init();
})(jQuery);
```

7. Let's test the `paddle` control of the game. Open the `index.html` page in the web browser. Try moving the mouse up and down within the playground area. The right paddle should follow your mouse's movement.

What just happened?

We handled the mouse events to move the paddle based on the mouse position. You can play the current work-in-progress version of the game at `http://makzan.net/html5-games/pingpong-wip-step3/`.

Getting the mouse event

jQuery provides several handy mouse events, and the most basic ones are click, mouse down and mouse up. We track the mouse enter and mouse leave event to start and pause the game. We also use the mouse move event to get the mouse position and update the paddle position based on the mouse position on the playground section.

We need to get the *y* position of the cursor based on the playground's top left edge. The value of Y in the mouse event is the mouse cursor from the page's top left edge. We then subtract the position of the playground via `$("#playground").offset().top`.

We update the data of paddle's Y value by using the mouse's X and Y values. This value will eventually reflect on the screen when the paddle view is updated in the `render` function during the browser redraw.

RequestAnimationFrame

The time interval is used to execute the game loop. The `game` loop calculates the game logic, which calculates the movement of the game objects.

The `requestAnimationFrame` feature is used to update the view according to the data. We use the `requestAnimationFrame` feature to update the view because the view only needs to update in an optimal scenario, where the browser decides.

The interval of `requestAnimationFrame` is not fixed. When the browser is at the front end, the `requestAnimationFrame` feature would run often. When the battery is low or the browser is in the background, the browser would slow down the frequency of execution of the `requestAnimationFrame` feature.

We are using `RequestAnimationFrame` only on view-related logic. In a later section, we will need to handle game data calculation. For data calculation, we will use `setInterval` because the `setInterval` function always executes in a fixed time interval. That's why we use the `setInterval` function for the game logic calculation and animation frame for view rendering.

Checking the console window

We are writing more complicated logic code now. It is good practice to keep an eye on the console of the **Developers Tools**. You may toggle between the developer tools by pressing *F12* in Windows or *command + option + I* on Mac OS. If the code contains any error or warning, the error message will appear there. It reports any found error and the line of code that contains the error. It is very useful and important to have the console window open when testing HTML5 games. I have often seen people get stuck and have no idea as to why the code is not working. The reason for this is that they have a typo or syntax error, and they did not check the console window before fighting with the code for hours.

The following screenshot shows that there is an error in the twenty-fifth line of the js/pingpong.js file. The error message is **Invalid left-hand side in assignment**. After inspecting the code, I found that I wrongly used an equal sign (=) when setting the CSS top property in jQuery:

```
$("#paddleA").css("top"=top+5);

// instead of the correct code:
// $("#paddleA").css("top", top+5);
```

The error is displayed as follows:

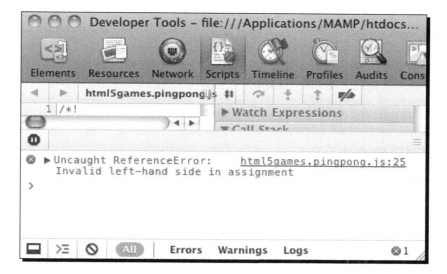

Moving a DOM object with JavaScript Interval

Imagine now we can make the little red ball move around the playground. The ball will bounce away when it hits the paddles. The player will win a score when the ball passes the opponent's paddle and hits the playground edge behind the paddle. All these actions manipulate the position of the DIVs inside the HTML page by jQuery. To complete this Ping Pong game, our next step is to move the ball.

Time for action – Moving the ball with JavaScript Interval

We will use the function to create a timer. The timer moves the ball a little bit every 30 milliseconds. We are going to also change the direction of the ball movement once it hits the playground edge. Let's make the ball move now:

1. We will use our last example, listening to multiple keyboard inputs, as the starting point.

2. Open the `js/pingpong.js` file in the text editor.

3. In the existing `pingpong.playground` object, we change to the following code that adds height and width to the playground.

```
playground: {
  offsetTop: $("#playground").offset().top,
  height: parseInt($("#playground").height()),
  width: parseInt($("#playground").width()),
},
```

4. We are now moving the ball, and we need to store the ball's status globally. We will put the ball-related variable inside the `pingpong` object:

```
var pingpong = {
  //existing data
  ball: {
    speed: 5,
    x: 150,
    y: 100,
    directionX: 1,
    directionY: 1
  }
}
```

5. We define a `gameloop` function and move the ball on each game loop iteration:

```
function gameloop() {
  moveBall();
}
```

6. We define the functions to check whether the ball is hitting the four boundary walls of the playground:

```
function ballHitsTopBottom() {
  var y = pingpong.ball.y + pingpong.ball.speed *
    pingpong.ball.directionY;
  return y < 0 || y > pingpong.playground.height;
}
function ballHitsRightWall() {
```

```
    return pingpong.ball.x + pingpong.ball.speed *
      pingpong.ball.directionX > pingpong.playground.width;
}
function ballHitsLeftWall() {
  return pingpong.ball.x + pingpong.ball.speed * pingpong.ball.
directionX < 0;
}
```

7. Then, we define two functions that reset the game after either player wins.

```
function playerAWin() {
  // reset the ball;
  pingpong.ball.x = 250;
  pingpong.ball.y = 100;

  // update the ball location variables;
  pingpong.ball.directionX = -1;
}
function playerBWin() {
  // reset the ball;
  pingpong.ball.x = 150;
  pingpong.ball.y = 100;

  pingpong.ball.directionX = 1;
}
```

8. It is time to define the moveBall function. The function checks the boundaries of the playground, changes the direction of the ball when it hits the boundaries, and sets the new ball position after all these calculations. Let's put the following moveBall function definition in the JavaScript file:

```
function moveBall() {
  // reference useful varaibles
  var ball = pingpong.ball;

  // check playground top/bottom boundary
  if (ballHitsTopBottom()) {
    // reverse direction
    ball.directionY *= -1;
  }
  // check right
  if (ballHitsRightWall()) {
    playerAWin();
  }
  // check left
  if (ballHitsLeftWall()) {
```

```
        playerBWin();
    }

    // check paddles here

    // update the ball position data
        ball.x += ball.speed * ball.directionX;
        ball.y += ball.speed * ball.directionY;
    }
```

9. We have calculated the ball's movement. Next, we want to render the view to update the ball's position based on the data. To do this, define a new `renderBall` function with the following code.

```
function renderBall() {
    var ball = pingpong.ball;
    $("#ball").css({
        "left" : ball.x + ball.speed * ball.directionX,
        "top" : ball.y + ball.speed * ball.directionY
    });
}
```

10. Now, we need to update the `render` function to render the ball's update based on the updated game data:

```
function render() {
    renderBall();
    renderPaddles();
    window.requestAnimationFrame(render);
}
```

11. The following lines of code is the new `init` function where we added a `gameloop` logic with the `setInterval` function:

```
function init() {
    // set interval to call gameloop logic in 30 FPS
    pingpong.timer = setInterval(gameloop, 1000/30);

    // view rendering
    window.requestAnimationFrame(render);

    // inputs
    handleMouseInputs();
}
```

12. We have prepared the code to move the ball every 33.3 milliseconds. Save all the files and open `index.html` in the web browser to test it. The paddles work just as in the last example, and the ball should be moving around the playground.

What just happened?

We just successfully made the ball move around the playground. We have a loop to run routine game logic 30 times per second. Inside that game loop, we moved the ball five pixels at a time. You can try the game and view the code in progress at `http://makzan.net/html5-games/pingpong-wip-step6/`.

There are three properties of the ball: speed, and the *x* and *y* directions. Speed defines how many pixels the ball moves in each step. The direction X/Y is either 1 or -1. We move the ball using the following equation:

```
new_ball_x = ball_x_position + speed * direction_x
new_ball_y = ball_y_position + speed * direction_y
```

The direction value is multiplied by the movement. When the direction is 1, the ball moves to the positive direction of the axis. When the direction is `-1`, the ball moves to the negative direction. By toggling the *x* and *y* directions, we can move the ball in four directions.

We compare the ball's X and Y values with the four edges of the playground DIV element. This checks whether the ball's next position is beyond the boundary, and then, we toggle the direction between 1 and -1 to create the bouncing effect.

Creating a JavaScript timer with the setInterval function

We have a timer to loop and move the ball periodically. This can be done by the `setInterval` function in JavaScript.

Here is the general definition of the `setInterval` function:

```
setInterval(expression, milliseconds)
```

The `setInterval` takes two required arguments. Additional arguments are passed into the function as parameters:

Argument	Definition	Discussion
`expression`	The function callback or code expression to be executed	The expression can be a reference of a function callback or an inline code expression. The inline code expression is quoted and a reference of function callback is not.
		For example, the following code calls the `hello` function every 100 milliseconds:
		`setInterval(hello, 100);`
		The following code calls the `hi` function with parameters every 100 milliseconds:
		`setInterval("hi('Makzan')", 100);`
`milliseconds`	The duration between every execution of the expression, in milliseconds	The unit of the interval is in milliseconds. Therefore, setting it to 1000 means running the expression every second.

Understanding the game loop

We have a timer to execute some game-related code every 33.3 milliseconds, so this code is executed 30 times per second. This frequency is known as frames per second, or FPS. In game development, this timer is called the **game loop**.

There are several common things that we will execute inside a game loop:

◆ Processing user input, which we just did

◆ Updating game objects' status, including position and appearance

◆ Checking game over

What is actually executing in the game loop differs in different types of games, but the purpose is the same. The game loop is executed periodically to calculate the game data.

Separating the data and the view logic

We have separated the data and the view logic. We used `setInterval` for data and `requestAnimationFrame` for view rendering. The data focuses on all the game data calculation, including an object's dimension and position based on the calculation. The `view` logic focuses on updating the interface based on the keep-updating game data.

In our render function, the view updates the CSS of the DOM elements. Imagine later if we are rendering the game in the Canvas, or using any other techniques, that our view rendering logic can use a specific method to render the view based on the same game data. The game data's calculation is independent to the techniques we use to render the game interface.

Beginning collision detection

We have checked the boundary of the playground when moving the ball in the previous section. Now, we can control the paddles with the keyboard and watch the ball move around the playground. What is missing now? We cannot interact with the ball. We control the paddles but the ball just passes through them as if they are not there. This is because we missed the collision detection between the paddles and the moving ball.

Time for action – hitting the ball with the paddles

We will use an approach, similar to that of checking the boundary, to check the collision:

1. Open the js/pingpong.js file that we used in the previous section.

2. In the moveBall function, we have already reserved the place to put the collision detection code there. Find the line with // check paddles here.

3. Let's put the following code there. The code checks whether the ball is overlapping with either paddle and bounces the ball away when they overlap:

```
// Variables for checking paddles
var ballX = ball.x + ball.speed * ball.directionX;
var ballY = ball.y + ball.speed * ball.directionY;

// check moving paddle here, later.
// check left paddle
if (ballX >= pingpong.paddleA.x && ballX < pingpong.paddleA.x +
  pingpong.paddleA.width) {
  if (ballY <= pingpong.paddleA.y + pingpong.paddleA.height &&
ballY >= pingpong.paddleA.y) {
    ball.directionX = 1;
  }
}

// check right paddle
if (ballX + pingpong.ball.radius >= pingpong.paddleB.x && ballX
  < pingpong.paddleB.x + pingpong.paddleB.width) {
  if (ballY <= pingpong.paddleB.y + pingpong.paddleB.height &&
ballY >= pingpong.paddleB.y) {
```

```
        ball.directionX = -1;
    }
}
```

4. Test the game in a browser and the ball will now bounce away after hitting the left or right paddle. It will also reset to the center of the playground when it hits the left or right edge of the playground.

What just happened?

We have modified the ball by making it bounce away when it overlaps with the paddles. Let's see how we check the collision between the ball and the left paddle.

At first, we check whether the ball's *x* position is less than the left paddle's right edge. The right edge is the `left` value plus the `width` of the paddle.

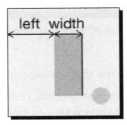

Then, we check whether the ball's *y* position is between the top edge and bottom edge of the paddle. The top edge is the `top` value and the bottom edge is the `top` value plus the `height` of the paddle.

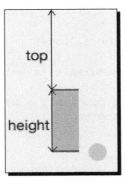

We bounce the ball away if the ball's position passes both the checks. This is how we check it, and it is just a basic collision detection.

We determine that the two objects are overlapped by checking their position and width/ height. This type of collision detection works well in rectangle objects but is not good for circles and other shapes. The following screenshot illustrates the issue. The collision areas shown in the following graph are false positive. Their bounding box collides but the actual shapes do not overlap each other. This is a classic and efficient way to check for collisions. It may not be very accurate but its calculation is fast.

For special shapes, we will need more advanced collision detection techniques, which we will discuss later.

Have a go hero

We have placed two paddles on the playground. How about we make the game more challenging by having an alternative paddle in the middle field? It's like having the goalkeeper and forwards in a soccer machine.

Controlling the left paddle movement

The computer controls the left paddle. We would like to create a function that makes the left paddle chase the ball.

Time for action – auto moving the left paddle

Perform the following set of actions for automoving our paddle:

1. Let's continue with our `pingpong.js` JavaScript file. We create a function that follows the ball's *y* position.

```
function autoMovePaddleA() {
  var speed = 4;
  var direction = 1;

  var paddleY = pingpong.paddleA.y + pingpong.paddleA.height/2;
  if (paddleY > pingpong.ball.y) {
    direction = -1;
  }

  pingpong.paddleA.y += speed * direction;
}
```

2. Then, inside the game loop function, we call our `autoMovePaddleA` function.

```
autoMovePaddleA();
```

What just happened?

We created a logic that moves the left paddle based on the ball's *y* position. You may try the game with its current progress at `http://makzan.net/html5-games/pingpong-wip-step6/`.

Since we have already implemented the view rendering in the `renderPaddles` function, in this section, we only need to update the paddle's data and the view will get updated automatically.

We make the paddle speed slower than the ball's speed. Otherwise, the player can never win against the computer, because the computer-controlled paddle can always catch the ball and bounce it back if they have the same speed.

Showing text dynamically in HTML

We have implemented the basic game mechanics in the previous sections. Our Ping Pong game is missing a scoring board that shows both players' scores. We discussed how to use jQuery to modify the CSS styles of the selected elements. Can we also alter the content of the selected elements with jQuery? Yes, we can.

Time for action – Showing the score of both players

We are going to create a text-based scoreboard and update the scores when either player scores a goal:

1. We are making improvements on our existing game so that we can use the last example as the starting point.

2. Open the `index.html` in the text editor. We are going to add the scoreboard's DOM elements.

3. Add the `#scoreboard` HTML structure to our `#game` DIV inside index.html. The `#game` DIV becomes the following:

```html
<div id="game">
  <div id="playground">
    <div class="paddle-hand right"></div>
    <div class="paddle-hand left"></div>
    <div id="paddleA" class="paddle"></div>
    <div id="paddleB" class="paddle"></div>
    <div id="ball"></div>
  </div>
  <div id="scoreboard">
    <div class="score"> A : <span id="score-a">0</span></div>
    <div class="score"> B : <span id="score-b">0</span></div>
  </div>
</div>
```

4. Now, let's move onto the JavaScript part. Open the `js/pingpong.js` file.

5. We need two more variables to store the players' scores. Add their score variables inside the existing `pingpong` data object:

```javascript
var pingpong = {
  scoreA : 0,  // score for player A
  scoreB : 0,  // score for player B

  // existing pingpong data goes here.
}
```

6. Find the `playerAWin` function. We increment player A's score there and update the scoreboard with the following code:

```javascript
// player B lost.
pingpong.scoreA += 1;
$("#score-a").text(pingpong.scoreA);
```

7. We can add a code similar to that in the previous step to update player B's score when player A is lost in the `playerBWin` function:

```
// player A lost.
pingpong.scoreB += 1;
$("#score-b").text(pingpong.scoreB);
```

8. Let's move onto the `css/pingpong.css` file. Put the following styles in the file to make the score board look nicer:

```css
/* Score board */
#scoreboard {
  position: absolute;
  bottom: 0;
  left: 0;
  width: 100%;
  padding: 5px;
  color: lightgrey;
}
```

9. It is time to test our latest code. Open the `index.html` in a web browser. Try playing by controlling both paddles and lose some points. The scoreboard should be counting the scores correctly.

What just happened?

We just used another common jQuery function: `text()` to alter the content of the game on the fly.

The `text()` function gets or updates the text content of the selected element. Here is a general definition of the `text()` function:

```
.text()
.text(string)
```

When we use the `text()` function without an argument, it returns the text content of the match elements. When we use it with an argument, it sets the text content to all the matched elements with the given string.

For example, provide the following HTML structure:

```html
<p>My name is <span id="myname" class="name">Makzan</span>.</p>
<p>My pet's name is <span id="pet" class="name">
  Co-co</span>.</p>
```

The following jQuery calls return Makzan:

```
$("#myname").text(); // returns Makzan
```

However, in the following jQuery call, it sets all matched elements to the given HTML content:

```
$(".name").text("Mr. Mystery")
```

Executing the jQuery command gives the following HTML result:

```
<p>My name is <span id="myname" class="name">Mr. Mystery</span></p>
<p>My pet's name is <span id="pet" class="name">Mr. Mystery</span></p>
```

Have a go hero – winning the game

Imagine that the game is an advertisement. We set the entire game playground with pointer cursor so that the user knows the game is clickable and links to some other place. Try to use jQuery's `click` event and handle the advertisement that's linked to the `handleMouseInputs` function.

Summary

You learned a lot in this chapter about the basic techniques of creating a simple Ping Pong game with HTML5 and JavaScript. Specifically, we created our first HTML5 game—Ping Pong. In the game, we used jQuery to manipulate DOM objects. We were able to use the mouse event to get the cursor position. We used a very simple method to detect collisions with the bounding box. In the logic, we separated data manipulation and view rendering. We also discussed how to create a game loop and move the ball and paddles.

Now that we've warmed up by creating a simple DOM-based game, we are ready to create more advanced DOM-based games with new features from CSS3. In the next chapter, we will create games with CSS3 transition and transformation.

3
Building a Card-matching Game in CSS3

CSS3 introduces many exciting features. In this chapter, we will explore and use some of them to create a card-matching game. CSS3 styles how the game objects look and animate, while the jQuery library helps us to define the game logic.

In this chapter, we will:

- Transform a playing card with animation
- Flip a playing card with new CSS3 properties
- Create the whole memory matching game
- Embed a custom web font to our game

You can try the card-matching game at the following URL to have a glimpse of what we are going to achieve in this chapter:

```
http://makzan.net/html5-games/card-matching/
```

So, let's get on with it.

Moving game objects with CSS3 transition

We had a glimpse of the CSS3 transition and transformation modules in *Chapter 1, Introducing HTML5 Games,* when we were overviewing the new CSS3 features. We often want to animate the game objects by easing the properties. Transition is the CSS property designed for this purpose. Suppose that we have a playing card on the web page and want to move it to another position in five seconds. We would have to use JavaScript to set up a timer and write our own function to change the position every few milliseconds. By using the `transition` property, we just need to specify the start and end styles and the duration. The browser optimizes the output and does all the easing and in-between animations.

Let's take a look at some examples to understand this.

Time for action – moving a playing card around

In this example, we will place two playing cards on a web page and transform them to a different position, scale, and rotation. We will tween the transformation by setting the transition:

1. To do this, create a new project folder with the following hierarchy. The `css3transition.css` and `index.html` files are empty now and we will add the code later. The `jquery-2.1.3.min.js` file is the jQuery library that we used in the previous chapter.

```
index.html
js/
   js/jquery-2.1.3.js
css/
   css/css3transition.css
images/
```

2. We are using two playing card graphic images in this example. They are `AK.png` and `AQ.png`. The images are available in the code bundle or you can download them from the book assets website at `http://mak.la/book-assets/`.

3. Put the two card images inside the `images` folder.

4. The next thing is to code the HTML with two card DIV elements. We will apply CSS transition style to these two cards elements when the page is loaded:

```
<!DOCTYPE html>
<html lang="en">
<head>
  <meta charset="utf-8">
  <title>Getting Familiar with CSS3 Transition</title>
  <link rel="stylesheet" href="css/css3transition.css" />
```

```
</head>
<body>
  <header>
    <h1>Getting Familiar with CSS3 Transition</h1>
  </header>

  <section id="game">
    <div id="cards">
      <div id="card1" class="card cardAK"></div>
      <div id="card2" class="card cardAQ"></div>
    </div> <!-- #cards -->
  </section> <!-- #game -->
  <footer>
    <p>This is an example of transitioning cards.</p>
  </footer>
<script src="js/jquery-2.1.3.min.js"></script>
<script>
$(function(){
  $("#card1").addClass("move-and-scale");
  $("#card2").addClass("rotate-right");
});
</script>
</body>
</html>
```

5. It is time to define the visual styles of the playing cards via CSS. This contains basic CSS 2.1 properties and CSS3's new properties. In the following code, the new CSS3 properties are highlighted:

```
body {
  background: LIGHTGREY;
}
/* defines styles for each card */
.card {
  width: 80px;
  height: 120px;
  margin: 20px;
  position: absolute;
  transition: all 1s linear;
}

/* set the card to corresponding playing card graphics */
.cardAK {
  background: url(../images/AK.png);
}
```

```
.cardAQ {
  background: url(../images/AQ.png);
}
/* rotate the applied DOM element 90 degree */
.rotate-right {
  transform: rotate3d(0, 0, 1, 90deg);
}

/* move and scale up the applied DOM element */
.move-and-scale {
  transform: translate3d(150px, 150px, 0) scale3d(1.5, 1.5, 1);
}
```

6. Let's save all the files and open the `index.html` file in the browser. The two cards should animate as shown in the following screenshot:

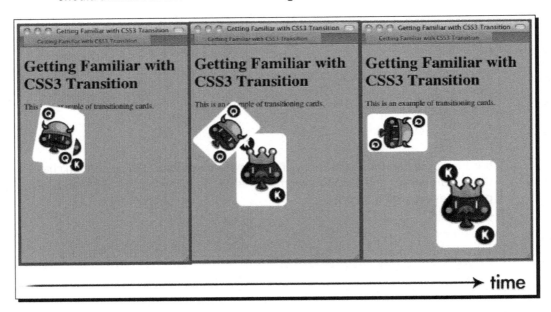

What just happened?

We just created two animation effects by using the CSS3 transition to tween the `transform` property.

Here is the usage of CSS transform:

```
transform: transform-function1 transform-function2;
```

The arguments of the `transform` property are functions. There are two sets of functions: the 2D and 3D transform functions. **CSS transform** functions are designed to move, scale, rotate, and skew the target DOM elements. The following sections show the usage of the transform functions.

2D transform functions

The 2D `rotate` function rotates the element clockwise on a given positive argument and counter-clockwise on a given negative argument:

```
rotate(angle)
```

The `translate` function moves the element by the given *x* and *y* displacement:

```
translate (tx, ty)
```

We can translate the *x* or *y* axis independently by calling the `translateX` and `translateY` function as follows:

```
translateX(number)
translateY(number)
```

The `scale` function scales the element by the given `sx` and `sy` vectors. If we only pass the first argument, then `sy` will be of the same value as `sx`:

```
scale(sx, sy)
```

In addition, we can independently scale the *x* and *y* axis as follows:

```
scaleX(number)
scaleY(number)
```

3D transform functions

The 3D rotation function rotates the element in 3D space by the given [x, y, z] unit vector. For example, we can rotate the *y* axis 60 degrees by using `rotate3d(0, 1, 0, 60deg)`:

```
rotate3d(x, y, z, angle)
```

We can also rotate one axis only by calling the following handy functions:

```
rotateX(angle)
rotateY(angle)
rotateZ(angle)
```

Similar to the 2D `translate` function, `translate3d` allows us to move the element in all the three axes:

```
translate3d(tx, ty, tz)
translateX(tx)
translateY(ty)
translateZ(tz)
```

Also, the `scale3d` scales the element in the 3D spaces:

```
scale3d(sx, sy, sz)
scaleX(sx)
scaleY(sy)
scaleZ(sz)
```

The `transform` functions that we just discussed are common, and we will use them many times. There are several other `transform` functions that are not discussed; they are `matrix`, `skew`, and `perspective`.

If you want to find the latest CSS Transforms working spec, you can visit the W3C website of CSS Transforms Modules at: `http://www.w3.org/TR/css3-3d-transforms/`.

Tweening the styles using CSS3 transition

There are tons of new features in CSS3. Transition module is one among them that affects us most in game designing.

What is **CSS3 transition**? W3C explains it in one sentence:

> *CSS transitions allows property changes in CSS values to occur smoothly over a specified duration.*

Normally, when we change any properties of the element, the properties are updated to the new value immediately. Transition slows down the changing process. It creates smooth in-between easing from the old value towards the new value in the given duration.

Here is the usage of the `transition` property:

```
transition: property_name duration timing_function delay
```

The following table explains each of the parameters used in the `transition` property:

Argument	Definition
property_name	This is the name of the property where the transition applies. It can be set to `all`.
duration	This is the duration that the transition takes.
timing_function	The `timing` function defines the interpolation between the start and end values. The default value is `ease`. Normally, we will use `ease`, `ease-in`, `ease-out`, and `linear`.
delay	The `delay` argument delays the start of the transition by the given seconds.

We can put several `transition` properties in one line. For example, the following code transitions the opacity in 0.3 seconds and background color in 0.5 seconds:

```
transition: opacity 0.3s, background-color 0.5s
```

We can also define each transition property individually by using the following properties:

```
transition-property, transition-duration, transition-timing-function
and transition-delay
```

Modules of CSS3

According to W3C, CSS3 is unlike CSS 2.1 in that there is only one CSS 2.1 spec. CSS3 is divided into different modules. Each module is reviewed individually. For example, there is a transition module, 2D/3D transforms module, and the Flexible Box Layout module.

The reason for dividing the spec into modules is because the pace at which the work of each part of the CSS3 progresses is not the same. Some CSS3 features are rather stable, such as border radius, while some have not yet settled down. Dividing the whole spec into different parts allows the browser vendor to support modules that are stable. In this scenario, slow-paced features will not slow down the whole spec. The aim of the CSS3 spec is to standardize the most common visual usage in web designing and this module fits this aim.

Have a go hero

We have translated, scaled, and rotated the playing cards. How about we try to change different values in the example? There are three axes in the `rotate3d` function. What will happen if we rotate the other axis? Experiment with the code yourself to get familiar with the transform and transition modules.

Creating a card-flipping effect

Imagine now that we are not just moving the playing card around, but we also want to flip the card element, just like we flip a real playing card. By using the `rotation transform` function, it is now possible to create the card-flipping effect.

Time for action – flipping a card with CSS3

We are going to start a new project and create a card-flipping effect when we click on the playing card:

1. Let's continue with our previous code example.

2. The card now contains two faces: a front face and a back face. Replace the following code in the `body` tag in the HTML code:

```html
<section id="game">
  <div id="cards">
    <div class="card">
      <div class="face front"></div>
      <div class="face back cardAK"></div>
    </div> <!-- .card -->
    <div class="card">
      <div class="face front"></div>
      <div class="face back cardAQ"></div>
    </div> <!-- .card -->
  </div> <!-- #cards -->
</section> <!-- #game -->
<script src="js/jquery-2.1.3.min.js"></script>
```

3. Then, create a new `css3flip.css` file in the `css` folder to test the flipping effect.

4. In the `index.html` file, change the CSS external link to the `css3flip.css` file:

```html
<link rel="stylesheet" href="css/css3flip.css" />
```

5. Now, let's add the styles to the `css3flip.css`:

```css
#game {
  background: #9c9;
  padding: 5px;
}
/* Define the 3D perspective view and dimension of each card. */
.card {
  perspective: 600px;
  width: 80px;
  height: 120px;
}
```

6. There are two faces on each card. We are going to slowly rotate the face of the card. Therefore, we define how the face transitions by CSS3's `transition` property. We also hide the back face's visibility. We will look at the detail of this property later:

```css
.face {
  border-radius: 10px;
  width: 100%;
  height: 100%;
  position: absolute;
  transition: all .3s;
  backface-visibility: hidden;
}
```

7. Now, it is time to style each individual face. The front face has a higher z-index than the back face:

```css
.front {
  background: #966;
}
.back {
  background: #eaa;
  transform: rotate3d(0,1,0,-180deg);
}
```

8. When we flip the card, we rotate the front face to the back and the back face to the front. We also swap the z-index of the front and back faces:

```css
.card-flipped .front {
  transform: rotate3d(0,1,0,180deg);
}
.card-flipped .back {
  transform: rotate3d(0,1,0,0deg);
}
.cardAK {
  background: url(../images/AK.png);
}
.cardAQ {
  background: url(../images/AQ.png);
}
```

9. Next, we will add logic after loading the jQuery library to toggle the card-flipped status when we click on the card:

```html
<script>
(function($){
  $(function(){
    $("#cards").children().each(function(index) {
```

```
      // listen the click event on each card DIV element.
      $(this).click(function() {
        // add the class "card-flipped".
        // the browser will animate the styles
        // between current state and card-flipped state.
        $(this).toggleClass("card-flipped");
      });
    });
  });
})(jQuery);
</script>
```

10. The styles and the scripts are now ready. Let's save all the files and preview it in our web browser. Click on the playing card to flip it over, and click on it again to flip it back.

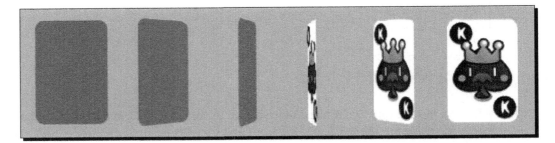

What just happened?

We have created a card-flipping effect that can be toggled by a mouse click. You can try out the example at `http://makzan.net/html5-games/simple-card-flip/`.

The example made use of several CSS transform properties and JavaScript to handle the mouse click event.

Toggling a class with jQuery's toggleClass function

We apply the `card-flipped` class to the card element when the mouse is clicked on the card. On the second click, we want to remove the applied card-flipped style so that the card flips back again. This is called **toggling a class** style.

jQuery provides us with a handy function named `toggleClass` to add or remove classes automatically, depending on whether the class is applied or not.

To use the function, we simply pass the classes that we want to toggle as an argument.

For example, the following code adds or removes the `card-flipped` class to an element with the ID as `card1`:

```
$("#card1").toggleClass("card-flipped");
```

The `toggleClass` function accepts the toggle instruction from more than one class at the same time. We can pass in several class names and separate them by using a space. Here is an example of toggling two classes at the same time:

```
$("#card1").toggleClass("card-flipped scale-up");
```

Introducing CSS' perspective property

CSS3 lets us present elements in 3D, and we have been able to transform the elements in the 3D space. The `perspective` property defines how the 3D perspective view looks. You can treat the value as far as you are looking at the object. The closer you are, the more perspective distortion there is on the viewing object.

The following two 3D cubes demonstrate how different perspective values change the perspective view of the element:

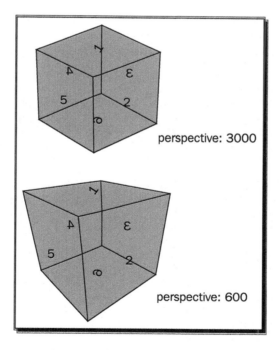

Have a go hero

The cube is created by putting six faces together with 3D transforms applied to each face. It used the techniques that we've discussed. Try to create a cube and experiment with the `perspective` property.

The following web page gives a comprehensive explanation on creating the CSS3 cube, and it also explains how to control the rotation of the cube with the keyboard:

`http://paulrhayes.com/experiments/cube-3d/`

Introducing backface-visibility

Before the `backface-visibility` property was introduced, all the elements on the page presented their front face to the visitor. Actually, there was no concept of the front face or the back face of the element because presenting the front face was the only choice. While CSS3 introduces the rotation in three axes, we can rotate an element so that its face is on the back. Try looking at your palm and rotating your wrist, your palm turns and you see the back of your palm. This happens to the rotated elements too.

CSS3 introduces a property named `backface-visibility` to define whether or not we can see the back face of the element. By default, it is visible. The following figure demonstrates the two different behaviors of the `backface-visibility` property:

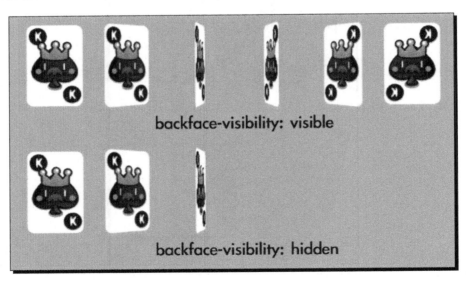

You can read more detailed information about different properties
and functions in CSS 3D transforms on its official Webkit blog at
`http://webkit.org/blog/386/3d-transforms/`.

Creating a card-matching memory game

We have gone through some basic techniques in CSS. Now, let's make a game using the
techniques. We are going to make a card game. The card game will make use of transform
to flip the card, transition to move the card, JavaScript to hold the logic, and a new HTML5
feature called **custom data attribute** to store custom data. Don't worry, we will discuss each
component step by step.

Downloading the sprite sheet of playing cards

In the card-flipping example, we were using the graphics of two different playing cards.
Now, we will prepare graphics for the whole deck of playing cards. Although we will only
use six playing cards in the matching game, we will prepare the whole deck so that we can
reuse these graphics in other card games that we may create.

There are 52 playing cards in a deck and we have one more graphic for the backside.
Instead of using 53 separate files, it is good practice to put separate graphics into one
big sprite sheet file. Sprite sheet is a graphics technique that loads one graphic's texture
into memory and displays part of the graphics for each game component.

One benefit of using a big sprite sheet instead of separate image files is that we can reduce
the amount of **HTTP requests**. When the browser loads the web page, it creates a new
HTTP request to load each external resource, including JavaScript files, CSS files, and images.
It takes quite a lot of time to establish a new HTTP request for each separated small file.
Combining the graphics into one file, greatly reduces the amount of requests and thus
improves the responsiveness of the game when it is loading in the browser.

Another benefit of placing graphics in one file is to avoid the overhead of the file format
header and reduce the amount of HTTP requests. The time to load a sprite sheet with 53
images is faster than loading 53 different images with the file header in each file.

The following deck of playing cards' graphics is drawn and aligned in Adobe Illustrator.
You can download it from `http://mak.la/deck.png`.

You can create your own sprite sheet with Instant Sprite Generator (http://instantsprite.com). The article at http://css-tricks.com/css-sprites/ explains in detail why and how we can create and use the CSS sprite sheet.

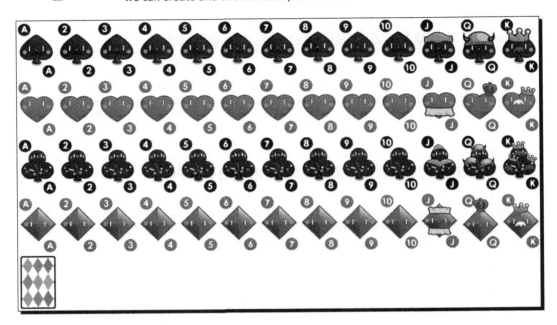

Setting up the game environment

Once the graphics are ready, we will need to set up a static page with the game objects that are prepared and placed on the game area. It is then easier to add game logic and interaction later:

Time for action – preparing the card-matching game

Before adding the complicated game logic to our matching game, let's prepare the HTML game structure and all the CSS styles:

1. Let's continue with our project. Create a new file named matchgame.js inside the js folder.

2. Replace the index.html file with the following HTML code:

```
<!DOCTYPE html>
<html lang="en">
<head>
  <meta charset=utf-8>
```

```
    <title>CSS3 Matching Game</title>
    <link rel="stylesheet" href="css/matchgame.css" />
</head>
<body>
    <header>
        <h1>CSS3 Matching Game</h1>
    </header>

    <section id="game">
        <div id="cards">
            <div class="card">
                <div class="face front"></div>
                <div class="face back"></div>
            </div> <!-- .card -->
        </div> <!-- #cards -->
    </section> <!-- #game -->

    <footer>
        <p>This is an example of creating a matching game with CSS3.</p>
    </footer>

<script src="js/jquery-2.1.3.min.js"></script>
<script src="js/matchgame.js"></script>
</body>
</html>
```

3. In order to make the game more appealing, I prepared background images for the game table and the page. These graphic assets can be found in the code example bundle. The background images are optional, and they will not affect the gameplay and the logic of the matching game.

4. We will also place the deck's sprite sheet graphics into the images folder. Then, we will download the deck.png file from http://mak.la/deck.png and save it within the images folder.

5. Create a dedicated CSS file named matchgame.css for our game and put it inside the css folder.

6. Now, let's add style to the matching game before writing any logic. Open matchgame.css and add the following body styles:

```
body {
  text-align: center;
  background: BROWN url(../images/bg.jpg);
}
```

7. We will continue to add the styles to the `game` element. This will be the main area of the game:

```
#game {
  border-radius: 10px;
  border: 1px solid GRAY;
  background: DARKGREEN url(../images/table.jpg);
  width: 500px;
  height: 460px;
  margin: 0 auto;
  display: flex;
  justify-content: center;
  align-items: center;
}
```

8. We will put all card elements into a parent DOM named `cards`. By doing this, we can easily center all the cards in the game area:

```
#cards {
  position: relative;
  width: 380px;
  height: 400px;
}
```

9. For each card, we define a `perspective` property to give it a visual depth effect:

```
.card {
  perspective: 600px;
  width: 80px;
  height: 120px;
  position: absolute;
  transition: all .3s;
}
```

10. There are two faces on each card. The back face will be rotated later, and we will define the transition properties to animate the style changes. We also want to make sure that the back face is hidden:

```
.face {
  border-radius: 10px;
  width: 100%;
  height: 100%;
  position: absolute;
  transition-property: opacity, transform, box-shadow;
  transition-duration: .3s;

  backface-visibility: hidden;
}
```

11. Now, we will set the styles for the front and back faces. They are almost the same as the flipping card example, except that we are now giving them background images and box shadows:

```
.front {
  background: GRAY url(../images/deck.png) 0 -480px;
}
.back {
  background: LIGHTGREY url(../images/deck.png);
  transform: rotate3d(0,1,0,-180deg);
}
.card:hover .face, .card-flipped .face {
  box-shadow: 0 0 10px #aaa;
}
.card-flipped .front {
  transform: rotate3d(0,1,0,180deg);
}
.card-flipped .back {
  transform: rotate3d(0,1,0,0deg);
}
```

12. When any card is removed, we want it to fade out. Therefore, we declare a card-removed class with 0 opacity:

```
.card-removed {
  opacity: 0;
}
```

13. In order to show different playing card graphics from the sprite sheet of the card deck, we clip the background of the card into different background positions:

```
.cardAJ {background-position: -800px 0;}
.cardAQ {background-position: -880px 0;}
.cardAK {background-position: -960px 0;}
.cardBJ {background-position: -800px -120px;}
.cardBQ {background-position: -880px -120px;}
.cardBK {background-position: -960px -120px;}
.cardCJ {background-position: -800px -240px;}
.cardCQ {background-position: -880px -240px;}
.cardCK {background-position: -960px -240px;}
.cardDJ {background-position: -800px -360px;}
.cardDQ {background-position: -880px -360px;}
.cardDK {background-position: -960px -360px;}
```

14. We have defined a lot of CSS styles. It is now time for JavaScript's logic. We will open the js/matchgame.js file and put the following code inside:

```
$(function(){
  // clone 12 copies of the card
  for(var i=0; i<11; i++){
    $(".card:first-child").clone().appendTo("#cards");
  }
  // initialize each card's position
  $("#cards").children().each(function(index) {
    // align the cards to be 4x3 ourselves.
    var x = ($(this).width() + 20) * (index % 4);
    var y = ($(this).height() + 20) * Math.floor(index / 4);
    $(this).css("transform", "translateX(" + x + "px)
      translateY(" + y + "px)");
  });
});
```

15. Now, we will save all the files and preview the game in the browser. The game should be well styled, and 12 cards should appear in the center. However, we cannot click on the cards yet because we have not set any interaction logic for the cards.

What just happened?

We created the game structure in HTML and applied styles to the HTML elements. You can find the working example of the game with the current progress at http://makzan.net/html5-games/card-matching-wip-step1/.

We also used jQuery to create 12 cards on the game area once the web was loaded and ready. The styles to flip and remove the cards were also prepared and will be applied to the card by using the game logic later.

Since we are using absolute positioning for each card, we need to align the cards into 4x3 tiles ourselves. In the JavaScript logic, we loop through each card and align it by calculating the position with the looping index:

```
$("#cards").children().each(function(index) {
  // align the cards to be 4x3 ourselves.
  var x = ($(this).width() + 20) * (index % 4);
  var y = ($(this).height() + 20) * Math.floor(index / 4);
  $(this).css("transform", "translateX(" + x + "px) translateY(
    " + y + "px)");
});
```

The % character in JavaScript is the **modulus operator** that returns the remainder left after division. The remainder is used to get the column count when we loop the cards. The following diagram shows the row/column relationship with the index number:

0	1	2	3
4	5	6	7
8	9	10	11

The division, on the other hand, is used to get the row count so that we can position the card on the corresponding row.

Take index 3 as an example; 3 % 4 is 3. So, the card at index 3 is on the third column. And 3 / 4 is 0, so it is on the first row.

Let's pick another number to see how the formula works. Let's see index 8; 8 % 4 is 0, and it is on the first column. 8 / 4 is 2 so it is on the third row.

Cloning DOM elements with jQuery

In our HTML structure, we only have one card and in the result, we have 12 cards. This is because we used the `clone` function in jQuery to clone the card element. After cloning the target element, we called the `appendTo` function to append the cloned card element as a child in the cards element:

```
$(".card:first-child").clone().appendTo("#cards");
```

Selecting the first child of an element in jQuery using child filters

When we selected the card element and cloned it, we used the following selector:

```
$(".card:first-child")
```

The `:first-child` filter is a **child filter** that selects the first child of the given parent element.

Besides `:first-child`, we can also select the last child by using `:last-child`.

 You can also check other child-related selectors on the jQuery document at: `http://api.jquery.com/category/selectors/child-filter-selectors/`.

Vertically aligning a DOM element

We put the cards DIV in the center of the game element. **CSS3 flexible box layout module** introduces an easy method to achieve the **vertical center alignment**, as follows:

```
display: flex;
justify-content: center;
align-items: center;
```

The flexible box module defines the alignment of the element when there are extra spaces in the container. We can set the element to certain behaviors as a flexible box container by using the display, a CSS2 property, with the `box` value, and a new CSS3 property value.

`justify-content` and `align-items` are two properties to define how it aligns and uses the extra free space horizontally and vertically. We can center the element by setting both properties to `center`.

Vertical alignment is just a small part of the flexible box layout module. It is very powerful when you make layouts in web design. You may find further information on the W3C page of the module (`http://www.w3.org/TR/css3-flexbox/`) or the CSS3 tricks website (`http://css-tricks.com/snippets/css/a-guide-to-flexbox/`).

Using CSS sprite with a background position

The CSS sprite sheet is a big image that contains many individual graphics. The big sprite sheet image is applied as the background image for the elements. We can clip each graphic out by moving the background position to a fixed width and height element.

Our deck's image contains a total of 53 graphics. In order to demonstrate the background position easily, let's assume that we have an image that contains three card images, as shown in the following screenshot:

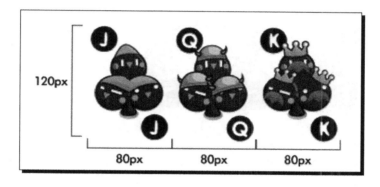

In the CSS style, we set the card element to a width of 80 px and a height of 120 px, with the background image set to the big deck image. If we want the top-left graphic, we change the values of both the *x* and *y* axes of the background position to 0. If we want the second graphic, we move the background image 80px to the left. This means setting the X position to `-80px` and Y to 0. Since we have a fixed width and height, only the clipped 80 x 120 area shows the background image. The rectangle in the following screenshot shows the viewable area:

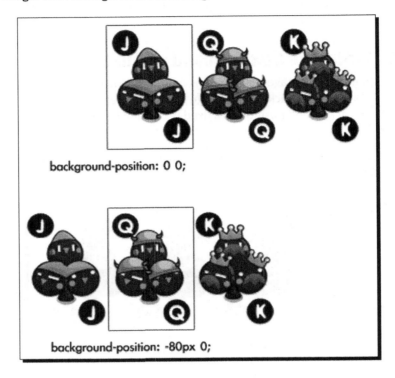

Adding game logic to the matching game

Let's now imagine holding a real deck in our hand and setting up the matching game.

We would first shuffle the cards in our hands and then we would put each card on the table with the back facing up. For an easier gameplay, we align the cards into a 4 x 3 array. Now, the game is set up and we are going to play it.

We pick up one card and flip it to make it face up. We pick another one and face it upwards. Afterwards, we have two possible actions. We take away the two cards if they have the same pattern. Otherwise, we put them back facing down, as if we had not touched them. The game continues until we pair all of the cards.

The code flow will be much clearer after we have this step-by-step scenario in our mind. Actually, the code in this example is exactly the same as the procedure we play with a real deck. We just need to replace the human language into the JavaScript code.

Time for action – adding game logic to the matching game

We have prepared the game environment in the last example and decided the game logic should be the same as playing a real deck. It is time to code the JavaScript logic now:

1. Let's begin from our last matching game example. We have styled the CSS, and now, it is time to add the game logic in the `js/matchgame.js` file.

2. The game is to match pairs of playing cards. We have 12 cards now, so we need six pairs of playing cards. Put the following code in the `js/matchgame.js` file. The array declares six pairs of card patterns:

```
var matchingGame = {};
matchingGame.deck = [
  'cardAK', 'cardAK',
  'cardAQ', 'cardAQ',
  'cardAJ', 'cardAJ',
  'cardBK', 'cardBK',
  'cardBQ', 'cardBQ',
  'cardBJ', 'cardBJ',
];
```

3. We aligned the cards in jQuery's `ready` function in the previous chapter. Now we need to prepare and initialize more code in the `ready` function. To do this, change the `ready` function into the following code. The changed code is highlighted here:

```
$(function(){
  matchingGame.deck.sort(shuffle);

  for(var i=0;i<11;i++){
    $(".card:first-child").clone().appendTo("#cards");
  }

  $("#cards").children().each(function(index) {
    var x = ($(this).width() + 20) * (index % 4);
    var y = ($(this).height() + 20) * Math.floor(index / 4);
    $(this).css("transform", "translateX(" + x + "px)
      translateY(" + y + "px)");

    // get a pattern from the shuffled deck
    var pattern = matchingGame.deck.pop();
```

```
    // visually apply the pattern on the card's back side.
    $(this).find(".back").addClass(pattern);

    // embed the pattern data into the DOM element.
    $(this).attr("data-pattern",pattern);

    // listen the click event on each card DIV element.
    $(this).click(selectCard);
  });
});
```

4. Similar to playing a real deck, the first thing we want to do is shuffle the deck.
   To do this, we need to add the following `shuffle` function to the JavaScript file:

```
function shuffle() {
  return 0.5 - Math.random();
}
```

5. When we click on the card, we flip it and schedule the checking function. So, we
   must append the following codes to the JavaScript file:

```
function selectCard() {
  // we do nothing if there are already two card flipped.
  if ($(".card-flipped").size() > 1) {
    return;
  }
  $(this).addClass("card-flipped");
  // check the pattern of both flipped card 0.7s later.
  if ($(".card-flipped").size() === 2) {
    setTimeout(checkPattern,700);
  }
}
```

6. When two cards are opened, the following function is executed. It controls whether
   we remove the card or flip it back:

```
function checkPattern() {
  if (isMatchPattern()) {
    $(".card-flipped").removeClass("card-flipped").addClass
      ("card-removed");
    $(".card-removed").bind("transitionend",
      removeTookCards);
  } else {
    $(".card-flipped").removeClass("card-flipped");
  }
}
```

7. It is time for the pattern-checking function. The following function accesses the custom pattern attribute of the opened cards and compares them to see whether they are in the same pattern:

```
function isMatchPattern() {
  var cards = $(".card-flipped");
  var pattern = $(cards[0]).data("pattern");
  var anotherPattern = $(cards[1]).data("pattern");
  return (pattern === anotherPattern);
}
```

8. After the matched cards fade out, we execute the following function to remove the cards:

```
function removeTookCards() {
  $(".card-removed").remove();
}
```

9. The game logic is ready now. Let's open the game's HTML file in a browser and play. Remember to check the console window in **Developer Tools** to see whether there is any error.

The following screenshot shows the CSS3 Card Matching game:

What just happened?

We coded the game logic of the CSS3 matching game. The logic adds the mouse click interaction to the playing cards, and it controls the flow of pattern checking. You can try the game and view the full source code at `http://makzan.net/html5-games/card-matching-wip-step2/`.

Executing code after the CSS transition has ended

We remove the paired cards after playing the fade out transition. We can schedule a function to be executed after the transition has ended by using the `transitionend` event. The following code snippet from our code example adds a `card-removed` class to the paired card to start the transition. Then, it binds the `transitionend` event to remove the card complete with the DOM, afterwards:

```
$(".card-flipped").removeClass("card-flipped").addClass("card-removed");
$(".card-removed").bind("transitionend", removeTookCards);
```

Delaying code execution on flipping cards

The game logic flow is designed in the same way as playing a real deck. One big difference is that we used several `setTimeout` functions to delay the execution of the code. When the second card is clicked, we schedule the `checkPattern` function to be executed 0.7 seconds later by using the following code example snippet:

```
if ($(".card-flipped").size() == 2) {
  setTimeout(checkPattern, 700);
}
```

The reason we delay the function call is to give time to the player to memorize the card pattern.

Randomizing an array in JavaScript

There is no built-in array randomize function in JavaScript. We have to write our own. Luckily, we can get help from the built-in array sorting function.

Here is the usage of the `sort` function:

```
sort(compare_function);
```

The `sort` function takes one optional argument:

Argument	Definition	Discussion
compare_function	A function that defines the sort order of the array. The `compare_function` requires two arguments.	The `sort` function compares two elements in the array by using the `compare` function. Therefore, the `compare` function requires two arguments. When the `compare` function returns any value that is bigger than 0, it puts the first argument at a lower index than the second argument. When the return value is smaller than 0, it puts the second argument at a lower index than the first argument.

The trick here is that we used the `compare` function that returns a random number between -0.5 and 0.5:

```
anArray.sort(shuffle);
function shuffle(a, b) {
  return 0.5 - Math.random();
}
```

By returning a random number in the `compare` function, the `sort` function sorts the same array in an inconsistent way. In other words, we shuffle the array.

The following link from the Mozilla Developer Network provides a detailed explanation on using the `sort` function with examples:

```
https://developer.mozilla.org/en/JavaScript/
Reference/Global_Objects/Array/sort
```

Storing internal custom data with an HTML5 custom data attribute

We can store custom data inside the DOM element by using the **custom data attribute**. We can create a custom attribute name with the `data-` prefix and assign a value to it.

For instance, we can embed custom data to the list elements in the following code:

```
<ul id="games">
  <li data-chapter="2" data-difficulty="easy">Ping-Pong</li>
  <li data-chapter="3" data-difficulty="medium">Matching Game</li>
</ul>
```

This is a new feature proposed in the HTML5 spec. According to the W3C, the custom data attributes are intended to store custom data that is private to a page or an application for which there are no more appropriate attributes or elements.

W3C also states that this custom data attribute is "intended for use by the site's own script and not a generic extension mechanism for publicly-usable metadata."

We are coding our matching game and embedding our own data to the card elements; therefore, custom data attribute fits our usage.

We use the custom attribute to store the card pattern inside each card so that we can check by comparing the pattern value whether the two flipped cards match in JavaScript. In addition, the pattern is used to style the playing cards into corresponding graphics as well:

```
$(this).find(".back").addClass(pattern);
$(this).attr("data-pattern",pattern);
```

Pop quiz

Q1. According to W3C's guidelines about the custom data attribute, which of the following statements is true?

1. We can create a `data-link` attribute to store the link of the `css` tag.

2. We can access the custom data attribute in a third-party game portal website.

3. We can store a `data-score` attribute in each player's DOM element to sort the ranking in our web page.

4. We can create a `ranking` attribute in each player's DOM element to store the ranking data.

Accessing custom data attribute with jQuery

In the matching game example, we used the `attr` function from the jQuery library to access our custom data:

```
pattern = $(this).attr("data-pattern");
```

The `attr` function returns the value of the given attribute name. For example, we can get the links in all the `a` tags by calling the following code:

```
$("a").attr("href");
```

For the HTML5 custom data attribute, jQuery provides us with another function to access the HTML5 custom data attribute. This is the `data` function.

`Data` function was designed to embed custom data into the jQuery object of the HTML elements. It was designed before the HTML5 custom data attribute.

Here is the usage of the `data` function:

```
.data(key)
.data(key,value)
```

The `data` function accepts two types of functions:

Function type	Arguments definition	Discussion
`.data(key)`	The `key` argument is a string that names the entry of the data.	When only the `key` argument is given, the `data` function reads the data associated with the jQuery object and returns the corresponding value. In the recent jQuery update, this function is extended to support the HTML5 custom data attribute.
`.data(key, value)`	The `key` argument is a string that names the entry of the data. The `value` argument is the data to be associated with the jQuery object.	When both the `key` and `value` arguments are given, the `data` function sets a new data entry to the jQuery object. The `value` argument can be any JavaScript type, including an array and an object.

In order to support the HTML5 custom data attribute, jQuery extends the `data` function to let it access the custom data that is defined in the HTML code.

Now, let's see how we use the `data` function. Consider the following line of an HTML code:

```
<div id="target" data-custom-name="HTML5 Games"></div>
```

Now, using the preceding line of code, we can access the `data-custom-name` attribute by calling the `data` function in jQuery:

```
$("#target").data("customName")
```

This will return "HTML5 Games".

 Keep in mind that `attr` would always return a string value. However, the `data` method will attempt to convert the HTML string value into a JavaScript value, such as a number or a Boolean.

Pop quiz

Q1. Given the following HTML code, which jQuery statements read the custom score data and return 100 in the integer format?

```
<div id="game" data-score="100"></div>
```

1. `$("#game").attr("data-score");`
2. `$("#game").attr("score");`
3. `$("#game").data("data-score");`
4. `$("#game").data("score");`

Have a go hero

We have created the CSS3 matching game. So, what is missing here? The game logic does not check whether the game is over. Try adding a "You won!" text when the game is over. You can also animate the text by using the techniques that we discussed in this chapter.

Making other playing card games

This CSS3 playing card approach is suitable to create card games. There are two sides on a card that fit the flipping. The transition feature is suitable to move the cards. With both moving and flipping, we can just define the playing rule and make the most of the card games.

Have a go hero

Can you use the playing card graphics and flipping techniques to create another game? How about poker?

Embedding web fonts into our game

Over the years, we have been using limited fonts to design web pages. We could not use whatever fonts we wanted because the browser loaded the font from the visitor's local machine, and we cannot control or ensure that visitors have our desired fonts.

Although we can embed **web fonts** to Internet Explorer 5 with a limited type format, we have to wait until browser vendors support embedding the most common TrueType font format.

Imagine that we can control the mood of the game by embedding different styles of web fonts. We can then design the games with our desired fonts and have more control over the appeal of the game. Let's try to embed a web font into our memory matching game.

Time for action – embedding a font from the Google Fonts directory

Google Fonts directory is a web font service that lists free-to-use web fonts. We will embed a web font chosen from the Google Fonts directory:

1. Go to the Google Fonts directory site at `http://google.com/fonts`.
2. In the font directory, there is a list of web fonts that are available under an open source license and can be used freely.
3. Choose one of them and click on the font name to proceed to the next step. In this example, I used **Droid Serif**.
4. After you click on a font, the font directory displays detailed information about the font. There are several actions that we can carry out here, such as preview the font, choose from variants, and most importantly, get the font embedding code.

5. In MAC, click on the **Get the code** tab and you will see the following screenshot; this shows a guide on how to embed this font into our web page. Alternatively, in Windows, you can click on the **Use** tab and you will find instructions to get the code:

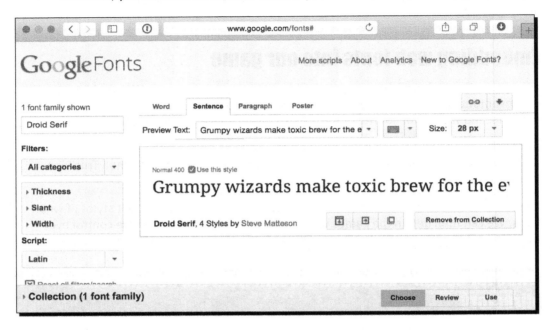

6. Copy the `link` tag provided by Google, and then paste it into the HTML code. This should be placed before any other style definition:

```
<link href='http://fonts.googleapis.com/css?family=
    Droid+Serif:regular,bold&subset=latin' rel='stylesheet'
        type='text/css'>
```

7. Now, we can use the font to style our text. Set the body's font family property as the following code:

```
body {
    font-family: 'Droid Serif', Arial, serif;
}
```

8. Save all the files and open the `index.html` file. The browser will download the font from the Google server and embed it into the web page. Keep an eye on the fonts; they should be loaded and rendered as our selected Google font.

What just happened?

We have just styled our game with an uncommon web font. The font is hosted and delivered through the Google Fonts directory.

Besides using the font directory, we can embed our font file by using `@font face`. The following link provides a bulletproof approach to embed a font ourselves:

`http://www.fontspring.com/blog/the-new-bulletproof-font-face-syntax`

Check the font license before embedding

Normally, the font license does not cover its usage on web pages. Be sure to check the license before embedding the font. All the fonts listed in the Google Fonts directory are licensed under the open source license and can be used on any website. You can check the license of individual fonts listed in the directory at `https://www.google.com/fonts/attribution`.

Choosing different font delivery services

Google Fonts directory is just one of the font delivery services. Typekit (`http://typekit.com`) and Fontdeck (`http://fontdeck.com`) are two other font services that provide hundreds of high quality fonts via yearly subscription plans.

Summary

In this chapter, you learned about using different new properties of CSS3 to create games.

Specifically, we covered how you can build a card game that is based on CSS3 styles and animation. You learned how to transform and animate the game object by using the transition module. We can flip a card back and forth with perspective depth illusion. We also embedded web fonts from an online font delivery service.

Now that you've learned about creating DOM-based HTML5 games with the help of CSS3 features, we are going to explore another approach—using the new `canvas` tag and the drawing API—to create HTML5 games in the next chapter.

4

Building the Untangle Game with Canvas and the Drawing API

One new highlighted feature in HTML5 is the `canvas` *element. We can treat it as a dynamic area where we can draw graphics and shapes with scripts.*

Images in websites have been static for years. There are animated GIFs, but they cannot interact with visitors. Canvas is dynamic. We draw and modify the context in the Canvas, dynamically through the JavaScript drawing API. We can also add interaction to the Canvas and thus make games.

In the previous two chapters, we discussed DOM-based game development with CSS3 and a few HTML5 features. In the coming two chapters, we will focus on using new HTML5 features to create games. In this chapter, we will take a look at a core feature, Canvas, and some basic drawing techniques.

In this chapter, we will cover the following topics:

- ◆ Introducing the HTML5 `canvas` element
- ◆ Drawing a circle in Canvas
- ◆ Drawing lines in the `canvas` element
- ◆ Interacting with drawn objects in Canvas with mouse events
- ◆ Detecting a line intersection
- ◆ Supporting the drag-n-drop feature in touch devices

The Untangle puzzle game is a game where players are given circles with some lines connecting them. The lines may intersect the others and the players need to drag the circles so that no line intersects anymore.

The following screenshot previews the game that we are going to achieve through this chapter:

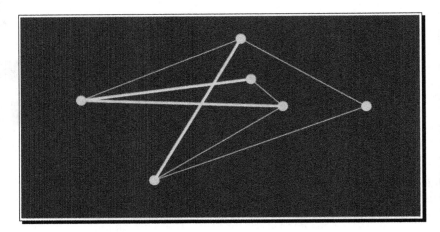

You can also try the game at the following URL:

`http://makzan.net/html5-games/untangle-wip-dragging/`

So let's start making our Canvas game from scratch.

Introducing the HTML5 canvas element

W3C community states that the `canvas` element and the drawing functions are as follows:

A resolution-dependent bitmap canvas, which can be used for rendering graphs, game graphics, or other visual images on the fly.

The `canvas` element contains context for drawing and the actual graphics and shapes are drawn by the JavaScript drawing API. There is one key difference between using `canvas` and the usual HTML DOM elements. Canvas is an immediate mode while DOM is a retained mode. We describe the DOM tree with elements and attributes, and the browser renders and tracks the objects for us. In Canvas, we have to manage all the attributes and rendering ourselves. The browser doesn't keep the information of what we draw. It only keeps the drawn pixel data.

Drawing a circle in the Canvas

Let's start our drawing in the Canvas from the basic shape—circle.

Time for action – drawing color circles in the Canvas

1. First, let's set up the new environment for the example. That is, an HTML file that will contain the `canvas` element, a jQuery library to help us in JavaScript, a JavaScript file containing the actual drawing logic, and a style sheet:

```
index.html
js/
  js/jquery-2.1.3.js
  js/untangle.js
  js/untangle.drawing.js
  js/untangle.data.js
  js/untangle.input.js
css/
  css/untangle.css
images/
```

2. Put the following HTML code into the `index.html` file. It is a basic HTML document containing the `canvas` element:

```html
<!DOCTYPE html>
<html lang="en">
<head>
  <meta charset="utf-8">
  <title>Drawing Circles in Canvas</title>
  <link rel="stylesheet" href="css/untangle.css">
</head>
<body>
  <header>
    <h1>Drawing in Canvas</h1>
  </header>

  <canvas id="game" width="768" height="400">
    This is an interactive game with circles and lines connecting
them.
  </canvas>

<script src="js/jquery-2.1.3.min.js"></script>
<script src="js/untangle.data.js"></script>
<script src="js/untangle.drawing.js"></script>
<script src="js/untangle.input.js"></script>
```

```
<script src="js/untangle.js"></script>
</body>
</html>
```

3. Use CSS to set the background color of the Canvas inside `untangle.css`:

```
canvas {
  background: grey;
}
```

4. In the `untangle.js` JavaScript file, we put a jQuery `document ready` function and draw a color circle inside it:

```
$(document).ready(function(){
  var canvas = document.getElementById("game");
  var ctx = canvas.getContext("2d");
  ctx.fillStyle = "GOLD";
  ctx.beginPath();
  ctx.arc(100, 100, 50, 0, Math.PI*2, true);
  ctx.closePath();
  ctx.fill();
});
```

5. Open the `index.html` file in a web browser and we will get the following screenshot:

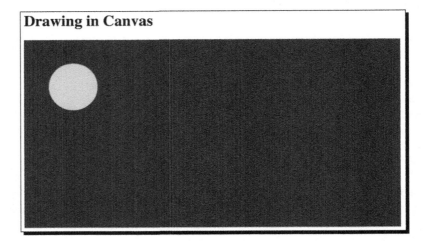

What just happened?

We have just created a simple **Canvas context** with circles on it. There are not many settings for the `canvas` element itself. We set the width and height of the Canvas, the same as we have fixed the dimensions of real drawing paper. Also, we assign an ID attribute to the Canvas for an easier reference in JavaScript:

```
<canvas id="game" width="768" height="400">
    This is an interactive game with circles and lines connecting them.
</canvas>
```

Putting in fallback content when the web browser does not support the Canvas

Not every web browser supports the `canvas` element. The `canvas` element provides an easy way to provide **fallback content** if the `canvas` element is not supported. The content also provides meaningful information for any screen reader too. Anything inside the open and close tags of the `canvas` element is the fallback content. This content is hidden if the web browser supports the element. Browsers that don't support `canvas` will instead display that fallback content. It is good practice to provide useful information in the fallback content. For instance, if the `canvas` tag's purpose is a dynamic picture, we may consider placing an `<img>` alternative there. Or we may also provide some links to modern web browsers for the visitor to upgrade their browser easily.

The Canvas context

When we draw in the Canvas, we actually call the drawing API of the **canvas rendering context**. You can think of the relationship of the Canvas and context as Canvas being the frame and context the real drawing surface. Currently, we have `2d`, `webgl`, and `webgl2` as the context options. In our example, we'll use the 2D drawing API by calling `getContext("2d")`.

```
var canvas = document.getElementById("game");
var ctx = canvas.getContext("2d");
```

Drawing circles and shapes with the Canvas arc function

There is no circle function to draw a circle. The Canvas drawing API provides a function to draw different arcs, including the circle. The arc function accepts the following arguments:

Arguments	Discussion
X	The center point of the arc in the *x* axis.
Y	The center point of the arc in the *y* axis.
radius	The radius is the distance between the center point and the arc's perimeter. When drawing a circle, a larger radius means a larger circle.
startAngle	The starting point is an angle in radians. It defines where to start drawing the arc on the perimeter.
endAngle	The ending point is an angle in radians. The arc is drawn from the position of the starting angle, to this end angle.
counter-clockwise	This is a Boolean indicating the arc from startingAngle to endingAngle drawn in a clockwise or counter-clockwise direction. This is an optional argument with the default value false.

Converting degrees to radians

The angle arguments used in the arc function are in **radians** instead of **degrees**. If you are familiar with the degrees angle, you may need to convert the degrees into radians before putting the value into the arc function. We can convert the angle unit using the following formula:

```
radians = π/180 x degrees
```

Executing the path drawing in the Canvas

When we are calling the arc function or other path drawing functions, we are not drawing the path immediately in the Canvas. Instead, we are adding it into a list of the paths. These paths will not be drawn until we execute the drawing command.

There are two drawing executing commands: one command to fill the paths and the other to draw the stroke.

We fill the paths by calling the fill function and draw the stroke of the paths by calling the stroke function, which we will use later when drawing lines:

```
ctx.fill();
```

Beginning a path for each style

The fill and stroke functions fill and draw the paths in the Canvas but do not clear the list of paths. Take the following code snippet as an example. After filling our circle with the color red, we add other circles and fill them with green. What happens to the code is both the circles are filled with green, instead of only the new circle being filled by green:

```
var canvas = document.getElementById('game');
var ctx = canvas.getContext('2d');
ctx.fillStyle = "red";
ctx.arc(100, 100, 50, 0, Math.PI*2, true);
ctx.fill();

ctx.arc(210, 100, 50, 0, Math.PI*2, true);
ctx.fillStyle = "green";
ctx.fill();
```

This is because, when calling the second fill command, the list of paths in the Canvas contains both circles. Therefore, the fill command fills both circles with green and overrides the red color circle.

In order to fix this issue, we want to ensure we call beginPath before drawing a new shape every time.

The beginPath function empties the list of paths, so the next time we call the fill and stroke commands, they will only apply to all paths after the last beginPath.

Have a go hero

We have just discussed a code snippet where we intended to draw two circles: one in red and the other in green. The code ends up drawing both circles in green. How can we add a beginPath command to the code so that it draws one red circle and one green circle correctly?

Closing a path

The `closePath` function will draw a straight line from the last point of the latest path to the first point of the path. This is called closing the path. If we are only going to fill the path and are not going to draw the stroke outline, the `closePath` function does not affect the result. The following screenshot compares the results on a half circle with one calling `closePath` and the other not calling `closePath`:

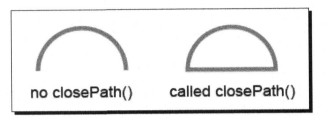

no closePath()   called closePath()

Pop quiz

Q1. Do we need to use the `closePath` function on the shape we are drawing if we just want to fill the color and not draw the outline stroke?

1.   Yes, we need to use the `closePath` function.

2.   No, it does not matter whether we use the `closePath` function.

Wrapping the circle drawing in a function

Drawing a circle is a common function that we will use a lot. It is better to create a function to draw a circle now instead of entering several code lines.

Time for action – putting the circle drawing code into a function

Let's make a function to draw the circle and then draw some circles in the Canvas. We are going to put code in different files to make the code simpler:

1.   Open the `untangle.drawing.js` file in our code editor and put in the following code:

```
if (untangleGame === undefined) {
  var untangleGame = {};
}

untangleGame.drawCircle = function(x, y, radius) {
  var ctx = untangleGame.ctx;
  ctx.fillStyle = "GOLD";
```

```
    ctx.beginPath();
    ctx.arc(x, y, radius, 0, Math.PI*2, true);
    ctx.closePath();
    ctx.fill();
};
```

2. Open the `untangle.data.js` file and put the following code into it:

```
if (untangleGame === undefined) {
  var untangleGame = {};
}

untangleGame.createRandomCircles = function(width, height) {
  // randomly draw 5 circles
  var circlesCount = 5;
  var circleRadius = 10;
  for (var i=0;i<circlesCount;i++) {
    var x = Math.random()*width;
    var y = Math.random()*height;
    untangleGame.drawCircle(x, y, circleRadius);
  }
};
```

3. Then open the `untangle.js` file. Replace the original code in the JavaScript file with the following code:

```
if (untangleGame === undefined) {
  var untangleGame = {};
}

// Entry point
$(document).ready(function(){
  var canvas = document.getElementById("game");
  untangleGame.ctx = canvas.getContext("2d");

  var width = canvas.width;
  var height = canvas.height;

  untangleGame.createRandomCircles(width, height);

});
```

4. Open the HTML file in the web browser to see the result:

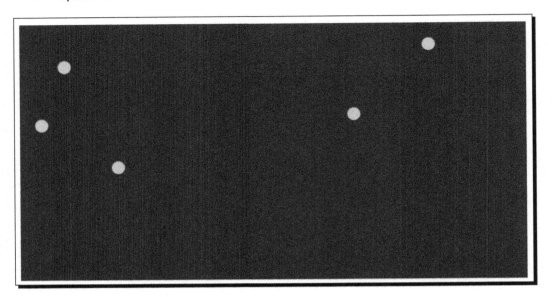

What just happened?

The code of drawing circles is executed after the page is loaded and ready. We used a loop to draw several circles in random places in the Canvas.

Dividing code into files

We are putting the code into different files. Currently, there are the `untangle.js`, `untangle.drawing.js`, and `untangle.data.js` files. The `untangle.js` is the entry point of the game. Then we put logic that is related to the context drawing into `untangle.drawing.js` and logic that's related to data manipulation into the `untangle.data.js` file.

We use the `untangleGame` object as the global object that's being accessed across all the files. At the beginning of each JavaScript file, we have the following code to create this object if it does not exist:

```
if (untangleGame === undefined) {
  var untangleGame = {};
}
```

Generating random numbers in JavaScript

In game development, we often use `random` functions. We may want to randomly summon a monster for the player to fight, we may want to randomly drop a reward when the player makes progress, and we may want a random number to be the result of rolling a dice. In this code, we place the circles randomly in the Canvas.

To generate a random number in JavaScript, we use the `Math.random()` function. There is no argument in the `random` function. It always returns a floating number between 0 and 1. The number is equal or bigger than 0 and smaller than 1. There are two common ways to use the `random` function. One way is to generate random numbers within a given range. The other way is generating a true or false value.

Usage	Code	Discussion
Getting a random integer between A and B	`Math.floor(Math.random()*B)+A`	`Math.floor()` function cuts the decimal point of the given number.
		Take `Math.floor(Math.random()*10)+5` as an example.
		`Math.random()` returns a decimal number between 0 to 0.9999....
		`Math.random()*10` is a decimal number between 0 to 9.9999....
		`Math.floor(Math.random()*10)` is an integer between 0 to 9.
		Finally, `Math.floor(Math.random()*10) + 5` is an integer between 5 to 14.
Getting a random Boolean	`(Math.random() > 0.495)`	`(Math.random() > 0.495)` means 50 percent `false` and 50 percent `true`.
		We can further adjust the true/false ratio. `(Math.random() > 0.7)` means almost 70 percent `false` and 30 percent `true`.

Saving the circle position

When we are developing a DOM-based game, such as the games we built in previous chapters, we often put the game objects into DIV elements and accessed them later in code logic. It is a different story in the Canvas-based game development.

In order to access our game objects after they are drawn in the Canvas, we need to remember their states ourselves. Let's say now we want to know how many circles are drawn and where they are, and we will need an array to store their position.

Time for action – saving the circle position

1. Open the `untangle.data.js` file in the text editor.

2. Add the following `circle` object definition code in the JavaScript file:

    ```
    untangleGame.Circle = function(x,y,radius){
       this.x = x;
       this.y = y;
       this.radius = radius;
    }
    ```

3. Now we need an array to store the circles' positions. Add a new array to the `untangleGame` object:

    ```
    untangleGame.circles = [];
    ```

4. While drawing every circle in the Canvas, we save the position of the circle in the `circles` array. Add the following line before calling the `drawCircle` function, inside the `createRandomCircles` function:

    ```
    untangleGame.circles.push(new untangleGame.
    Circle(x,y,circleRadius));
    ```

5. After the steps, we should have the following code in the `untangle.data.js` file:

    ```
    if (untangleGame === undefined) {
      var untangleGame = {};
    }

    untangleGame.circles = [];

    untangleGame.Circle = function(x,y,radius){
       this.x = x;
       this.y = y;
       this.radius = radius;
    };

    untangleGame.createRandomCircles = function(width, height) {
       // randomly draw 5 circles
    ```

```
var circlesCount = 5;
var circleRadius = 10;
for (var i=0;i<circlesCount;i++) {
  var x = Math.random()*width;
  var y = Math.random()*height;
  untangleGame.circles.push(new
    untangleGame.Circle(x,y,circleRadius));
  untangleGame.drawCircle(x, y, circleRadius);
}
};
```

6. Now we can test the code in the web browser. There is no visual difference between this code and the last example when drawing random circles in the Canvas. This is because we are saving the circles but have not changed any code that affects the appearance. We just make sure it looks the same and there are no new errors.

What just happened?

We saved the position and radius of each circle. This is because Canvas drawing is an immediate mode. We cannot directly access the object drawn in the Canvas because there is no such information. All lines and shapes are drawn on the Canvas as pixels and we cannot access the lines or shapes as individual objects. Imagine that we are drawing on a real canvas. We cannot just move a house in an oil painting, and in the same way we cannot directly manipulate any drawn items in the `canvas` element.

Defining a basic class definition in JavaScript

We can use **object-oriented programming** in JavaScript. We can define some object structures for our use. The `Circle` object provides a data structure for us to easily store a collection of *x* and *y* positions and the radii.

After defining the `Circle` object, we can create a new `Circle` instance with an *x*, *y*, and radius value using the following code:

```
var circle1 = new Circle(100, 200, 10);
```

 For more detailed usage on object-oriented programming in JavaScript, please check out the Mozilla Developer Center at the following link:
https://developer.mozilla.org/en/Introduction_to_Object-Oriented_JavaScript

Have a go hero

We have drawn several circles randomly on the Canvas. They are in the same style and of the same size. How about we randomly draw the size of the circles? And fill the circles with different colors? Try modifying the code and then play with the drawing API.

Drawing lines in the Canvas

Now we have several circles here, so how about connecting them with lines? Let's draw a straight line between each circle.

Time for action – drawing straight lines between each circle

1. Open the `index.html` file we just used in the circle-drawing example.

2. Change the wording in h1 from **drawing circles in Canvas** to **drawing lines in Canvas**.

3. Open the `untangle.data.js` JavaScript file.

4. We define a `Line` class to store the information that we need for each line:

```
untangleGame.Line = function(startPoint, endPoint, thickness) {
   this.startPoint = startPoint;
   this.endPoint = endPoint;
   this.thickness = thickness;
}
```

5. Save the file and switch to the `untangle.drawing.js` file.

6. We need two more variables. Add the following lines into the JavaScript file:

```
untangleGame.thinLineThickness = 1;
untangleGame.lines = [];
```

7. We add the following `drawLine` function into our code, after the existing `drawCircle` function in the `untangle.drawing.js` file.

```
untangleGame.drawLine = function(ctx, x1, y1, x2, y2, thickness) {
   ctx.beginPath();
   ctx.moveTo(x1,y1);
   ctx.lineTo(x2,y2);
   ctx.lineWidth = thickness;
   ctx.strokeStyle = "#cfc";
   ctx.stroke();
}
```

8. Then we define a new function that iterates the circle list and draws a line between each pair of circles. Append the following code in the JavaScript file:

```
untangleGame.connectCircles = function() {
  // connect the circles to each other with lines
  untangleGame.lines.length = 0;
  for (var i=0;i< untangleGame.circles.length;i++) {
    var startPoint = untangleGame.circles[i];
    for(var j=0;j<i;j++) {
      var endPoint = untangleGame.circles[j];
      untangleGame.drawLine(startPoint.x, startPoint.y,
        endPoint.x,
        endPoint.y, 1);
      untangleGame.lines.push(new untangleGame.Line(startPoint,
        endPoint,
        untangleGame.thinLineThickness));
    }
  }
};
```

9. Finally, we open the `untangle.js` file, and add the following code before the end of the jQuery document `ready` function, after we have called the `untangleGame.createRandomCircles` function:

```
untangleGame.connectCircles();
```

10. Test the code in the web browser. We should see there are lines connected to each randomly placed circle:

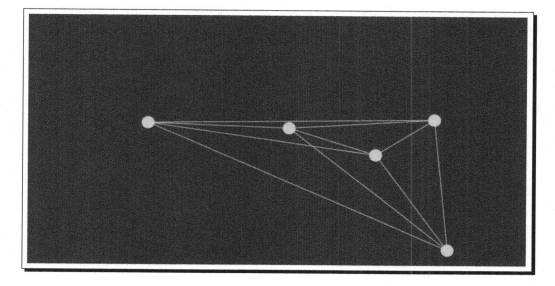

What just happened?

We have enhanced our code with lines connecting each generated circle. You may find a working example at the following URL:

`http://makzan.net/html5-games/untangle-wip-connect-lines/`

Similar to the way we saved the circle position, we have an array to save every line segment we draw. We declare a line class definition to store some essential information of a line segment. That is, we save the start and end point and the thickness of the line.

Introducing the line drawing API

There are some drawing APIs for us to draw and style the line stroke:

Line drawing functions	Discussion
moveTo	The moveTo function is like holding a pen in our hand and moving it on top of the paper without touching it with the pen.
lineTo	This function is like putting the pen down on the paper and drawing a straight line to the destination point.
lineWidth	The lineWidth function sets the thickness of the strokes we draw afterwards.
stroke	The stroke function is used to execute the drawing. We set up a collection of moveTo, lineTo, or styling functions and finally call the stroke function to execute it on the Canvas.

We usually draw lines by using the moveTo and lineTo pairs. Just like in the real world, we move our pen on top of the paper to the starting point of a line and put down the pen to draw a line. Then, keep on drawing another line or move to the other position before drawing. This is exactly the flow in which we draw lines on the Canvas.

 We just demonstrated how to draw a simple line. We can set different line styles to lines in the Canvas. For more details on line styling, please read the styling guide in W3C at `http://www.w3.org/TR/2dcontext/#line-styles` and the Mozilla Developer Center at `https://developer.mozilla.org/en-US/docs/Web/API/Canvas_API/Tutorial/Applying_styles_and_colors`.

Using mouse events to interact with objects drawn in the Canvas

So far, we have shown that we can draw shapes in the Canvas dynamically based on our logic. There is one part missing in the game development, that is, the input.

Now, imagine that we can drag the circles around on the Canvas, and the connected lines will follow the circles. In this section, we will add mouse events to the canvas to make our circles **draggable**.

Time for action – dragging the circles in the Canvas

1. Let's continue with our previous code. Open the `html5games.untangle.js` file.

2. We need a function to clear all the drawings in the Canvas. Add the following function to the end of the `untangle.drawing.js` file:

```
untangleGame.clear = function() {
  var ctx = untangleGame.ctx;
  ctx.clearRect(0,0,ctx.canvas.width,ctx.canvas.height);
};
```

3. We also need two more functions that draw all known circles and lines. Append the following code to the `untangle.drawing.js` file:

```
untangleGame.drawAllLines = function(){
  // draw all remembered lines
  for(var i=0;i<untangleGame.lines.length;i++) {
    var line = untangleGame.lines[i];
    var startPoint = line.startPoint;
    var endPoint = line.endPoint;
    var thickness = line.thickness;
    untangleGame.drawLine(startPoint.x, startPoint.y,
      endPoint.x,
    endPoint.y, thickness);
  }
};

untangleGame.drawAllCircles = function() {
  // draw all remembered circles
  for(var i=0;i<untangleGame.circles.length;i++) {
    var circle = untangleGame.circles[i];
    untangleGame.drawCircle(circle.x, circle.y, circle.radius);
  }
};
```

4. We are done with the `untangle.drawing.js` file. Let's switch to the `untangle.js` file. Inside the jQuery document-ready function, before the ending of the function, we add the following code, which creates a game loop to keep drawing the circles and lines:

```
// set up an interval to loop the game loop
setInterval(gameloop, 30);

function gameloop() {
  // clear the Canvas before re-drawing.
  untangleGame.clear();
  untangleGame.drawAllLines();
  untangleGame.drawAllCircles();
}
```

5. Before moving on to the input handling code implementation, let's add the following code to the jQuery document ready function in the `untangle.js` file, which calls the `handleInput` function that we will define:

```
untangleGame.handleInput();
```

6. It's time to implement our input handling logic. Switch to the `untangle.input.js` file and add the following code to the file:

```
if (untangleGame === undefined) {
  var untangleGame = {};
}

untangleGame.handleInput = function(){
  // Add Mouse Event Listener to canvas
  // we find if the mouse down position is on any circle
  // and set that circle as target dragging circle.
  $("#game").bind("mousedown", function(e) {
    var canvasPosition = $(this).offset();
    var mouseX = e.pageX - canvasPosition.left;
    var mouseY = e.pageY - canvasPosition.top;

    for(var i=0;i<untangleGame.circles.length;i++) {
      var circleX = untangleGame.circles[i].x;
      var circleY = untangleGame.circles[i].y;
      var radius = untangleGame.circles[i].radius;
      if (Math.pow(mouseX-circleX,2) + Math.pow(
        mouseY-circleY,2) < Math.pow(radius,2)) {
        untangleGame.targetCircleIndex = i;
        break;
      }
    }
  }
```

```
  });

  // we move the target dragging circle
  // when the mouse is moving
  $("#game").bind("mousemove", function(e) {
    if (untangleGame.targetCircleIndex !== undefined) {
      var canvasPosition = $(this).offset();
      var mouseX = e.pageX - canvasPosition.left;
      var mouseY = e.pageY - canvasPosition.top;
      var circle = untangleGame.circles[
        untangleGame.targetCircleIndex];
      circle.x = mouseX;
      circle.y = mouseY;
    }
    untangleGame.connectCircles();
  });

  // We clear the dragging circle data when mouse is up
  $("#game").bind("mouseup", function(e) {
    untangleGame.targetCircleIndex = undefined;
  });
};
```

7. Open `index.html` in a web browser. There should be five circles with lines connecting them. Try dragging the circles. The dragged circle will follow the mouse cursor and the connected lines will follow too.

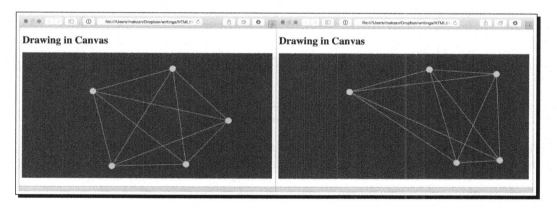

What just happened?

We have set up three mouse event listeners. They are the mouse down, move, and up events. We also created the game loop, which updates the Canvas drawing based on the new position of the circles. You can view the example's current progress at: http://makzan. net/html5-games/untangle-wip-dragging-basic/.

Detecting mouse events in circles in the Canvas

After discussing the difference between DOM-based development and Canvas-based development, we cannot directly listen to the mouse events of any shapes drawn in the Canvas. There is no such thing. We cannot monitor the event in any shapes drawn in the Canvas. We can only get the mouse event of the canvas element and calculate the relative position of the Canvas. Then we change the states of the game objects according to the mouse's position and finally redraw it on the Canvas.

How do we know we are clicking on a circle? We can use the **point-in-circle** formula. This is to check the distance between the center point of the circle and the mouse position. The mouse clicks on the circle when the distance is less than the circle's radius. We use this formula to get the distance between two points: *Distance = (x2-x1)2 + (y2-y1)2.*

The following graph shows that when the distance between the center point and the mouse cursor is smaller than the radius, the cursor is in the circle:

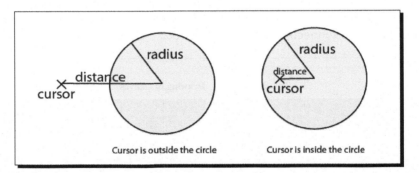

Cursor is outside the circle   Cursor is inside the circle

The following code we used explains how we can apply distance checking to know whether the mouse cursor is inside the circle in the mouse down event handler:

```
if (Math.pow(mouseX-circleX,2) + Math.pow(mouseY-circleY,2) < Math.
pow(radius,2)) {
  untangleGame.targetCircleIndex = i;
  break;
}
```

Please note that Math.pow is an expensive function that may hurt performance in some scenarios. If performance is a concern, we may use the bounding box collision checking, which we covered in *Chapter 2, Getting Started with DOM-based Game Development*.

When we know that the mouse cursor is pressing the circle in the Canvas, we mark it as the targeted circle to be dragged on the mouse move event. During the mouse move event handler, we update the target dragged circle's position to the latest cursor position. When the mouse is up, we clear the target circle's reference.

Pop quiz

Q1. Can we directly access an already drawn shape in the Canvas?

1. Yes
2. No

Q2. Which method can we use to check whether a point is inside a circle?

1. The coordinate of the point is smaller than the coordinate of the center of the circle.
2. The distance between the point and the center of the circle is smaller than the circle's radius.
3. The *x* coordinate of the point is smaller than the circle's radius.
4. The distance between the point and the center of the circle is bigger than the circle's radius.

Game loop

In *Chapter 2, Getting Started with DOM-based Game Development*, we discussed the **game loop** approach. In the Ping Pong game, the game loop manipulates the keyboard input and updates the position of the DOM-based game objects.

Here, the game loop is used to redraw the Canvas to present the later game states. If we do not redraw the Canvas after changing the states, say the position of the circles, we will not see it.

Clearing the Canvas

When we drag the circle, we redraw the Canvas. The problem is the already drawn shapes on the Canvas won't disappear automatically. We will keep adding new paths to the Canvas and finally mess up everything in the Canvas. The following screenshot is what will happen if we keep dragging the circles without clearing the Canvas on every redraw:

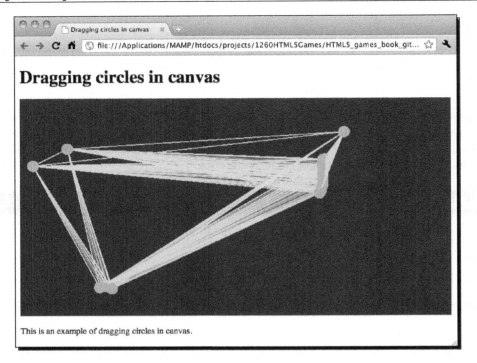

This is an example of dragging circles in canvas.

Since we have saved all game statuses in JavaScript, we can safely clear the entire Canvas and draw the updated lines and circles with the latest game status. To clear the Canvas, we use the `clearRect` function provided by Canvas drawing API. The `clearRect` function clears a rectangle area by providing a rectangle clipping region. It accepts the following arguments as the clipping region:

```
context.clearRect(x, y, width, height)
```

Argument	Definition
x	The top left point of the rectangular clipping region, on the *x* axis.
y	The top left point of the rectangular clipping region, on the *y* axis.
width	The width of the rectangular region.
height	The height of the rectangular region.

The `x` and `y` values set the top left position of the region to be cleared. The `width` and `height` values define how much area is to be cleared. To clear the entire Canvas, we can provide (0,0) as the top left position and the width and height of the Canvas to the `clearRect` function. The following code clears all things drawn on the entire Canvas:

```
ctx.clearRect(0, 0, ctx.canvas.width, ctx.canvas.height);
```

Pop quiz

Q1. Can we clear a portion of the Canvas by using the clearRect function?

1. Yes

2. No

Q2. Does the following code clear things on the drawn Canvas?

```
ctx.clearRect(0, 0, ctx.canvas.width, 0);
```

1. Yes

2. No

Detecting line intersection in the Canvas

We have draggable circles and connected lines in the Canvas. Some lines intersect others and some do not. Now imagine we want to distinguish the intersected lines. We need some mathematics formula to check them and then thicken those intersected lines.

Time for action – distinguishing the intersected lines

Let's increase the thickness of those intersected lines so we can distinguish them in the Canvas

1. Open the `untangle.drawing.js` file in the text editor.

2. We have the `thinLineThickness` variable as the default line thickness. We add the following code to define a thickness for bold lines:

   ```
   untangleGame.boldLineThickness = 5;
   ```

3. Open the `untangle.data.js` file. We create a function to check whether the given two lines intersect. Add the following functions to the end of the JavaScript file:

   ```
   untangleGame.isIntersect = function(line1, line2) {
       // convert line1 to general form of line: Ax+By = C
       var a1 = line1.endPoint.y - line1.startPoint.y;
       var b1 = line1. startPoint.x - line1.endPoint.x;
       var c1 = a1 * line1.startPoint.x + b1 * line1.startPoint.y;

       // convert line2 to general form of line: Ax+By = C
       var a2 = line2.endPoint.y - line2.startPoint.y;
       var b2 = line2. startPoint.x - line2.endPoint.x;
   ```

```
  var c2 = a2 * line2.startPoint.x + b2 * line2.startPoint.y;

  // calculate the intersection point
  var d = a1*b2 - a2*b1;

  // parallel when d is 0
  if (d === 0) {
    return false;
  }

  // solve the interception point at (x, y)
  var x = (b2*c1 - b1*c2) / d;
  var y = (a1*c2 - a2*c1) / d;

  // check if the interception point is on both line segments
  if ((isInBetween(line1.startPoint.x, x, line1.endPoint.x) ||
isInBetween(line1.startPoint.y, y, line1.endPoint.y)) &&
    (isInBetween(line2.startPoint.x, x, line2.endPoint.x) ||
isInBetween(line2.startPoint.y, y, line2.endPoint.y))) {
      return true;
    }

    // by default the given lines is not intersected.
    return false;
};

// return true if b is between a and c,
// we exclude the result when a==b or b==c
untangleGame.isInBetween = function(a, b, c) {
  // return false if b is almost equal to a or c.
  // this is to eliminate some floating point when
  // two value is equal to each other
  // but different with 0.00000...0001
  if (Math.abs(a-b) < 0.000001 || Math.abs(b-c) < 0.000001) {
    return false;
  }

  // true when b is in between a and c
  return (a < b && b < c) || (c < b && b < a);
};
```

4. Let's continue on with the `untangle.data.js` file. We define the following function to check whether our lines intersect and mark that line in bold. Append the following new function to the end of the file:

```
untangle.updateLineIntersection = function() {
  // checking lines intersection and bold those lines.
  for (var i=0;i<untangleGame.lines.length;i++) {
    for(var j=0;j<i;j++) {
      var line1 = untangleGame.lines[i];
      var line2 = untangleGame.lines[j];

      // we check if two lines are intersected,
      // and bold the line if they are.
      if (isIntersect(line1, line2)) {
        line1.thickness = untangleGame.boldLineThickness;
        line2.thickness = untangleGame.boldLineThickness;
      }
    }
  }
}
```

5. Finally, we update the line intersection by adding the following function call in two places. Open the `untangle.js` file. Add the following line of code inside the jQuery document-ready function, probably before the game-loop function:

```
untangleGame.updateLineIntersection();
```

6. Then, open the `untangle.input.js` file and add the same code inside the mouse move event handler.

7. It is time to test the intersection in the web browser. When viewing the circles and lines in Canvas, the lines with an intersection should be thicker than those without an intersection. Try dragging the circles to change the intersection relationship and the lines will become thin or thick.

What just happened?

We have just added some code checking for line intersections to our existing circle-dragging example. The line intersection code involves some mathematical formula to get the **intersection point** of two lines and checks whether the point is inside the line segment we provide. You can view the example's current progress at: `http://makzan.net/html5-games/untangle-wip-intersected-lines/`.

Let's look at the mathematics element and see how it works.

Determining whether two line segments intersect

According to the intersection equation we learned from geometry, with two given lines in a general form, we can get the intersection point.

What is a **general form**? In our code, we have the starting point and ending point of a line in *x* and *y* coordinates. This is a **line segment** because it is just a segment part of the line in mathematics. A general form of a line is represented by $Ax + By = C$.

The following graph explains the line segment on a line in a general form:

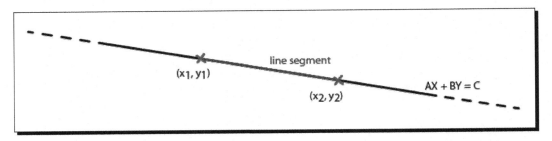

We can transform the line segment with point 1 in **x1, y1** and point 2 in **x2, y2** into general form by the following equation:

```
A = y2-y1
B = x1-x2
C = A * x1 + B * y2
```

Now we have a line equation $AX+BY = C$ where A, B, C are known and X and Y are unknown.

We are checking two lines intersecting. We can transform both lines into a general form and get two line equations:

```
Line 1: A1X+B1Y = C1
Line 2: A2X+B2Y = C2
```

By putting the two general form equations together, X and Y are two variables that are unknown. We can then solve these two equations and get the intersection point of *x* and *y*.

If A1 * B2 - A2 * B1 is zero, then two lines are parallel and there is no intersection point. Otherwise we get the interception point by using the following equation:

```
X = (B2 * C1 - B1 * C2) / (A1 * B2 - A2 * B1)
Y = (A1 * C2 - A2 * C1) / (A1 * B2 - A2 * B1)
```

The intersection point of these general forms only provides that the two lines are not parallel to each other and will intersect each other at some point. It does not guarantee that the intersection point is on both line segments.

The following graphs show two possible results of the intersection point and the given line segments. The intersection point is not in between both line segments in the left graph; in this case, the two line segments are not intersecting with each other. In the right-hand side graph, the point is in between both line segments so these two line segments intersect with each other:

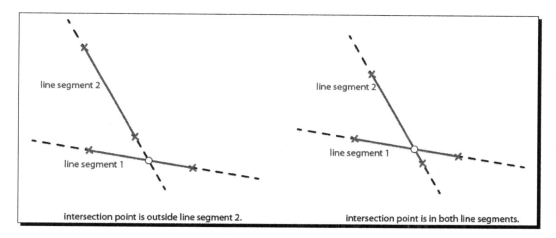

Therefore, we need another function named isInBetween to determine whether a provided value is in between the beginning and ending value. Then we use this function to check whether the intersection point from the equation is in between both line segments that we are checking.

After getting the result of the lines intersection, we draw the thick line to indicate those intersected lines.

Adding touch support for tablets

Drag-and-drop is a common gesture in touch devices in tablets and mobile devices. Currently, our game doesn't support these touch devices. We want to add touch support for our game in this section.

Time for action – adding the touch input support

Let's allow our tablet users to drag-n-drop our circles with the following steps:

1. By default, there is a selection highlighted in the `canvas` element in iOS devices. We want to get rid of this highlighted part to make the dragging interaction smooth. Add the following CSS rules to the `canvas` CSS. Please note that we use the `webkit` vendor prefix here because this rule is specific for `webkit` at the time of writing this book:

```
canvas {
  /* for iOS devices */
  -webkit-tap-highlight-color: transparent;
}
```

2. Open the `untangle.input.js file`. We bind the mouse events on the Canvas in the previous step. Now we add the support for touch events. We used `MouseEvent.pageX` and `pageY` to calculate the mouse position. With touch devices, there can be multiple touches. We modify our code to add the touch support:

```
$("#game").bind("mousedown touchstart", function(e) {
  // disable default drag to scroll behavior
  e.preventDefault();

  // touch or mouse position
  var touch = e.originalEvent.touches && e.originalEvent.
touches[0];
  var pageX = (touch||e).pageX;
  var pageY = (touch||e).pageY;

  var canvasPosition = $(this).offset();
  var mouseX = pageX - canvasPosition.left;
  var mouseY = pageY - canvasPosition.top;

  // existing code goes here.

}
```

3. We modify the `mousemove` event similarly. We bind both the `mousemove` and `touchmove` events and calculate the touch position:

```
$("#game").bind("mousemove touchmove", function(e) {
  // disable default drag to scroll behavior
  e.preventDefault();

  // touch or mouse position
  var touch = e.originalEvent.touches && e.originalEvent.
touches[0];
  var pageX = (touch||e).pageX;
  var pageY = (touch||e).pageY;

  var canvasPosition = $(this).offset();
  var mouseX = pageX - canvasPosition.left;
  var mouseY = pageY - canvasPosition.top;

  // existing code goes here.
}
```

4. For the original `mouseup` event handler, we add the `touchend` handling:

```
$("#game").bind("mouseup touchend", function(e) {
 // existing code goes here.
}
```

What just happened?

We just added touch support to our untangle game. You may find the code and example at: `http://makzan.net/html5-games/untangle-wip-dragging/`.

In the CSS, we disable the default tap highlight by setting the `-webkit-tap-highlight-color` to transparent. We need the vendor prefix `-webkit-` because this is a WebKit-only rule especially designed for their touch devices.

Handling touches

We get the `touch` event object by using the following code:

```
var touch = e.originalEvent.touches && e.originalEvent.touches[0];
```

The touches array holds all the current touches on the screen. Since we are handling the touch events in jQuery, we need to access the `originalEvent` to access the touches because these are browser native events, instead of a jQuery event.

We only care about one touch in this game, that's why we only check the `touches[0]` parameter. We also confirm that `originalEvent.touches` exists before using the array notation, otherwise, the browser throws errors on non-touch devices.

Then we access the `pageX` property of either the `touch` object or the mouse event object. If the `touch` object presents, JavaScript uses the `touch.pageX`. Otherwise, JavaScript uses the mouse event's `pageX` property:

```
var pageX = (touch||e).pageX;
```

Mouse move and Touch move

We reuse the same logic for our `mousedown`/`touchstart`, `mousemove`/`touchmove`, and `mouseup`/`touchend` event. Often `mousedown` and `touchstart` share very similar logic for dragging starts. The `mouseup` and `touchend` events also share similar logic for dragging ends. The `mousemove` and `touchmove` events, however, have a subtle difference. In desktop devices with mouse input, the `mousemove` event is always firing whenever the mouse moves, regardless of the pressing of mouse button. That was why we needed to use a variable `targetCircleIndex` to determine whether the button was pressed and then selected a certain circle when the mouse moves. The `touchmove` event, on the other hand, happens only when a finger is actually down on the screen and dragging. This difference may sometimes affect the different ways we handle the logic.

Summary

You learned a lot in this chapter about drawing shapes and creating interaction with the new HTML5 `canvas` element and the drawing API.

Specifically, you learned to draw circles and lines in the Canvas. We added mouse events and touch dragging interaction with the paths drawn in the Canvas. We determined line intersection with the help of mathematics formulas. We separated a complex code logic into different files to make the code maintainable. We divided the logic into data, drawing, and inputs.

Now that you've learned about basic drawing functions in the Canvas and the drawing API, you're ready to learn some advanced drawing techniques in Canvas. In the next chapter, we will create a puzzle solving game by continuing the code example. You will also learn more Canvas drawing techniques, such as drawing text, drawing images, and creating multiple drawing layers.

5
Building a Canvas Game's Masterclass

In the previous chapter, we explored some basic Canvas context drawing APIs and created a game named Untangle. In this chapter, we are going to enhance the game by using some other context drawing APIs.

In this chapter, you will learn how to do the following:

- ◆ Implement the Untangle game logic
- ◆ Fill text in the Canvas with a custom web font
- ◆ Draw images in the Canvas
- ◆ Animate a sprite sheet image
- ◆ Build multiple Canvas layers

The following screenshot is a preview of the final result that we are going to build through this chapter. It is a Canvas-based Untangle game with an animated game guideline and several subtle details:

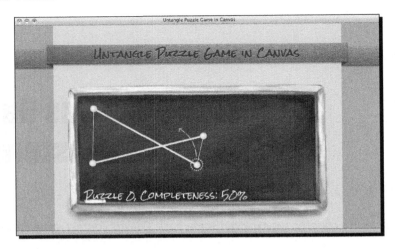

You can also try the final game example at: http://makzan.net/html5-games/untangle/.

So let's get on with it.

Making the Untangle puzzle game

Now that we have created an interactive Canvas, we can drag the circles, and the lines connecting the circles which are intersecting with other lines. How about we make it a game? There are some predefined circles and lines and our aim is to drag the circles so that there are no lines intersecting with others. This is called an **Untangle puzzle game**.

Time for action – making the Untangle puzzle game in Canvas

Let's add the game logic to our line intersection code:

1.   We need two more files for the game logic. Create two new files named untangle.game.js and untangle.levels.js file. Put them into the js folder.

2.   Open the index.html file in a text editor. Add the following code to include our newly created file. Put the code in the file before including the js/untangle.js file:

```
<script src="js/untangle.levels.js"></script>
<script src="js/untangle.game.js"></script>
```

3. Still in the `index.html` file, we add the following code after the `canvas` element. It displays the game level information:

```
<p>Puzzle <span id="level">0</span>, Completeness:
  <span id="progress">0</span>%</p>
```

4. Open the `untangle.levels.js` file. Put the following level data definition code into the file. It is a predefined level data for the players to play. It is a collection of data that defines where the circles are placed and how they connect to each other initially:

```
if (untangleGame === undefined) {
  var untangleGame = {};
}
untangleGame.levels = [
  {
    circles : [
          {x : 400, y : 156},
          {x : 381, y : 241},
          {x : 84, y : 233},
          {x : 88, y : 73}],
    relationship : [
          {connectedPoints : [1,2]},
          {connectedPoints : [0,3]},
          {connectedPoints : [0,3]},
          {connectedPoints : [1,2]}
    ]
  },
  {
    circles : [
          {x : 401, y : 73},
          {x : 400, y : 240},
          {x : 88, y : 241},
          {x : 84, y : 72}],
    relationship : [
          {connectedPoints : [1,2,3]},
          {connectedPoints : [0,2,3]},
          {connectedPoints : [0,1,3]},
          {connectedPoints : [0,1,2]}
    ]
  },
  {
    circles : [
          {x : 192, y : 155},
          {x : 353, y : 109},
```

```
            {x : 493, y : 156},
            {x : 490, y : 236},
            {x : 348, y : 276},
            {x : 195, y : 228}],
    relationship : [
            {connectedPoints : [2,3,4]},
            {connectedPoints : [3,5]},
            {connectedPoints : [0,4,5]},
            {connectedPoints : [0,1,5]},
            {connectedPoints : [0,2]},
            {connectedPoints : [1,2,3]}
    ]
  }
];
```

5. Open the `untangle.game.js` file in text editor. We will put game logic into this file.

6. This is a new file, so we define the `untangleGame` object at the beginning of the file:

```
if (untangleGame === undefined) {
  var untangleGame = {};
}
```

7. Continue in the `untangle.game.js` file. Add the following variables to the file. They store the current level and level progress of the game:

```
untangleGame.currentLevel = 0;
untangleGame.levelProgress = 0;
```

8. When starting on each level, we need to set up the initial level data. To help make the code more readable, we create a function. Append the following code to the `untangle.game.js` JavaScript file:

```
untangleGame.setupCurrentLevel = function() {
  untangleGame.circles = [];
  var level = untangleGame.levels[untangleGame.currentLevel];
  for (var i=0; i<level.circles.length; i++) {
    untangleGame.circles.push(new untangleGame.
      Circle(level.circles[i].x, level.circles[i].y, 10));
  }

  untangleGame.levelProgress = 0;

  untangleGame.connectCircles();
  untangleGame.updateLineIntersection();
```

```
    untangleGame.checkLevelCompleteness();
    untangleGame.updateLevelProgress();
}
```

9. This is a game with several levels. We need to check whether the player solves the puzzle in the current level and jumps to the next puzzle. Add the following function to the end of the untangle.game.js file:

```
untangleGame.checkLevelCompleteness = function () {
  if (untangleGame.levelProgress === 100) {
    if (untangleGame.currentLevel+1 < untangleGame.
      levels.length) {
      untangleGame.currentLevel+=1;
    }
    untangleGame.setupCurrentLevel();
  }
}
```

10. We need another function to update the game progress. Add the following function to the end of untangle.game.js file:

```
untangleGame.updateLevelProgress = function() {
  // check the untangle progress of the level
  var progress = 0;
  for (var i=0; i<untangleGame.lines.length; i++) {
    if (untangleGame.lines[i].thickness === untangleGame.
      thinLineThickness) {

      progress+=1;
    }
  }
  var progressPercentage = Math.floor(
    progress/untangleGame.lines.length*100);

  untangleGame.levelProgress = progressPercentage;
  $("#progress").text(progressPercentage);

  // display the current level
  $("#level").text(untangleGame.currentLevel);
}
```

11. Open the untangle.input.js file. We add the following code to the mouse move event handler, which updates the level progress:

```
untangleGame.updateLevelProgress();
```

12. We add the following code to the mouse up event handler to check whether the player completes the level:

```
untangleGame.checkLevelCompleteness();
```

13. Now open the `untangle.js` file in an editor. Inside the jQuery document's `ready` function, we had code to set up the circles and lines. They are now replaced by our level setup code. Delete the call to `untangleGame.createRandomCircles` and `untangleGame.connectCircles` functions. Replace them with the following code:

```
untangleGame.setupCurrentLevel();
```

14. Finally, open the `untangle.drawing.js` file in the code editor. We replace the `connectCircles` function to connect circles based on the level data:

```
untangleGame.connectCircles = function() {
  // set up all lines based on the circles relationship
  var level = untangleGame.levels[untangleGame.currentLevel];
  untangleGame.lines.length = 0;
  for (var i in level.relationship) {
    var connectedPoints = level.relationship[i].connectedPoints;
    var startPoint = untangleGame.circles[i];
    for (var j in connectedPoints) {
      var endPoint = untangleGame.circles[connectedPoints[j]];
      untangleGame.lines.push(new untangleGame.Line(startPoint,
        endPoint, untangleGame.thinLineThickness));
    }
  }
}
```

15. Save all files and test the game in the browser. We can drag the circles and the line thickness will indicate whether it is intersected with other lines. During the mouse dragging, the level completeness percentage should change when more or less line intersections are detected. If we solve the puzzle, that is when no lines are intersected, the game will jump to the next level. When the game reaches the last level, it will keep showing the last level again. This is because we have not yet added the game over screen.

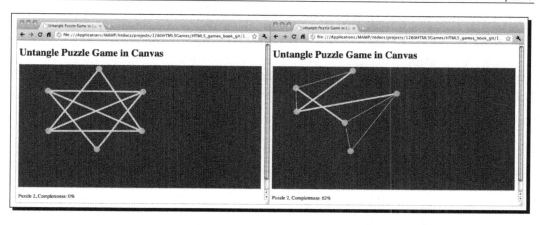

What just happened?

We have added the game logic to our Canvas so that we can play our circle dragging code that has been created throughout this chapter. This section changes quite a lot of code. You may find the working example with uncompressed source code at: `http://makzan.net/html5-games/untangle-wip-gameplay/`.

Let's recall the variables we added to the `untangleGame` object. The following table lists the description and usage of these:

Variable	Description
`circleRadius`	The radius setting of all drawing circles.
`thinLineThickness`	The line thickness when drawing thin lines.
`boldLineThickness`	The line thickness when drawing bold lines.
`circles`	An array to store all drawn circles in the Canvas.
`lines`	An array to store all drawn lines in the Canvas.
`targetCircle`	Keeps track of the circle that we are dragging.
`levels`	Stores all initial data of each level in the JSON format.
`currentLevel`	A number to help you remember the current level.
`levelProgress`	The percentage of non-intersected lines over all the lines.

Defining the leveling data

In each level, we have an initial position of the circles for the Untangle puzzle. The level data is designed as an array of objects. Each object contains every level's data. Inside each level's data, there are three properties: level number, circles, and lines connecting the circles. The following table shows the properties in each level's data:

Level property	Definition	Discussion
`circles`	An array of circles' positions in the level.	This defines how the circles are placed initially when the level is set up.
`relationships`	An array of relationships defining which circles connect to each other.	There are some lines connecting the circles in each level. We design the line connections so that there is a solution in each level. The array index of each relationship indicates the target circle. The value of the line relationship defines which circle connects to the target circle. For example, the following code means the target circle is connected to both circle 1 and circle 2: `{"connectedPoints" : [1,2]}`

Determining level-up

The level is complete when there are no lines intersecting with each other. We loop through each line and see how many lines are thin. Thin lines mean they are not intersected with others. We can use the thin lines for all line ratios to get the percentage of the level of completeness:

```
var progress = 0;
for (var i in untangleGame.lines) {
  if (untangleGame.lines[i].thickness === untangleGame.
    thinLineThickness) {
    progress+=1;
  }
}
var progressPercentage = Math.floor(progress/
  untangleGame.lines.length * 100);
```

We can then simply determine that the level has been completed when the progress is 100 percent.

Displaying the current level and completeness progress

We have displayed a sentence below the Canvas game describing the current level status and progress. It is used to display the game status to the players so they know that they are making progress in the game:

```
<p>Puzzle <span id="level">0</span>, Completeness:
  <span id="progress">0</span>%</p>
```

We use the jQuery `text` function that we discussed in *Chapter 2, Getting Started with DOM-based Game Development*, to update the completeness progress:

```
$("#progress").text(progressPercentage);
```

Have a go hero

We have only defined three levels in the example Untangle puzzle game so far. But it is not fun enough to play with just three levels. How about adding more levels to the game? If you cannot come up with a level, try searching for similar untangle games on the Internet and get some inspiration on the levels.

Drawing text in the Canvas

Imagine that now we want to show the progress level directly inside the Canvas. Canvas provides us with methods to draw text inside the Canvas.

Time for action – displaying the progress level text inside the canvas element

1. We will continue using our Untangle game. Open the `untangle.drawing.js` JavaScript file in text editor. Add the following code after the Canvas drawing code in the `gameloop` function, which draws the current level and progress text inside the Canvas:

```
untangleGame.drawLevelProgress = function() {
  var ctx = untangleGame.ctx;
  ctx.font = "26px Arial";
  ctx.fillStyle = "WHITE";
  ctx.textAlign = "left";
  ctx.textBaseline = "bottom";
  ctx.fillText("Puzzle "+untangleGame.currentLevel+",
    Completeness: " + untangleGame.levelProgress + "%",
      60, ctx.canvas.height-60);
}
```

2. Open the `untangle.js` file. We put the following code inside the `gameloop` function:

    ```
    untangleGame.drawLevelProgress();
    ```

3. Save the file and preview the `index.html` in a web browser. We will see that the text is now drawn inside the Canvas.

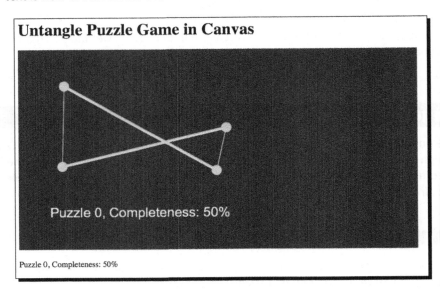

What just happened?

We have just drawn the title and the level progress text in our Canvas-based game. We draw text in the Canvas by using the `fillText` function. The following table shows how we use the function:

```
fillText(string, x, y);
```

Argument	Definition
String	The text that we are going to draw
X	The *x* coordinate that the text draws
Y	The *y* coordinate that the text draws

This is the basic setting to draw some text. There are several more drawing context properties to set up the text drawing:

Context properties	Definition	Discussion
`context.font`	The font style of the text	This shares the same syntax we used to declare the font style in CSS. For example, the following code sets the font style to 20 pixels bold with the Arial typeface: `ctx.font = "bold 20px Arial";`
`context.textAlign`	The text alignment	The **alignment** defines how the text is aligned. It can be one of the following values: ◆ `start` ◆ `end` ◆ `left` ◆ `right` ◆ `center` For instance, if we are going to place some text on the right edge of the Canvas, using the `left` alignment means we need to calculate the text's width in order to know the x coordinate of the text. When using right alignment in this case, all we need to do is set the x position directly to the Canvas width. The text will then automatically be placed on the right edge of the Canvas.
`context.textBaseline`	The text baseline	The following lists the common value of a `textBaseline` property: ◆ `top` ◆ `middle` ◆ `bottom` ◆ `alphabet` Similar to text alignment, the `bottom` baseline is useful when we want to place our text at the bottom of the Canvas. The y position of the `fillText` function is based on the bottom baseline of the text instead of the top. The `alphabet` baseline aligns the y position based on the lowercase alphabet. The following screenshot shows our text drawing with the **alphabet** baseline.

Please be aware that the text drawing in Canvas is treated as bitmap image data. This means visitors cannot select the text; search engines cannot index the text; we cannot search the text. For this reason, we should think carefully about whether we want to draw the text inside the Canvas or just place it directly in the DOM. Alternatively, we should change the fallback text inside the `canvas` element to reflect the drawing text.

Pop quiz – drawing text in the Canvas

Q1. If we are going to draw some text close to the bottom-right corner of the Canvas, which alignment and baseline setting is better?

1. Left alignment, bottom baseline.
2. Center alignment, alphabet baseline.
3. Right alignment, bottom baseline.
4. Center alignment, middle baseline.

Q2. We are going to make a realistic book with a flipping effect with the latest open web standard. Which of the following settings is better?

1. Draw the realistic book in Canvas, including all the text and the flipping effect.
2. Put all text and content in the DOM and draw the realistic page-flipping effect in Canvas.

Using embedded web font inside the Canvas

We used a custom font in our memory, matching the game in the previous chapter. Custom font embedding also works in the Canvas. Let's conduct an experiment on drawing a custom font in our Untangle game in the Canvas.

Time for action – embedding a Google web font into the canvas element

Let's draw the Canvas texts with a handwriting style font:

1. First, go to the Google font directory and choose a handwriting style font. I used the font **Rock Salt** and you can get it from the following URL:

   `http://www.google.com/fonts/specimen/Rock+Salt`.

2. The Google font directory provides a CSS link code that we can add to our game in order to embed the font. Add the following CSS link to the head of `index.html`:

```
<link href='http://fonts.googleapis.com/css?family=Rock+Salt'
  rel='stylesheet' type='text/css'>
```

3. The next thing is to use the font. We open the `untangle.drawing.js` JavaScript file and modify the context `font` property in the `drawLevelProgress` function to the following:

```
ctx.font = "26px 'Rock Salt'";
```

4. It is time to open our game in the web browser to test the result. The text drawn in the Canvas is now using the font we chose in the Google font directory.

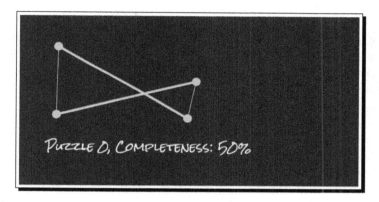

What just happened?

We just chose a web font and embedded it into the Canvas when drawing text. This shows that we can style the font family of the filled text in the Canvas just like other DOM elements.

Sometimes the width of the text varies in different font families although they have the same word count. In this case, we can use the `measureText` function to get the width of the text we draw. The Mozilla Developer Network explains how we can use the function at: `https://developer.mozilla.org/en/Drawing_text_using_a_canvas#measureText()`.

Drawing images in the Canvas

We have drawn some text inside the Canvas. What about drawing an image? Yes. Drawing images and image manipulation is a big feature of the Canvas.

Time for action – adding graphics to the game

We are going to draw a blackboard background to the game:

1. Download the graphics files from the code example bundle or the following URL: `http://mak.la/book-assets`. The graphics files include all the graphics that we need in this chapter.

2. Put the newly downloaded graphics files into a folder named `images`.

3. Now it is time to really load the image. There is a `board.png` file in the graphics file we just downloaded. It is a blackboard graphic that we will draw in the Canvas as a background. Add the following code after the code we just added in the previous step:

```
untangleGame.loadImages = function() {
  // load the background image
  untangleGame.background = new Image();

  untangleGame.background.onerror = function() {
    console.log("Error loading the image.");
  }
  untangleGame.background.src = "images/board.png";
};
```

4. Since the image loading takes time, we also need to ensure it is loaded before drawing it:

```
untangleGame.drawBackground = function() {
  // draw the image background
  untangleGame.ctx.drawImage(untangleGame.background, 0, 0);
};
```

5. Open the `untangle.js` file, in the jQuery document `ready` function:

```
untangleGame.loadImages();
```

6. In the `gameloop` function in the `untangle.js` file, we draw the image in the Canvas after clearing the context and before drawing anything else:

```
untangleGame.drawBackground();
```

7. Next, we do not want a background color set to the Canvas because we have a PNG background with a transparent border. Open the `untangle.css` file and remove the background property in Canvas.

8. Now, save all files and open the `index.html` file in the web browser. The background should be there and the handwritten fonts should match our blackboard theme.

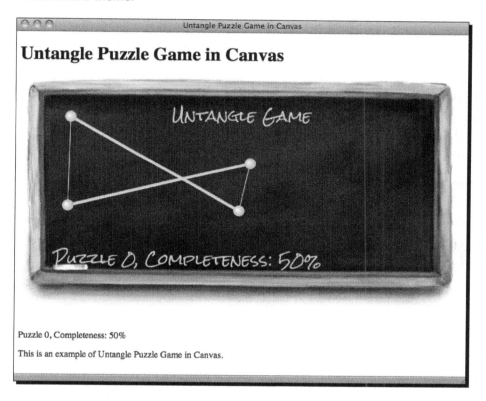

What just happened?

We just drew an image inside the `canvas` element. You can find the working example at the following URL:

`http://makzan.net/html5-games/untangle-wip-graphics1/`

There are two common ways to draw an image in the Canvas. We can either reference an existing `<img>` tag or load the image on the fly in JavaScript.

Here is how we reference the existing image tag in `canvas`, assuming that we have the following `img` tag in HTML:

```
<img id="board" src="img/board.png">
```

We can draw the image in the Canvas by using the following JavaScript code:

```
var img = document.getElementById('board');
context.drawImage(img, x, y);
```

Here is another code snippet to load the image without attaching the `<img>` tag into the DOM. If we load the image inside JavaScript, we need to make sure the image is loaded before drawing it in the Canvas. Therefore, we draw the image after the `onload` event of the image:

```
var board = new Image();
board.onload = function() {
   context.drawImage(board, x, y);
}
board.src = "images/board.png";
```

The order matters when setting the `onload` event handler and assigning the image `src`.

When we assign the `src` property to the image and if the image is cached by the browser, some browsers fire the `onload` event immediately. If we place the `onload` event handler after assigning the `src` property, we may miss it because it is fired before we set the event handler.

In our example, we used the latter approach. We create an `Image` object and loaded the background.

Another event that we should handle when loading the image is the `onerror` event. It is especially useful when we are accessing extra network data. We use the following code snippet to check the errors in our example:

```
untangleGame.background.onerror = function() {
   console.log("Error loading the image.");
}
```

Have a go hero

The error loading now only displays a message in the console. The console is normally not viewed by players. How about writing a message to the Canvas to tell players that the game failed to load the game's assets?

Using the drawImage function

There are three ways to draw an image in the Canvas using the `drawImage` function. We can draw the image without any modification on a given coordinate, we can also draw the image with a scaling factor on a given coordinate, or we can even crop the image and draw only the clipping region.

The `drawImage` function accepts several arguments:

◆ Every argument present in `drawImage(image, x, y);` is explained in the following table:

Argument	Definition	Discussion
image	The reference of the image that we are going to draw.	We either get the image reference by using an existing `img` element or creating a JavaScript `Image` object.
x	The position of x where the image will be placed in the Canvas coordinates.	The x and y coordinate is where we place the image with respect to its top-left corner.
y	The position of y where the image will be placed in the Canvas coordinates.	

◆ Every argument present in `drawImage(image, x, y, width, height);` is explained in the following table:

Argument	Definition	Discussion
image	The image reference that we are going to draw.	We either get the image reference by using an existing `img` element or creating a JavaScript `Image` object.
x	The position of x where the image will be placed in the Canvas coordinates.	The x and y coordinate is where we place the image with respect to its top-left corner.
y	The position of y where the image will be placed in the Canvas coordinates.	
width	The width of the final drawn image.	We apply scale to the image if the width and height is not the same as the original image.
height	The height of the final drawn image.	

◆ Every argument present in `drawImage(image, sx, sy, sWidth, sHeight, dx, dy, width, height);` is explained in the following table:

Argument	Definition	Discussion
image	The image reference that we are going to draw.	We either get the image reference by getting an existing img element or creating a JavaScript Image object.
sx	The *x* coordinate of the top-left corner of the clipping region.	Clipping *x*, *y*, width, height together defines a rectangular clipping area. The given image is clipped by this rectangle.
sy	The *y* coordinate of the top-left corner of the clipping region.	
sWidth	The width of the clipping region.	
sHeight	The height of the clipping region.	
dx	The position of *x* where the image will be placed in the Canvas coordinates.	The *x* and *y* coordinate is where we place the image with respect to its top-left corner.
dy	The position of *y* where the image will be placed in the Canvas coordinates.	
width	The width of the final drawn image.	We are applying scale to the clipped image if the width and height is not the same as the clipping dimension.
height	The height of the final drawn image.	

Have a go hero – optimizing the background image

In the example, we draw the blackboard image as the background in every call to the `gameloop` function. Since our background is static and does not change with time, clearing it and redrawing it again and again is wasting CPU resources. How can we optimize this performance issue? In a later section, we will divide the game into multiple layers to avoid redrawing the static background image.

Decorating the Canvas-based game

We have enhanced the Canvas game with gradients and images. Before moving forward, let's decorate the web page of our Canvas game.

Time for action – adding CSS styles and image decoration to the game

We are going to build a center-aligned layout with a game title:

1. Open `index.html` in a text editor. It is easier for us to style the layout with one grouping DOM element. We put all the elements inside the body into a section with the id page. Replace the contents of the HTML file with the following:

```
<section id="page">
  <header>
    <h1>Untangle Puzzle Game in Canvas</h1>
  </header>

  <canvas id="game" width="768" height="400">
    This is an interactive game with circles and lines connecting
      them.
  </canvas>
  <p>Puzzle <span id="level">0</span>, Completeness: <span id=
    "progress">0</span>%</p>

  <footer>
    <p>This is an example of Untangle Puzzle Game in Canvas.</p>
  </footer>
</section>
```

2. Let's apply CSS to the page layout. Replace existing content in the `untangle.css` file with the following code:

```
html, body {
  background: url(../images/title_bg.png) 50% 0 no-repeat,
      url(../images/bg_repeat.png) 50% 0 repeat-y #889ba7;
  margin: 0;
  color: #111;
}

#game{
  position:relative;
}

#page {
  width: 820px;
  min-height: 800px;
```

```
    margin: 0 auto;
    padding: 0;
    text-align: center;
    text-shadow: 0 1px 5px rgba(60,60,60,.6);
}

header {
  height: 88px;
  padding-top: 36px;
  margin-bottom: 50px;
  font-family: "Rock Salt", Arial, sans-serif;
  font-size: 14px16px;
  text-shadow: 0 1px 0 rgba(200,200,200,.5);
  color: #121;
}
```

3. It is time to save all the files and preview the game in a web browser. We should see a title ribbon and a well-styled layout that is center-aligned. The following screenshot shows the result:

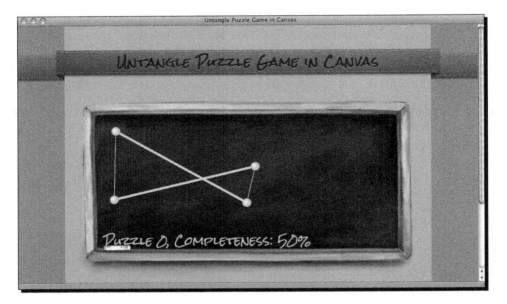

What just happened?

We just decorated the web page that contains our Canvas-based game. Although our game is based on a Canvas drawing, it does not restrict us from decorating the whole web page with graphics and CSS styles.

> **Default background of the canvas element**
>
> The default background of the `canvas` element is transparent. If we do not set any background CSS style for the Canvas, it will be transparent. This is useful when our drawing is not a rectangle. In this example, the textured layout background shows within the Canvas region.

Pop quiz – styling a Canvas background

Q1. How can we set the Canvas background to be transparent?

1. Set the background color to `#ffffff`.
2. Do nothing. It is transparent by default.

Animating a sprite sheet in Canvas

We first used **sprite sheet** images in *Chapter 3, Building a Card-matching Game in CSS3*, when displaying a deck of playing cards.

Time for action – making a game guide animation

There is a graphics file named `guide_sprite.png` in the images folder. It is a game guideline graphic that contains each step of the animation.

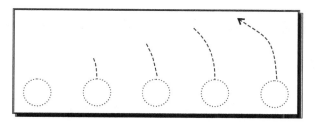

Let's draw this guide into our game with **animations**:

1. Open the `untangle.drawing.js` JavaScript file in the text editor.

2. In the `untangleGame.loadImages` function, add the following code:

```
// load the guide sprite image
untangleGame.guide = new Image();
untangleGame.guide.onload = function() {
  // setup timer to switch the display frame of the guide sprite
  untangleGame.guideFrame = 0;
  setInterval(untangleGame.guideNextFrame, 500);
}
untangleGame.guide.src = "images/guide_sprite.png";
```

3. Still in the `untangleGame.drawing.js` file, we add the following function to move the current frame to the next frame every 500 milliseconds:

```
untangleGame.guideNextFrame = function() {
  untangleGame.guideFrame++;
  // there are only 6 frames (0-5) in the guide animation.
  // we loop back the frame number to frame 0 after frame 5.
  if (untangleGame.guideFrame > 5) {
    untangleGame.guideFrame = 0;
  }
}
```

4. Next, we define the `drawGuide` function in the `untangleGame.drawing.js` file. This function draws the guide animation according to the current frame:

```
untangleGame.drawGuide = function() {
  var ctx = untangleGame.ctx;
  // draw the guide animation
  if (untangleGame.currentLevel === 0) {
    // the dimension of each frame is 80x130.
    var nextFrameX = untangleGame.guideFrame * 80;
    ctx.drawImage(untangleGame.guide, nextFrameX, 0, 80, 130,
      325, 130, 80, 130);
  }
};
```

5. Let's switch to the untangle.js file. In the gameloop function, we call the guide drawing function before ending the gameloop function.

```
untangleGame.drawGuide();
```

6. Let's watch the animation in the web browser by opening the index.html file. The following screenshot demonstrates the animation of the game guideline. The guideline animation will play and loop until the player levels up:

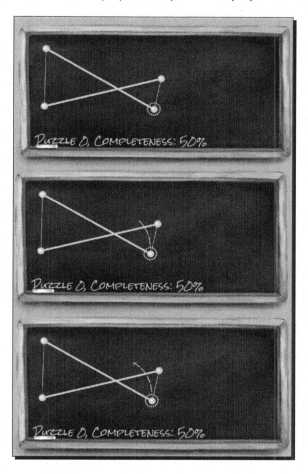

What just happened?

We can draw only a region of an image when using the `drawImage` context function.

The following screenshot demonstrates the process of animation step by step. The rectangle is the clipping region:

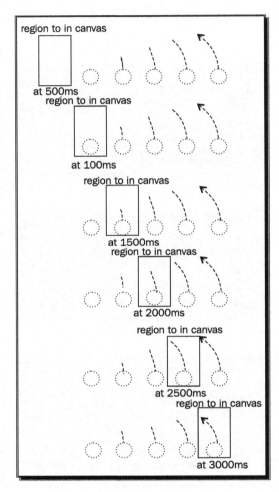

We used a variable named `guideFrame` to control which frame to show. The width of each frame is 80. Therefore, we get the x position of the clipping region by multiplying the width and the current frame number:

```
var nextFrameX = untangleGame.guideFrame * 80;
ctx.drawImage(untangleGame.guide, nextFrameX, 0, 80, 130, 325, 130,
    80, 130);
```

The `guideFrame` variable is updated every 500 milliseconds by the following `guideNextFrame` function:

```
untangleGame.guideNextFrame = function() {
  untangleGame.guideFrame += 1;
  // there are only 6 frames (0-5) in the guide animation.
  // we loop back the frame number to frame 0 after frame 5.
  if (untangleGame.guideFrame > 5) {
    untangleGame.guideFrame = 0;
  }
}
```

Animating a sprite is a commonly used technique when developing games. There are some benefits of using sprite animation when developing traditional video games. The reasons may not apply to web game development but there are other benefits of using sprite sheet animation:

- ◆ All frames are loaded as one file so the whole animation is ready once the sprite file is loaded.

- ◆ Putting all frames into one file means we can reduce the HTTP request from the web browser to the server. If each frame is a file, the browser requests the file many times, while now it just requests one file and uses one HTTP request.

- ◆ Putting different images into one file also reduces the duplication of files, which helps to reduce the duplicate file's header, footer, and metadata.

- ◆ Putting all frames into one image means we can easily clip the image to display any frame without complex code to change the image source.

Sprite sheet animation is usually used in character animation. The following screenshot is a **sprite animation** of an angry cat that I used in an HTML5 game named **Neighbours**.

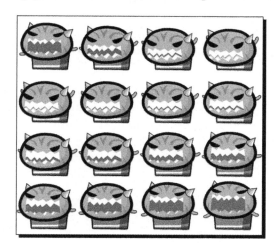

We built the sprite sheet animation by clipping the frame and setting up the timer ourselves in this example. When working with a lot of animations, we may want to use a third-party sprite animation plugin or create our own Canvas sprite animation to better reuse and manage the logic code.

Sprite animation is an important topic in HTML5 games development and there are many online resources discussing this topic. The following links are some of them:

The sprite animation tutorial (`http://simurai.com/blog/2012/12/03/step-animation/`) by Simurai discusses how we can make a sprite animation with CSS only.

Spritely (`http://www.spritely.net/`), on the other hand, provides sprite animation over the DOM element with CSS. It is useful when we want to animate a sprite without using Canvas.

Creating a multilayer Canvas game

Now all things are drawn into the context, which has no other state to distinguish the items drawn. We may split the Canvas game into different layers and code the logic to control and draw each layer at a time.

Time for action – dividing the game into four layers

We are going to separate our Untangle game into four layers:

1. In `index.html`, we need to change or replace the current `canvas` tag with the following code. It should contain several Canvases within a section:

```
<section id="layers">
  <canvas id="bg" width="768" height="440">
    This is an interactive game with circles and lines connecting
them.
  </canvas>
  <canvas id="guide" width="768" height="440"></canvas>
  <canvas id="game" width="768" height="440"></canvas>
  <canvas id="ui" width="768" height="440"></canvas>
</section>
```

2. We also need to apply some styles to the Canvases so they overlap with each other to create a multiple layers effect. Also we have to prepare a `fadeout` class and a `dim` class to make the target transparent. Add the following code into the `untangle.css` file:

```css
#layers {
  position: relative;
  margin: 0 auto;
  width:768px;
  height: 440px;
}
#layers canvas{
  top: 0;
  left: 0;
  position: absolute;
}
#guide {
  opacity: 0.7;
  transition: opacity 0.5s ease-out;
}
#guide.fadeout {
  opacity: 0;
}
#ui {
  transition: opacity 0.3s ease-out;
}
#ui.dim {
  opacity: 0.3;
}
```

3. Open the `untangle.js` JavaScript file. We modify the code to support the layers feature. First, we add an array to store the context reference of each Canvas. Add it at the beginning of the file, before the jQuery document ready function and after the `untangleGame` definition:

```javascript
untangleGame.layers = [];
```

4. Then, we remove the following lines of code in the jQuery document ready function.

```javascript
var canvas = document.getElementById("game");
untangleGame.ctx = canvas.getContext("2d");
```

5. We replace the code we deleted with the following code. We get the context reference of each Canvas layer and store them in the array:

```
// prepare layer 0 (bg)
var canvas_bg = document.getElementById("bg");
untangleGame.layers[0] = canvas_bg.getContext("2d");

// prepare layer 1 (guide)
var canvas_guide = document.getElementById("guide");
untangleGame.layers[1] = canvas_guide.getContext("2d");

// prepare layer 2 (game)
var canvas = document.getElementById("game");
var ctx = canvas.getContext("2d");
untangleGame.layers[2] = ctx;

// prepare layer 3 (ui)
var canvas_ui = document.getElementById("ui");
untangleGame.layers[3] = canvas_ui.getContext("2d");
```

6. Let's switch to `untangle.drawing.js` file. We are going to update the context references at several places to support multilayers.

7. There are now four Canvas contexts that we may clear. Find the existing `clear` function and replace it with the following:

```
untangleGame.clear = function(layerIndex) {
  var ctx = untangleGame.layers[layerIndex];
  ctx.clearRect(0,0,ctx.canvas.width,ctx.canvas.height);
};
```

8. In the `drawCircle` and `drawLine` function, replace `var ctx = untangleGame.ctx;` with the following code:

```
var ctx = untangleGame.layers[2];
```

9. In the `drawLevelProgress` function, replace `var ctx = untangleGame.ctx;` with the following code:

```
var ctx = untangleGame.layers[3];
```

10. In the `drawBackground` function, we replace the existing code with the following, which draws on the background layer with index 0:

```
untangleGame.drawBackground = function() {
  // draw the image background
  var ctx = untangleGame.layers[0];
  ctx.drawImage(untangleGame.background, 0, 0);
};
```

11. Then, we move to the `loadImages` function. Add the following code to the function. It draws the background once:

```
untangleGame.background.onload = function() {
  untangleGame.drawBackground();
}
```

12. In the `drawGuide` function, replace `var ctx = untangleGame.ctx;` with the following code:

```
var ctx = untangleGame.layers[1];
```

13. Actually, we fade out the guide layer in this function too. So we replace the entire `drawGuide` function with the following:

```
untangleGame.drawGuide = function() {
  var ctx = untangleGame.layers[1];
  // draw the guide animation
  if (untangleGame.currentLevel < 2) {
    // the dimension of each frame is 80x130.
    var nextFrameX = untangleGame.guideFrame * 80;
    ctx.drawImage(untangleGame.guide, nextFrameX, 0, 80, 130, 325,
    130, 80, 130);
  }

  // fade out the guideline after level 0
  if (untangleGame.currentLevel === 1)    {
    $("#guide").addClass('fadeout');
  }
};
```

14. Inside the `guideNextFrame` function, we clear the guide layer and redraw it. Add the following code to the end of the function:

```
untangleGame.clear(1);
untangleGame.drawGuide();
```

15. During the circle dragging, we don't want our progress text layer to block the game elements. So we will define an extra function that dims the opacity of the progress layer when there are any game circles overlapping the layer:

```
untangleGame.dimUILayerIfNeeded = function() {
  // get all circles,
  // check if the ui overlap with the game objects
  var isOverlappedWithCircle = false;
  for(var i in untangleGame.circles) {
    var point = untangleGame.circles[i];
```

```
      if (point.y > 280) {
        isOverlappedWithCircle = true;
      }
    }
    if (isOverlappedWithCircle) {
      $("#ui").addClass('dim');
    } else {
      $("#ui").removeClass('dim');
    }
};
```

16. We are done with the `untangle.drawing.js` file. Let's switch back to the `untangle.js` file. In the `gameloop` function, we remove the calls to the `drawBackground` and `drawGuide` functions. Then, we call the `dimUILayerIfNeeded` function. We also clear the layer 2 game elements and layer 3 level progress in every game loop. Now the `gameloop` function becomes the following:

```
function gameloop() {
    // clear the canvas before re-drawing.
    untangleGame.clear(2);
    untangleGame.clear(3);

    untangleGame.drawAllLines();
    untangleGame.drawAllCircles();
    untangleGame.drawLevelProgress();
    untangleGame.dimUILayerIfNeeded();
}
```

17. Finally, open the `untangle.input.js` file. We had mouse down, move, and up event listeners on the `#game` Canvas. Since the game Canvases are now overlapping, the mouse event listener we had in the `game` Canvas does not fire anymore. We can change the listener to listen to the events from its parent `#layers` DIV, which has the same position and dimension of the Canvas:

```
$("#layers"). bind("mousedown touchstart", function(e){
    // existing code that handles mousedown and touchstart.
});
$("#layers"). bind("mousemove touchmove", function(e) {
    // existing code that handles mousemove and touchmove.
});
$("#layers"). bind("mouseup touchend", function(e){

    // existing code that handles mouseup and touchend.

});
```

18. Save all the files and check our code changes in the web browser. The game should be displayed as if we haven't changed anything. Try dragging the circle down close to the bottom edge of the blackboard. The level progress text should dim to a low opacity. When you finish the first level, the guideline animation will fade out gracefully. The following screenshot shows the level progress in half opacity:

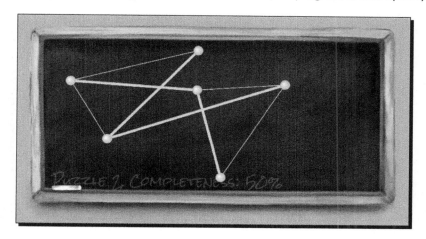

What just happened?

We divided our working game into four layers. There are quite a lot of changes in this section. You may try the working example at: `http://makzan.net/html5-games/untangle/`. By observing the source code, you can view the uncompressed code example.

There are four Canvases in total now. Each Canvas is in charge of one layer. The layers are divided into the background, game guideline, game itself, and the user interface showing the level progress.

By default, the Canvases, like other elements, are placed one after the other. In order to overlap all Canvases to construct the layer effect, we applied the `absolute` position to them.

The following screenshots show the four layers in our game. By default, the DOM that was added later is on top of the one added before. Therefore, the bg Canvas is at the bottom and ui is on the top:

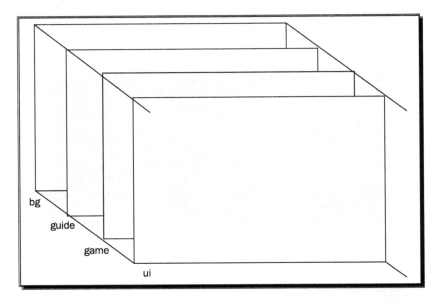

By using different layers, we can create specific logic for each layer. For example, the background in this game is static. We only draw it once. The guide layer is a 6-frames animation with 500 milliseconds for each frame. We redraw the guide layer in 500 milliseconds intervals. The game layer and UI layer are the core game logic, which we draw 30 times per second.

Mixing a CSS technique with Canvas drawing

We are creating a Canvas-based game but we are not restricted to use only a Canvas drawing API. Each layer is an individual Canvas layer. We can apply a CSS technique to any layer. The level progress information is now in another Canvas with the ID ui. In this example, we mixed the CSS technique we discussed in *Chapter 3, Building a Card-matching Game in CSS3*.

When we drag the circles around the Canvas, they may overlap the level information. When drawing the UI Canvas layer, we check whether any circle's coordinate is too low and is overlapping the text. We then fade the UI Canvas CSS opacity so it does not distract the player from the circles.

We also fade out the guideline animation after the player levels up. This is done by fading out the whole `guide` Canvas with CSS transition easing to 0 opacity. Since the `guide` Canvas is only in charge of that animation, hiding that Canvas does not affect other elements:

```
if (untangleGame.currentLevel === 1) {
  $("#guide").addClass('fadeout');
}
```

Clearing only the changed region to boost the canvas performance

We can use the clear function to only clear part of the Canvas context. This will give the performance some boost because it avoids redrawing the entire Canvas context every time. This is achieved by marking the 'dirty' region of the context that has changed state since last drawn.

In the guide Canvas layer in our example, we may consider clearing only the region of the sprite sheet image drawing instead of the whole Canvas.

We may not see significant differences in simple Canvas examples but it helps boost the performance when we have a complex Canvas game that includes many sprite image animations and complex shape drawings.

Have a go hero

We fade out the guide when the players advance to level 2. How about we fade out the guide animation once the player drags any circles? How can we do that?

Summary

You learned a lot in this chapter about drawing gradients, text, and images in a Canvas. Specifically, we built the Untangle game logic and used several advanced Canvas techniques, including sprite sheet animation using the clipping function when drawing images. We divided the game into several layers by stacking several `canvas` elements. This allows us to handle different parts of the game rendering in separated and specific logic. Finally, we mixed the CSS transition animation in a Canvas-based game.

One thing we haven't mentioned in this book is the bitmap manipulation in Canvas. Canvas context is a bitmap data where we can apply an operation on each pixel. For instance, we may draw an image in the Canvas and apply Photoshop-like filters to the image. We will not cover this in the book because image manipulation is an advanced topic and the application may not relate to game development.

Now that you've learned about building games in Canvas and making animation for game objects, such as game character, we are ready to add audio components and sound effects to our games in the next chapter.

We will get back to Canvas-based games in *Chapter 9, Building a Physics Car Game with Box2D and Canvas*.

6

Adding Sound Effects to Your Games

In the earlier chapters, we discussed several techniques to draw game objects visually. In this chapter, we will focus on using the `audio` *tag that is introduced in the HTML5 specification. We can add sound effects, background music, and control the audio through the JavaScript API. In addition, we will build a music game in this chapter. It is a game that requires players to hit the correct string at the right time to produce the music.*

In this chapter, you will learn the following topics:

◆ Adding a sound effect to the **Play** button

◆ Building a mini piano musical game

◆ Linking the music game and the **Play** button

◆ Adding keyboard and touch inputs to the game

◆ Creating a keyboard-driven music game

◆ Completing the musical game with a level data recording and the game over event

You can play the game example at: `http://makzan.net/html5-games/audiogame/`.

The following screenshot shows the final result we will create through this chapter:

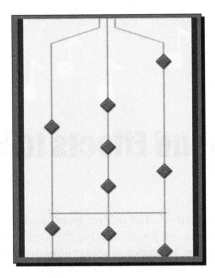

So, let's get on with it.

Adding a sound effect to the Play button

We had several mouse interactions in the Untangle game examples in previous chapters. Now imagine that we want to have sound effects with the mouse interaction. This requires us to instruct the game about the audio file to be used. We will use the `audio` tag to create a sound effect when a button is clicked.

Time for action – adding sound effects to the Play button

We will start with the code example available in the code bundle. We will have a folder structure similar to the one shown in the following screenshot:

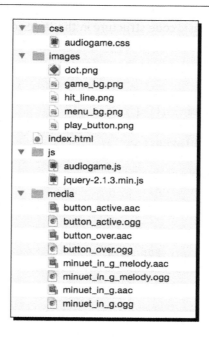

Perform the following set of steps to add sound effects to the **Play** button:

1. The `index.html` file contains the basic structure of the HTML. Now let's add the following code to the body section of the `index.html` file:

```
<div id="game">
  <section id="menu-scene" class="scene">
    <a href="#game"><span>Play</span></a>
  </section>
</div>
<audio id="buttonover">
  <source src="media/button_over.aac" />
  <source src="media/button_over.ogg" />
</audio>
<audio id="buttonactive">
  <source src="media/button_active.aac" />
  <source src="media/button_active.ogg" />
</audio>
```

2. The HTML file runs successfully with a stylesheet. The file can be found in the code bundle named `audiogame.css`.

3. Next, we create the basic code structure in the JavaScript file. Add the following JavaScript in the `audiogame.js` file:

```
(function($){
  var audiogame = {
    // game init method
    initGame: function() {
      this.initMedia();
      this.handlePlayButton();
    },
    // init medias
    initMedia: function() {
        // TODO: init media related logic
    },

    handlePlayButton: function() {
      // TODO: logic for the play button
    }

  };

  // init function when the DOM is ready
  $(function(){
    audiogame.initGame();
  });
})(jQuery);
```

4. Then we store the references of the audio tags. Add the following code inside the `initMedia` function:

```
initMedia: function() {
  // get the references of the audio element.
  this.buttonOverSound = document.getElementById("buttonover");
  this.buttonOverSound.volume = 0.3;
  this.buttonActiveSound = document.getElementById(
    "buttonactive");
  this.buttonActiveSound.volume = 0.3;
},
```

5. We add a sound effect to the button in the JavaScript file. Add the following JavaScript inside the `handlePlayButton` function:

```
handlePlayButton: function() {
  var game = this;

  // listen the button event that links to #game
```

```
$("a[href='#game']")
.hover(function(){
  game.buttonOverSound.currentTime = 0;
  game.buttonOverSound.play();
},function(){
  game.buttonOverSound.pause();
})
.click(function(){
  game.buttonActiveSound.currentTime = 0;
  game.buttonActiveSound.play();

  return false;
});
}
```

6. Open the `index.html` file in a browser. There, you should see a **PLAY** button on a yellow background, as shown in the following screenshot. Try to move the mouse on the button and click on it. You should be able to hear a sound when you hover over the button and another sound when you click on it:

What just happened?

We just created a basic HTML5 game layout with a play button placed in the middle of the page. The JavaScript file handles the mouse hover and clicks of the button and plays corresponding sound effects.

Defining an audio element

The easiest way to use the `audio` tag is by providing a source file. The following code snippet shows how we can define an audio element:

```
<audio>
  <source src="media/button_active.aac" >
  <source src="media/button_active.ogg" >
  <!-- Any code for browser that does not support audio tag -->
</audio>
```

Besides setting the source file of the `audio` tag, we can have additional controls by using several attributes. The following table shows the attributes we can set for the audio element:

Arguments	Definition	Explanation

src	Defines the source file of the audio element	When we use the `src` attribute in the `audio` tag, it specifies one source file for the audio file. For example, we load a sound effect Ogg file in the following code:
		
		`<audio src='sound.ogg'>`
		
		If we want to specify multiple files with different formats, then we use the `source` tag inside the audio element. The following code specifies the `audio` tag with different formats to support different web browsers:
		
		`<audio>`
		`    <source src='sound.ogg'>`
		`    <source src='sound.aac'>`
		`    <source src='sound.wav'>`
		`</audio>`

autoplay	Specifies that the audio plays automatically once it is loaded	Autoplay is used as a standalone attribute. This means that there is no difference in the following two lines of code:
		
		`<audio src='file.ogg'`
		`    autoplay>`
		`<audio src='file.ogg`
		`    autoplay="autoplay">`

loop	Specifies that the audio plays from the beginning again after playback finishes	This is also used as a standalone attribute.

Arguments	Definition	Explanation
preload	Specifies that the audio source is loaded once the page is loaded	The preload attribute takes either of the following values: ♦ preload="auto" ♦ preload="metadata" ♦ preload="none" When preload is used as a standalone attribute and set to auto, the browser will preload the audio. When preload is set as metadata, the browser will not preload the content of the audio. However, it will load the metadata of the audio, such as the duration and size. When preload is set to none, the browser will not preload the audio at all. The content and metadata is loaded once it is played.
controls	Shows the playback control of the audio	The controls attribute is a standalone attribute. It instructs the browser to show a playback control in the audio position.

The following screenshot shows the Chrome display controls:

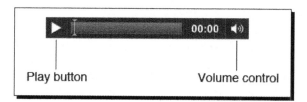

Playing a sound

We can get the reference of the audio element by calling the getElementById function. Then, we play it by calling the play function. The following code plays the buttonactive audio:

```
<audio id="buttonactive">
  <source src="media/button_active.aac" />
  <source src="media/button_active.ogg" />
</audio>
<script>
  document.getElementById("buttonactive").play();
</script>
```

The `play` function plays the audio from the elapsed time, which is stored in the `currentTime` property. The default value of `currentTime` is zero. The following code plays the audio from 3.5 seconds:

```
document.getElementById("buttonactive").currentTime = 3.5;
document.getElementById("buttonactive").play();
```

jQuery's selector versus browser selector

We were using jQuery's query selector `$("#buttonactive")` to select an element. We were applying DOM manipulation to those selected elements, such as toggling classes, or getting text content. In this example, we use `document.getElementById("buttonactive")` to get the reference of the element. That's because we are using the browser's Web Audio API on the element. We don't want the jQuery object, we want the browser DOM element.

An alternative way is to select the element via jQuery and use its `.get()` method to retrieve the DOM elements of the jQuery object.

Pausing a sound

Similar to the play button, we can also pause the playback of an audio element by using the `pause` function. The following code pauses the `buttonactive` audio element:

```
<script>
   document.getElementById("buttonactive").pause();
</script>
```

> There is no `stop` function to stop the audio element. Instead, we can pause the audio and reset the `currentTime` property of the element to zero. The following code shows how we can stop an audio element:
>
> ```
> function stopAudio(){
>    document.getElementById("buttonactive").pause();
>    document.getElementById("buttonactive").currentTime
> = 0;
> }
> ```

Adjusting the sound volume

We can also set the volume of the audio element. The volume must range between 0 and 1. We can set the volume to 0 to mute it, and set it to 1 for the maximum volume. The following code snippet sets the volume of the `buttonactive` audio to 30%:

```
document.getElementById("buttonactive").volume = 0.3;
```

Using the jQuery hover event

jQuery provides a `hover` function to define the behavior when we mouse over and mouse out a DOM element. Here is how we use the `hover` function:

```
.hover(handlerIn, handlerOut);
```

The arguments of the `hover` function are explained as follows:

Arguments	Discussion
`handlerIn`	The function is executed when the mouse moves in.
`handlerOut`	This is optional. The function is executed when the mouse moves out. When this function is not provided, the move out behavior is the same as the first function.

In the following code, we'll play the mouse over sound effect when moving the mouse in and will pause the sound during mouse out:

```
$("a[href='#game']").hover(function(){
    audiogame.buttonOverSound.currentTime = 0;
    audiogame.buttonOverSound.play();
},function(){
    audiogame.buttonOverSound.pause();
});
```

File format for WebAudio

We use an **AAC** format and the **Ogg** format file when we define the source of the audio element. Ogg is a free and open source media container format that is supported in Mozilla Firefox. There are applications that convert audio files into Ogg files. Audacity is one of these. Also, there are online tools that are convenient to use. Online-Convert (`http://audio.online-convert.com`) is one of them.

We didn't use the MP3 format because of the license costs. The royalty rates to use an MP3 in a distributed game is $2500 per game once there are more than 5,000 distributed copies, according to the MP3 license website (`http://www.mp3licensing.com/royalty/games.html`).

The following table shows the audio formats supported by the latest popular web browsers at the time of writing this book:

Browser	Ogg	AAC	WAV
Firefox	Yes	Yes	Yes
Safari	-	Yes	Yes
Chrome	Yes	Yes	Yes
Opera	Yes	Yes	Yes
Internet Explorer	-	Yes	-

Pop quiz – using the audio tag

Q1. How can we stop an `audio` element playing?

1. Use the `stop` function.
2. Use the `pause` function and reset the value of `currentTime` to 0.
3. Reset the value of `currentTime` to 0.

Q2. How can we put fallback content to display in browsers that do not support `audio` tags?

Building a mini piano musical game

Imagine now that we are not only playing a sound effect, but also playing a full song with the `audio` tag. Along with the song playing, there are some music dots moving downwards as a visualization of the music.

Time for action – creating a basic background for the music game

First, we will draw a few paths in the Canvas as the background of the music playback.

1. We will continue working with our example and draw the background. Open the `index.html` file in a text editor and add the following highlighted code that defines the game scene with two Canvases set up:

```
<div id="game">
  <div id="menu-scene" class="scene">
    <a href="#game"><span>Play</span></a>
  </div>
```

```
<div id="game-scene" class="scene">
  <canvas id="game-canvas" width="320" height="440">
     This is an interactive audio game with some music notes
moving from top to bottom.
  </canvas>
 </div>
</div>
```

2. We added a game scene in the HTML file. We want to put it on top of the menu scene, so we style the game scene to have an `absolute` position by adding the following to `audiogame.css`:

```css
#game {
  position: relative;
  width: 320px;
  height: 440px;
  overflow: hidden;
}
.scene {
  position: absolute;
  width: 100%;
  height: 100%;
}

#menu-scene {
  background: url(../images/menu_bg.png);
  display: flex;
  justify-content: center;
  align-items: center;
}

#game-scene {
  background: url(../images/game_bg.png);
  top: -440px;
}

#game-scene.show-scene {
  top: 0;
  transition: top 0.3s ease-out;
}
```

3. Now, we will move on to the JavaScript part. Open the `html5games.audio.js` JavaScript file.

4. In the **Play** button click handler, we add the following highlighted code:

```
$("a[href='#game']").click(function(){
    // existing code here.

    $("#game-scene").addClass('show-scene');
    return false;
});
```

Save all files and open the index.html in a browser. There should be a slide-in animation to show the music playback scene when we click on the **Play** button. The following screenshot sequence shows the slide-in animation:

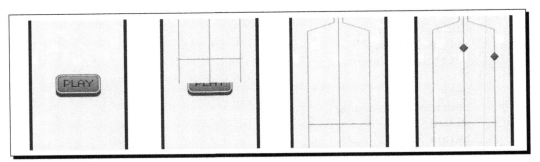

What just happened?

We created a game scene with Canvas. In this music game example, we introduced basic scene management in HTML5 games. We created a transition that links between the menu scene and the game scene.

Creating scenes in games

Creating **scenes** in a game is similar to creating **layers**, like we did in the last chapter. A scene is a DOM element that contains several children. All the children elements are positioned in absolute positions. We have two scenes in our example now. The following code snippet shows a possible scene structure in an entire game with a game over scene, credit scene, and leaderboard scene included:

```
<div id="game">
  <div id="menu-scene" class="scene"></div>
  <div id="game-scene" class="scene"></div>
  <div id="gameover-scene" class="scene"></div>
  <div id="credit-scene" class="scene"></div>
  <div id="leaderboard-scene" class="scene"></div>
</div>
```

The following screenshot shows that the scenes are placed in the same place on a web page. It is very similar to the layers structure. The difference is that we will control the scene by showing and hiding each scene:

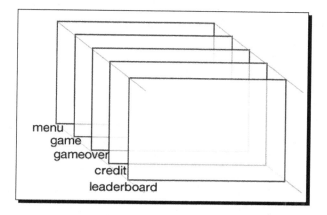

Creating a slide-in effect in CSS3

The game scene slides in from the top when the play button is clicked. This scene transition effect is done by moving the game scene using a CSS3 transition. The game scene position is initially placed with a negative top value. We then change the top position from negative value to zero with a transition, so it animates from the top to the correct position.

Another important thing to make the sliding effect work is to set the overflow of the parent DIV of the scenes to `hidden`. Without the hidden overflow, the game scene is visible even with a negative top position. Therefore, it is important to set the parent DIV of the scenes to the hidden overflow.

The following screenshot illustrates the slide-in transition of the game scene. The #game DIV is the parent of both the menu scene and the game scene. The game scene moves from the top when we add the .show-scene class, which sets the top value to 0 with a transition:

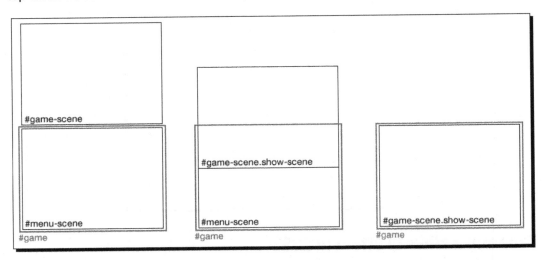

Have a go hero – creating different scene transition effects

We made a slide-in effect for the scene transition when showing the game. By using JavaScript and CSS3, we can make many different scene transition effects creatively. Try adding your own transition effect to the game, such as fading in, pushing in from the right, or even flipping with a 3D rotation.

Visualizing the music playback

If you have ever played the Dance Dance Revolution, Guitar Hero, or the Tap Tap Revenge games, then you may be familiar with the music dots moving downwards or upwards and the player hitting the music dots when they move to the right place. The following screenshot demonstrates the Tap Tap Revenge game:

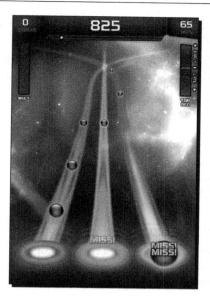

We will play a song in the `audio` tag with similar music visualization in the canvas.

Time for action – creating the playback visualization in the music game

In order to create the playback visualization in the music game, you'll need to carry out the following steps:

1. We need a song with both a melody part and a base part. Copy the `minuet_in_g. ogg`, `minuet_in_g.aac`, `minuet_in_g_melody.ogg`, and `minuet_in_g_ melody.aac` files from the downloaded files or from the code bundle in the `media` folder.

2. Then, add the `audio` tag with the song as a source file. Open the `index.html` file and add the following code:

```
<audio id="melody">
  <source src="media/minuet_in_g_melody.aac" />
  <source src="media/minuet_in_g_melody.ogg" />
</audio>

<audio id="base">
  <source src="media/minuet_in_g.aac" />
  <source src="media/minuet_in_g.ogg" />
</audio>
```

3. The music visualization is mainly done in JavaScript. Open the `audiogame.js` JavaScript file in a text editor.

4. Add a `MusicNote` object type to represent the music data and a `Dot` object type to represent the visual dot of the music note in the canvas as follows:

```
function MusicNote(time,line){
    this.time = time;
    this.line = line;
}
function Dot(distance, line) {
    this.distance = distance;
    this.line = line;
    this.missed = false;
}
```

5. Then, we need several game variables to store the `MusicNote` instances, the `Dot` instance, and other information. The level data is a sequence of time and the appearing line that is separated by a semicolon. We will record and create our own data in a later section. The level data represents the time and line at which the music note should appear:

```
var audiogame = {
  // an array to store all music notes data.
  musicNotes: [],
  leveldata: "1.592,3;1.984,2;2.466,1;2.949,2;4.022,3;",
  // the visual dots drawn on the canvas.
  dots: [],
  // for storing the starting time
  startingTime: 0,
  // reference of the dot image
  dotImage: new Image(),

  // existing code inside audiogame object.
}
```

6. The level data is serialized and stored in a string format. We have the following function to extract the string in the `MusicNote` object instances and store in an array:

```
var audiogame = {
  // existing code inside audiogame object.

  setupLevelData: function() {
    var notes = this.leveldata.split(";");
```

```
      // store the total number of dots
      this.totalDotsCount = notes.length;

      for(var i=0, len=notes.length; i<len; i++) {
        var note = notes[i].split(",");
        var time = parseFloat(note[0]);
        var line = parseInt(note[1]);
        var musicNote = new MusicNote(time,line);
        this.musicNotes.push(musicNote);
      }
    },
  }
```

7. Add the following code inside the `initMedia` function. It references the `melody` and `base` audio tags and loads the dot image for later use:

```
initMedia: function() {
  // existing code goes here.

  // melody and base
  this.melody = document.getElementById("melody");
  this.base = document.getElementById("base");

  // load the dot image
  this.dotImage.src = "images/dot.png";
}
```

8. Add the following code inside the `initGame` function. It references the canvas and `canvasContext` variables for later use:

```
initGame: function() {
  // existing code goes here.
  this.canvas = document.getElementById("game-canvas");
  this.canvasContext = this.canvas.getContext('2d');
}
```

9. Add the following two functions in the JavaScript file. The `startGame` function sets the starting time and executes the `playMusic` function with a delay. The latter function plays both the melody and base audios:

```
var audiogame = {
  // existing code goes here.
  startGame: function() {
    var date = new Date();
    this.startingTime = date.getTime();
```

```
      this.registerMusicPlayback();
   },

   registerMusicPlayback: function() {
      // play both the melody and base
     this.melody.play();
     this.base.play();

     // pause for 3550ms to sync with the music dots movement.
     this.melody.pause();
     this.base.pause();
     setTimeout(this.playMusic.bind(this), 3550);
   },

   playMusic: function() {
     this.melody.play();
     this.base.play();
   },
};
```

10. Add the following `gameloop` function to JavaScript. The `gameloop` function creates new dots at the top of the game and moves the existing notes down:

```
var audiogame = {
   // existing code goes here.

   gameloop: function() {
     var canvas = this.canvas;
     var ctx = this.canvasContext;

     // show new dots
     // if the game is started
     if (this.startingTime !== 0)  {
       for(var i=0, len=this.musicNotes.length; i<len; i++) {
         var date = new Date();
         var elapsedTime = (date.getTime() -
           this.startingTime)/1000;
         var note = this.musicNotes[i];

         var timeDiff = note.time - elapsedTime;

         // When time difference is short enough.
         if (timeDiff >= 0 && timeDiff <= 0.03)  {
           var dot = new Dot(ctx.canvas.height-150, note.line);
```

```
          this.dots.push(dot);
        }
      }
    }

    // loop again to remove dots that are out of the screen.
    for(var i=this.dots.length-1; i>=0; i--) {
      // remove missed dots after moved to the bottom
      if (this.dots[i].distance < -100)  {
        this.dots.splice(i, 1);
      }
    }

    // move the dots
    for(var i=0, len=this.dots.length; i<len; i++) {
      this.dots[i].distance -= 2.5;
    }

    // only clear the dirty area, that is the middle area
    ctx.clearRect(ctx.canvas.width/2-200, 0, 400,
      ctx.canvas.height);

    // draw the music note dots
    for(var i=0, len=this.dots.length; i<len; i++) {
      // draw the music dot.
      ctx.save();
      var center = canvas.width/2;
      var dot = this.dots[i];
      var x = center-100
      if (dot.line === 2) {
        x = center;
      } else if (dot.line === 3) {
        x = center+100;
      }
      ctx.translate(x, ctx.canvas.height-80-this.dots[i].
        distance);
      ctx.drawImage(this.dotImage, -this.dotImage.width/2,
        -this.dotImage.height/2);
      ctx.restore();
    }
  }
};
```

11. Now, add the following code at the end of the jQuery ready function:

```
audiogame.setupLevelData();
setInterval(audiogame.gameloop.bind(audiogame), 30);
```

12. Finally, we call the `startGame` function in the click event handler of the **Play** button:

```
game.startGame();
```

13. Save all files and open the `index.html` file in a web browser. The following screenshot shows the music playing with the music dots appearing on the top and moving downwards:

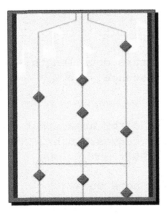

What just happened?

We just built a fully functional music game. This is the basic playback function. It plays the song with both the melody and the base part with some music dots moving downwards.

Choosing the right song for the music game

We have to be careful of copyright issues when choosing a song for the music game, as this usually requires you to pay a usage fee or make an agreement with the song copyright owner. This is fine if you are building a commercial music game that is going to be a hit in the game industry and the earnings can outweigh the copyright usage expense. As a book example here, however, we are going to use a copyright-free song. That is why we use the classical song *Minute in G*, which is in the public domain and free, and is also generated by computer software without a copyrighted performance.

 The performance of music can be copyrighted even if the song itself is free.

Playing audio on mobile devices

There are restrictions on playing audio on mobile devices, specifically iOS and Android. The latest Android with Chrome browser can only play audio that's triggered by the user. That's why we cannot play the audio plainly after a timeout. We need to play the audio right after the click handler, and then we pause the audio for a suitable time delay to sync the audio with our music dots. In iOS, there are similar user-triggering restrictions. We cannot control audio volume programmatically in mobile Safari. We may not be able to dim the melody in mobile Safari. Apart from this, the game is still playable.

Storing and extracting the song-level data

The level data shown in the *Time for action—creating the playback visualization in the music game* section is just a portion of the entire level data. It is a very long string storing music note information, including the time and the line. It is stored in the following format, which I came up with:

```
music_current_time, line; music_current_time, line; ...
```

Each music dot data contains two pieces of information: the time to show up, and the line that is shown. This data is separated by a comma. Every piece of music dot data is separated by a semicolon. You can choose any characters to separate the data as long as the splitter doesn't conflict with the data content. For example, choosing a number or full stop would be a bad choice here. The following code extracts the level string into a `MusicNote` object by splitting the semicolon and the comma:

```
musicNotes = [];
leveldata = "1.592,3;1.984,2;2.466,1;2.949,2;4.022,3;";
function setupLevelData() {
    var notes = audiogame.leveldata.split(";");
    for(var i=0, len=notes.length; i<len; i++) {
        var note = notes[i].split(",");
        var time = parseFloat(note[0]);
        var line = parseInt(note[1]);
        var musicNote = new MusicNote(time,line);
        musicNotes.push(musicNote);
    }
}
```

The level data string is recorded by the keyboard and we are going to discuss the recording later in this chapter.

 The level data contains only a few music notes here. In the code bundle, there is the entire level data of the complete song.

There is an optional second parameter for the JavaScript `parseInt` function. It defines the radix of the number to parse. By default, it uses a decimal but `parseInt` will parse the string as an octal when the string begins with zero. For example, `parseInt("010")` returns result 8 instead of 10. If we want the decimal number, then we can use `parseInt("010",10)` to specify the radix.

Getting the elapsed time of the game

Although we know the elapsed time of an audio element by accessing the `currentTime` property, we want to get the time from the start of the game.

We can get the elapsed time by storing the current computer time when starting the game and subtracting the current time value to get the elapsed time.

We get the current computer time by using the `Date` object. The following code snippet shows how we use `startingTime` to get the elapsed time, which is in milliseconds:

```
// starting game
var date = new Date();
audiogame.startingTime = date.getTime();

// some time later
var date = new Date();
var elapsedTime = (date.getTime() - audiogame.startingTime)/1000;
```

The following screenshot shows the preceding code snippet running in the console:

```
> var audiogame = {};
  undefined
> var date = new Date();
  undefined
> audiogame.startingTime = date.getTime();
  1306138121829
> // some time later
  undefined
> var date = new Date();
  undefined
> var elapsedTime = (date.getTime() - audiogame.startingTime) / 1000;
  undefined
> elapsedTime + "seconds"
  "39.608seconds"
> |
```

Creating music dots

In the `gameloop` function, we check all the `MusicNote` instances and see whether it is time to create the visual dot of that music note. The following code shows the logic we used to create the visual music dot:

```
if (audiogame.startingTime !== 0) {
  for(var i in audiogame.musicNotes) {
    // get the elapsed time from beginning of the melody
    var date = new Date();
    var elapsedTime = (date.getTime() - audiogame.startingTime)/1000;
    var note = audiogame.musicNotes[i];

    // check whether the dot appear time is as same as the elapsed
time
    var timeDiff = note.time - elapsedTime;
    if (timeDiff >= 0 && timeDiff <= 0.03) {
      // create the dot when the appear time is within one frame
        of the elapsed time
      var dot = new Dot(ctx.canvas.height-150, note.line);
      audiogame.dots.push(dot);
    }
  }
}
```

Basically, we get the elapsed time of the game and compare it with the current time of each music note. If the time difference between the note's current time and elapsed time is within 30 milliseconds, then we create the visual dot instance and let the `gameloop` function draw it.

Moving the music dots

There is a time difference between the game start and music start. The game starts several seconds before the song starts playing. This is because we need to show the music dots and move them down before the music starts.

The music dots should match the song when the dots are on the grey line. The music dots appear from the top of the game and move down towards the grey line. We delay the music play to wait as the dots move from top to bottom. This is around 3.55 seconds in this example, so we delay the music playing by 3.55 seconds. This delay may vary when playing different songs. So we may store this information later if we extend the game to support multiple songs playback.

When the dot is created, it is placed at a given distance. We decrease all the dots' distances by 2.5 every time the `gameloop` function is executed. The distance is stored in each `dot` object, representing how far away it is from the grey line:

```
for(var i=0, len=this.dots.length; i<len; i++) {
    audiogame.dots[i].distance -= 2.5;
}
```

The *y* position of the dot is calculated by the grey line, subtracting the distance as follows:

```
// draw the dot
ctx.save();
var x = ctx.canvas.width/2-100
if (audiogame.dots[i].line === 2) {
    x = ctx.canvas.width/2;
}
else if (audiogame.dots[i].line === 3) {
    x = ctx.canvas.width/2+100;
}
ctx.translate(x, ctx.canvas.height-80-audiogame.dots[i].distance);
ctx.drawImage(audiogame.dotImage, -audiogame.dotImage.width/2, -
    audiogame.dotImage.height/2);
```

The following screenshot shows the distance between the grey line and each dot. When the distance is zero, it is exactly on the grey line:

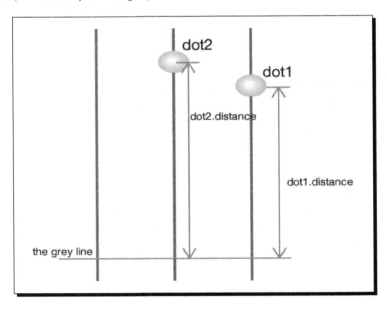

Creating a keyboard-driven mini piano musical game

Now we can click on the **Play** button. The music game slides in and plays the song with music notes dropping down. Our next step is adding interaction to the music notes. Therefore, we will add keyboard events to control the three lines to hit the music notes.

Time for action – creating a mini piano musical game

Carry out the following steps:

1. We want to show an indication when pressing the keyboard. Open the `index.html` file and add the following highlighted HTML:

```
<div id="game-scene" class="scene">
    <!-- existing code goes here -->
    <div id="hit-line-1" class="hit-line hide"></div>
    <div id="hit-line-2" class="hit-line hide"></div>
    <div id="hit-line-3" class="hit-line hide"></div>
</div>
```

2. Then, we may want to inform visitors that they can play the game by pressing the *J*, *K*, and *L* keys. Modify the footer content as follows:

```
<footer>
    <p>This is an example of making audio game in HTML5.
        Press J, K, L to play.
    </p>
</footer>
```

3. Now, we will move on to the stylesheet. Open the `css/audiogame.css` file and put the following code at the end of the file:

```
#hit-line-1 {
  left: 35px;
  top: 335px;
}

#hit-line-2 {
  left: 135px; /* 320/2-50/2 */
  top:  335px;
}

#hit-line-3 {
  left: 235px;
  top: 335px;
}
```

4. Next, we will add the keyboard event in the JavaScript part. Open the `audiogame.` `js` JavaScript file and add the following code inside the audiogame object:

```
initKeyboardListener: function() {
  var game = this;

  // keydown
  $(document).keydown(function(e){
    // our target is J(74), K(75), L(76)
    var line = e.which-73;

    game.hitOnLine(line);

  });
  $(document).keyup(function(e){
    var line = e.which-73;
    $('#hit-line-'+line).removeClass('show');
    $('#hit-line-'+line).addClass('hide');
  });
},

hitOnLine: function (lineNo) {
  $('#hit-line-'+lineNo).removeClass('hide');
  $('#hit-line-'+lineNo).addClass('show');

  // check if hit a music note dot
  for(var i=this.dots.length-1; i>=0; i--) {
    if (lineNo === this.dots[i].line && Math.abs(
      this.dots[i].distance) < 20) {
      // remove the hit dot from the dots array
      this.dots.splice(i, 1);
    }
  }
},
```

5. Finally, we call the `initKeyboardListener` function in the `initGame` function:

```
initGame: function() {
  // existing code goes here.
  this.initKeyboardListener();
},
```

6. Now save all the files and open the game in a browser. Try pressing the *J*, *K*, and *L* keys. The three hit line indicator should appear and fade out when the key is pressed. If the music dot passes by the horizontal line when hitting the right key, then it disappears:

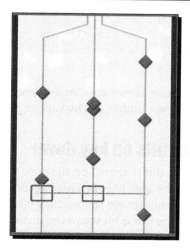

What just happened?

We just added keyboard interaction to our music game. There is a glow animation when hitting the keys. The music dot will disappear when the right key is pressed at the right moment. You can take a look at the following URL for an example of the current progress: http://makzan.net/html5-games/audiogame-wip-keyboard/.

Hitting the three music lines by key down

We use the *J*, *K*, and *L* keys to hit the three music lines in the game. The *J* key controls the left line, the *K* key controls the middle line, and the *L* key controls the right one.

There is also an indication showing that we just hit the music line. This is done by placing the following image at the intersection of the horizontal line and the vertical lines:

Next, we can control the showing and hiding of the hit indication graphics with the following jQuery code:

```
$(document).keydown(function(e){
    var line = e.which-73;
    $('#hit-line-'+line).removeClass('hide');
    $('#hit-line-'+line).addClass('show');
});
$(document).keyup(function(e){
```

```
    var line = e.which-73;
    $('#hit-line-'+line).removeClass('show');
    $('#hit-line-'+line).addClass('hide');
});
```

The *J*, *K*, and *L* keys control the music lines 1 to 3. As J, K, and L have the key code 74, 75, and 76 respectively, we know which line number it is by subtracting 73 from the key code.

Determining music dot hits on key down

The distance is close to zero if the dot is almost on the grey horizontal line. This helps us to determine whether the dots hit the grey line. By checking both the key down event and the dot distance, we can determine whether we successfully hit a music dot. The following code snippet shows that we consider the dot is hit when the distance is close enough; in this case it's within 20 pixels:

```
// check whether we hit a music note dot
  for(var i=this.dots.length-1; i>=0; i--) {
    if (lineNo === this.dots[i].line && Math.abs(
      this.dots[i].distance) < 20)    {
      // remove the hit dot from the dots array
      this.dots.splice(i, 1);
    }
  }
```

With determination, we remove the music dots when we hit them. The missed dots will still pass through the grey line and move toward the bottom. This creates basic game play where the player has to eliminate all the music dots by hitting them correctly at the right moment when the song is playing.

> When we remove elements in array inside an iteration, we usually iterate it backwards to avoid an error of null reference after elements are deleted in the array.

Removing an element in an array with the given index

We remove the music dot data from an array when it is hit (and thus it will not be drawn anymore). To remove an element in an array, we use the `splice` function. The following line of code removes one element from an array at the given index:

```
array.splice(index, 1);
```

The `splice` function is a little tricky to use. This is because it allows us to add or remove elements in an array. Then, it returns removed elements as another array.

This is how we use the `splice` function:

```
array.splice(index, length, element1, element2, …, elementN);
```

The following table shows how we use the arguments:

Argument	Definition	Discussion
index	Specifies the index of an element to be added or removed in the array	The index starts from 0. 0 means the first element, 1 means the second one, and so on. We can also use negative indexes, such as -1, which means the last element, -2, which means the second last element, and so on.
length	Specifies how many elements we want to remove	Putting 0 means we do not remove any element.
element1, element2, … elementN	The new elements to be added into the array	This is optional. Putting a list of elements here means we add the elements at the given index.

 The Mozilla Developer Network link discusses different usages of the `splice` function at: `https://developer.mozilla.org/en/JavaScript/Reference/Global_Objects/Array/splice`.

Have a go hero

In similar commercial music games, there are some words showing when the player hits or misses a music dot. How can we add this feature to our game?

Adding additional features to the mini piano game

We have created basic interaction in the game. We can go further to make the game better by adding melody volume feedback. This will make the performance playing realistic and count the success rate of the performance.

Adjusting the music volume according to the player

Imagine that now we are in a performance playing the music. We hit the music dots to play the melody. If we miss any of them, then we fail to perform it well and the melody disappears.

Time for action – removing missed melody notes

We will store some game play statistics and use them to adjust the melody volume. We will continue with our JavaScript file:

1. First, add the following variables in the variable declaration region:

```
var audiogame = {
  totalSuccessCount: 0,

  // storing the success count of last 5 results.
  successCount: 5,

  // existing code goes here.

};
```

2. We want to not only remove a dot but also keep track of the result when we hit it by using a keyboard. Add the following code inside the hitOnLine function:

```
// check if hit a music note dot
for(var i in audiogame.dots) {
    if (lineNo === audiogame.dots[i].line &&
      Math.abs(audiogame.dots[i].distance) < 20) {
      // remove the hit dot from the dots array
      audiogame.dots.splice(i, 1);

      // increase the success count
      audiogame.successCount+=1;

      // keep only 5 success count max.
      audiogame.successCount = Math.min(5,
        audiogame.successCount);

      // increase the total success count
      audiogame.totalSuccessCount +=1;
    }
}
```

3. In the `gameloop` function, we calculate all missed dots and store the result. Then, we can use these statistics to get the successful rate of the game. Add the following code to the `gameloop` function:

```
// loop again to remove dots that's out or the screen.
// existing code goes here.

// check missed dots
for(var i=this.dots.length-1; i>=0; i--) {
    if (!audiogame.dots[i].missed &&
       audiogame.dots[i].distance < -10) {
       // mark the dot as missed if it's not marked before
       audiogame.dots[i].missed = true;

       // reduce the success count
       audiogame.successCount -= 1;

       // reset the success count to 0 if it is lower than 0.
       audiogame.successCount = Math.max(0,
          audiogame.successCount);
    }

    // remove missed dots after moved to the bottom
    if (audiogame.dots[i].distance < -100) {
       audiogame.dots.splice(i, 1);
    }
}

// calculate the percentage of the success in last 5 music dots
var successPercent = audiogame.successCount / 5;

// prevent the successPercent to exceed range(fail safe)
successPercent = Math.max(0, Math.min(1, successPercent));

// move the dots
// existing code goes here.
```

4. Lastly, we adjust the melody volume by using the successful rate. Put the following code after the code we just added in the `gameloop` function:

```
audiogame.melody.volume = successPercent;
```

5. Save all files and test our game in a browser. When the player continues to play the game well, the melody keeps playing. When the player misses several music dots, the melody disappears and only the base plays.

What just happened?

We just used the player's performance as feedback on the melody volume. This gives the player the feeling that we are really performing the music. When we perform poorly, the melody volume is low and the song sounds poor too. You may try the working example at the following URL: `http://makzan.net/html5-games/audiogame-wip-volume/`.

Removing dots from the game

We want to remove the dots either after they drop under the bottom bound or when they are being hit by the player. The game loop displays all the dots in the dot list on the game canvas. We can remove the dot graphic by removing its data from the array of dots. We'll use the following `splice` function to remove an entry in the array of the target index:

```
audiogame.dots.splice(index, 1);
```

Storing the success count in the last five results

In our game, we need to store the success count in the last five results to calculate the success rate. We can do this by using a counter representing this. When a dot is successfully hit, the counter increases by one, but when the player fails to hit a dot, the counter decreases by 1.

The counter then represents the successful counts within the last few results if we limit the counter to have a range, 0 to 5 in our example.

Have a go hero

We discussed how to display the game progress in the Untangle game in the last chapter. Can we apply a similar technique in the music game? We have the player's success percentage during game play. How about displaying it as a percentage bar at the top of the game?

Recording music notes as level data

The game relies on the level data to play. The playback visualization will not work if there is no level data. We also cannot play it if the playback visualization is not working. So how can we record that level data?

Imagine that now the music is playing without any music dots appearing in the game. We listen to the music carefully and press the *J, K, L* keys when the music plays. After the music ends, we print out all the keys and time we pressed. This data will then be used in the playback visualization of the music.

Time for action – adding functionalities to record the music level data

Carry out the following steps:

1. First, we create a variable to toggle between the recording mode and normal playing mode. Open the `html5games.audio.js` file and add the code as follows:

```
var audiogame = {
  isRecordMode : true,
  //existing code here
```

2. Next, we add the following highlighted code in the `keydown` event handler. This code stores all our pressed keys in an array and prints them out to the console when the semicolon key is pressed:

```
if (game.isRecordMode) {
  // print the stored music notes data when press ";" (186)
  if (e.which === 186) {
    var musicNotesString = "";
    for(var i=0, len=game.musicNotes.length; i<len; i++)      {
      musicNotesString += game.musicNotes[i].time + "," +
        game.musicNotes[i].line+";";
    }
    console.log(musicNotesString);
  }

  var currentTime = game.melody.currentTime.toFixed(3);
  var note = new MusicNote(currentTime, e.which-73);
  game.musicNotes.push(note);
}
```

3. Finally, we want to make sure that the `setupLevelData` and `gameloop` functions are not executed during the recording mode. These functions are for the playing mode only:

```
if (!audiogame.isRecordMode) {
  audiogame.setupLevelData();
  setInterval(audiogame.gameloop.bind(audiogame), 30);
}
```

4. Now open the `index.html` file in a browser. After clicking on the **Play** button, the game starts and the music plays without the music notes. Try pressing the *J*, *K*, and *L* keys following the music beat. After finishing the music, press the semicolon to print the level data in the console. The following screenshot shows the console displaying the level data string:

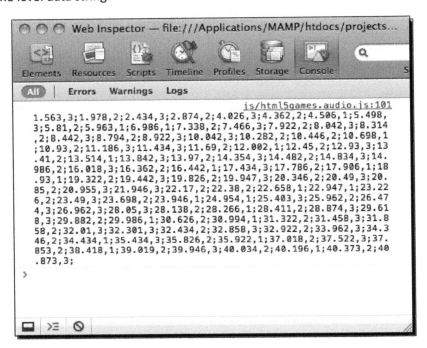

What just happened?

We just added a recording feature to our game. We can now record our music notes. We can toggle the record mode and playing mode by setting the `audiogame.isRecordMode` variable to `true` and `false`.

On every key press, we get the elapsed time of the melody and create a `MusicNote` instance with the time and line number. The following code shows how we record the pressed keys. The `currentTime` is cut to two decimal digits before saving:

```
var currentTime = audiogame.melody.currentTime.toFixed(3);
var note = new MusicNote(currentTime, e.which-73);
audiogame.musicNotes.push(note);
```

We also capture the semicolon key to print out all the recorded `MusicNote` data into a string. The string follows the `time,line;time,line;` format, so we can directly copy the printed string and paste it as level data to play.

The `toFixed` function formats the number with the given number of trailing decimals. In our example, we used it to get the current time with 3 trailing decimals.

Adding touch support

Now the game works well on a desktop browser. But we want to make the game playable on mobile devices too.

Time for action – indicating a game over event in the console

We target the 3-intersection point between the horizontal line and the vertical line.

1. We have defined three DIV elements there to display the graphics when hitting the *J*, *K*, and *L* keys. We modify the HTML to add a data-line-no attribute to these elements:

```
<div id="hit-line-1" data-line-no="1"
    class="hit-line hide"></div>
<div id="hit-line-2" data-line-no="2"
    class="hit-line hide"></div>
<div id="hit-line-3" data-line-no="3"
    class="hit-line hide"></div>
```

2. We move to JavaScript. We define a new function inside the `audiogame` object:

```
initTouchAndClick: function() {
  var game = this;
  $('.hit-line').bind('mousedown touchstart', function() {
    var line = $(this).data('lineNo') * 1; // parse in int
    game.hitOnLine(line);
    return false;
  });

  $('.hit-line').bind('mouseup touchend', function(){
    var line = $(this).data('lineNo') * 1; // parse in int
    $('#hit-line-'+line).removeClass('show');
    $('#hit-line-'+line).addClass('hide');
  });
},
```

3. We call our newly created `initTouchAndClick` function in the `initGame` function:

```
initGame: function() {
  // existing code goes here.

  this.initTouchAndClick();
},
```

4. We can now open the game in a mobile browser and play it with our fingers.

What just happened?

We have added a touch event to the game. The data-line-no attribute in the HTML elements lets us know which line the player is touching. Then we call the same `hitOnLine` function that the `keydown` event calls, which shares the some code that handles the hit-or-miss determination.

Handling the audio event in playback complete events

We can play the game now, but there is no indication when the game is over. Imagine that now we want to know how well we played when the game is completed. We will capture the melody-ending signal and display the success rate of the game.

Time for action – indicating a game over event in the console

Carry out the following steps:

1. Open the `audiogame.js` JavaScript file.

2. Add the following code in the jQuery ready function:

```
$(audiogame.melody).bind('ended', onMelodyEnded);
```

3. Add the following event handler function at the end of the file:

```
// show game over scene on melody ended.
function onMelodyEnded() {
  console.log('song ended');
  alert ('success percent: ' + audiogame.totalSuccessCount /
    audiogame.totalDotsCount * 100 + '%');
}
})(jQuery);
```

4. It is time to save all files and play the game in a web browser. When the game is over, we should see a pop-up alert with the successful rate.

What just happened?

We just listened to the `ended` event of the audio element and handled it with a handler function.

Handling audio events

There are many other events in the audio element. The following table lists a few commonly used audio events:

Event	Discussion
ended	Sent when the audio element finishes a playback
play	Sent when the audio element plays or resumes
pause	Sent when the audio element pauses
progress	Sent periodically when the audio element is downloading
timeupdate	Sent when the `currentTime` property changes

Here we just listed a few commonly used events; you can refer to the complete audio event list in the Mozilla Developer Center at: `https://developer.mozilla.org/En/Using_ audio_and_video_in_Firefox#Media_events`.

Have a go hero

In our music game, we print out the success rate in the console when the game is over. How about adding a game over scene to our game and showing it at the end of the game? It would be good to use animation transition when showing a game over scene too.

We have managed the sound assets and played the audio with the native JavaScript API. Sometimes it will get troublesome to manage a large amount of audio loading and playing. There are some JS libraries to help you manage HTML5 audio easier. Here are few of them:

- SoundJS (`http://www.createjs.com/SoundJS`)
- Buzz (`http://buzz.jaysalvat.com`)
- AudioJS (`http://kolber.github.io/audiojs/`)

Summary

You learned a lot in this chapter about using the HTML5 audio element and built a music game. Specifically, we managed and controlled audio playback by using the HTML audio tag and related JavaScript API. You learned different attributes that change the audio tag's behavior. We made use of the audio tag to create a keyboard-based canvas game. We also made the game work on touch devices by sharing the common logic between keyboard input and touch input. We created the game with a special mode that helps the game level designer to create the level data.

You learned about adding music and sound effects in our HTML5 games. Now we are ready to build a more complete game by adding a leaderboard to store game scores in the next chapter.

7
Saving the Game's Progress

Local storage is a new specification from HTML5. It allows a website to store information in the browser locally and access the stored data later. This is a useful feature in game development because we can use it as a memory slot to save any game data locally in a web browser.

We are going to add the feature of storing game data in the CSS3 card matching game we built in *Chapter 3, Building a Card-matching Game in CSS3*. Besides storing and loading the game data, we will also notify the player when they break a record with a nice 3D ribbon using pure CSS3 styling.

In this chapter, we will cover the following topics:

- Storing data by using HTML5 local storage
- Saving the object in the local storage
- Notifying players when they break a new record with a nice ribbon effect
- Saving the entire game's progress

You may try the final game at: `http://makzan.net/html5-games/card-matching/`.

The following screenshot shows the final result we will create in this chapter:

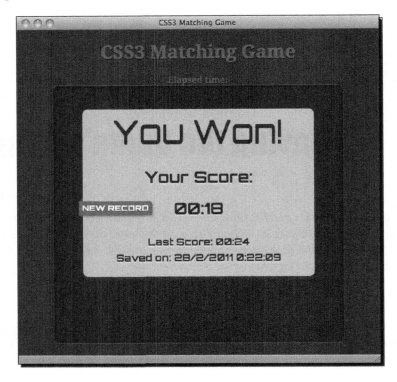

So, let's get on with it.

Storing data using HTML5 local storage

Remember the CSS3 card matching game we made in *Chapter 3, Building a Card-matching Game in CSS3*? Imagine now that we have published our game and players are trying their best to perform well in the game.

We want to show the players whether they played better or worse than the last time. We will save the latest score and inform players whether they are better or not this time, by comparing the scores.

The reasons we might want to do this are because it gives the player a sense of pride when they perform better, and they may become addicted to our game to try to get higher scores, which is good for us.

Creating a game over dialog

Before actually saving anything in the local storage, we need a game over screen. We made a few games in previous chapters. We made a Ping Pong game, the card matching game, the Untangle puzzle game, and a music game. In these games, we did not create any game over screen. Imagine now that we are playing the CSS3 card matching game that we built in *Chapter 3, Building a Card-matching Game in CSS3*. We successfully match and remove all cards. Once we finish a game a screen pops up and shows the time we took to complete the game.

Time for action – creating a game over dialog with the elapsed played time

We will continue with the code from the card matching game we made in *Chapter 3, Building a Card-matching Game in CSS3*. Carry out the following steps:

1. Open the CSS3 matching game folder as our working directory.

2. Download a background image from the following URL (we will use it as the background of the popup): `http://mak.la/book-assets`

3. Place the image in the `images` folder.

4. Open `index.html` in any text editor.

5. We will need a font for the game over popup. Add the following font embedding CSS into the `head` section:

   ```
   <link href="http://fonts.googleapis.com/css?family=
     Orbitron:400,700" rel="stylesheet" type="text/css">
   ```

6. Before the `game` section, we add a `div` named `timer` to show the elapsed playing time. In addition, we add a new `popup` section containing the HTML markup of the pop-up dialog:

   ```
   <div id="timer">
       Elapsed time: <span id="elapsed-time">00:00</span>
   </div>
   <section id="game">
       <div id="cards">
           <div class="card">
               <div class="face front"></div>
               <div class="face back"></div>
           </div> <!-- .card -->
       </div> <!-- #cards -->
   </section> <!-- #game -->
   ```

```
<section id="popup" class="hide">
  <div id="popup-bg">
  </div>
  <div id="popup-box">
    <div id="popup-box-content">
      <h1>You Won!</h1>
      <p>Your Score:</p>
      <p><span class='score'>13</span></p>
    </div>
  </div>
</section>
```

7. We will now move on to the style sheet. As it is just for styling and not related to our logic yet, we can simply copy the `matchgame.css` file from `01-gameover-dialog` in the code example bundle.

8. It is time to edit the game's logic part. Open the `matchgame.js` file in an editor.

9. In the jQuery `ready` function, we need a variable to store the elapsed time of the game. Then, we create a timer to count the game every second as follows:

```
$(document).ready(function(){
  ...
  // reset the elapsed time to 0.
  matchingGame.elapsedTime = 0;

  // start the timer
  matchingGame.timer = setInterval(countTimer, 1000);
}
```

10. Next, we add a `countTimer` function that will be executed every second. It displays the elapsed seconds in the minutes and seconds format:

```
function countTimer() {
  matchingGame.elapsedTime++;

  // calculate the minutes and seconds from elapsed time
  var minute = Math.floor(matchingGame.elapsedTime / 60);
  var second = matchingGame.elapsedTime % 60;

  // add padding 0 if minute and second is less than 10
  if (minute < 10) minute = "0" + minute;
  if (second < 10) second = "0" + second;

  // display the elapsed time
  $("#elapsed-time").html(minute+":"+second);
}
```

11. In the `removeTookCards` function that we wrote earlier, add the following highlighted code that executes the game over logic after removing all cards:

```
function removeTookCards() {
  $(".card-removed").remove();

  // check whether all cards are removed and show game over
  if ($(".card").length === 0) {
    gameover();
  }
}
```

12. And last, we create the following `gameover` function. It stops the counting timer, displays the elapsed time in the game over popup, and finally shows the popup:

```
function gameover() {
  // stop the timer
  clearInterval(matchingGame.timer);

  // set the score in the game over popup
  $(".score").html($("#elapsed-time").html());

  // show the game over popup
  $("#popup").removeClass("hide");
}
```

13. Now, save all files and open the game in a browser. Try finishing the card matching game and the game over screen will popup, as shown in the following screenshot:

What just happened?

We used the CSS3 transition animation to show the game over popup. We benchmark the score by using the time the player utilized to finish the game.

Counting time

We used the time interval to calculate elapsed time. We provide an interval, for instance, 1 second, and the browser executes our logic at the provided interval. Inside the logic, we count the elapsed seconds. We need to keep in mind that `setInterval` does not guarantee the execution of the logic precisely at the given time interval. It's an approximate value. If you need a more precise elapsed time, you may get the time stamp and subtract it from the start time.

Saving scores in the browser

Imagine now that we are going to display how well the player played last time. The game over screen includes the elapsed time as the last score alongside the current game score. Players can then see how well they do this time compared to last time.

Time for action – saving the game score

1. First, we need to add a few markups in the `popup` section to display the last score. Add the following HTML in `popup-box` in `index.html`. The changed code is highlighted:

```
<section id="popup" class="hide">
  <div id="popup-bg">
  </div>
  <div id="popup-box">
    <div id="popup-box-content">
      <h1>You Won!</h1>
      <p>Your Score:</p>
      <p><span class='score'>13</span></p>
      <p>
        <small>Last Score: <span class='last-score'>20</span>
        </small>
      </p>
    </div>
  </div>
</section>
```

2. Then, we open the `matchgame.js` to modify some game logic in the `gameover` function.

3. Add the following highlighted code in the `gameover` function. It loads the saved score from the local storage and displays it as the score last time. Then, we save the current score in the local storage:

```js
function gameover() {
  // stop the timer
  clearInterval(matchingGame.timer);

  // display the elapsed time in the game over popup
  $(".score").html($("#elapsed-time").html());

  // load the saved last score from local storage
  var lastElapsedTime = localStorage.getItem(
    "last-elapsed-time");

  // convert the elapsed seconds
  //into minute:second format
  // calculate the minutes and seconds
  // from elapsed time
  var minute = Math.floor(lastElapsedTime / 60);
  var second = lastElapsedTime % 60;

  // add padding 0
  if (minute < 10) minute = "0" + minute;
  if (second < 10) second = "0" + second;

  // display the last elapsed time in game over popup
  $(".last-score").html(minute+":"+second);

  // save the score in local storage
  localStorage.setItem("last-elapsed-time",
    matchingGame.elapsedTime);

  // show the game over popup
  $("#popup").removeClass("hide");
}
```

4. It is now time to save all the files and test the game in the browser. When you finish the game for the first time, the last score should be `00:00`. Then, try to finish the game for the second time. The game over popup will show the elapsed time when you played the last time. The following screenshot shows the game over screen with the current and last score:

What just happened?

We just built a basic scoring system that compares a player's score with their last score.

Storing and loading data with local storage

We can store data by using the `setItem` function from the `localStorage` object as follows:

```
localStorage.setItem(key, value);
```

The following table shows the usage of the function:

Argument	Definition	Description
key	The key is the name of the record that we used to identify an entry	The key is a string and each record has a unique key. Writing a new value to an existing key overwrites the old value.
value	The value is any data that will be stored	This can be any data, but the final storage is in a string. We will discuss this shortly.

In our example, we save the game elapsed time as the score with the following code by using the key `last-elapsed-item`:

```
localStorage.setItem("last-elapsed-time", matchingGame.elapsedTime);
```

Complementary to `setItem`, we get the stored data by using the `getItem` function in the following way:

```
localStorage.getItem(key);
```

The function returns the stored value of the given key. It returns `null` when trying to get a non-existent key. This can be used to check whether we have stored any data for a specific key.

The local storage saves the string value

The local storage stores data in a key-value pair. The key and value are both strings. If we save numbers, Boolean, or any type other than a string, then the browser will convert the value into a string while saving. For objects and arrays, we will do our conversion using JSON in a later section.

Usually, problems occur when we load a saved value from the local storage. The loaded value is a string regardless of the type we are saving. We need to explicitly parse the value into the correct type before using it.

For example, if we save a floating number into the local storage, we need to use the `parseFloat` function when loading it. The following code snippet shows how we can use `parseFloat` to retrieve a stored floating number:

```
var score = 13.234;

localStorage.setItem("game-score",score);
// result: stored "13.234".

var gameScore = localStorage.getItem("game-score");
// result: get "13.234" into gameScore;

gameScore = parseFloat(gameScore);
// result: 13.234 floating value
```

In the preceding code snippet, the manipulation may be incorrect if we forget to convert `gameScore` from a string to a float. For instance, if we increase `gameScore` by 1 without the `parseFloat` function, the result will be **13.2341** instead of **14.234**. So, be sure to convert the value from the local storage to its correct type.

Size limitations on local storage

There is a size limitation on the data stored through `localStorage` for each domain. This size limitation may be slightly different in different browsers. Normally, the size limitation is 5 MB. If the limit is exceeded, then the browser throws a `QUOTA_EXCEEDED_ERR` exception when setting a key-value into `localStorage`.

Treating the local storage object as an associative array

Besides using the `setItem` and `getItem` functions, we can treat the `localStorage` object as an associated array and access the stored entries by using square brackets. For instance, consider the following lines of code:

```
localStorage.setItem("last-elapsed-time", elapsedTime);
var lastElapsedTime = localStorage.getItem("last-elapsed-time");
```

We can replace the preceding block of code with the following one and access `localStorage` as an array:

```
localStorage["last-elapsed-time"] = elapsedTime;
var lastElapsedTime = localStorage["last-elapsed-time"];
```

Saving objects in the local storage

Now, imagine that we are saving not only the score, but also the date and time when the ranking is created. We can either save two separate keys for the score and date time of playing, or pack the two values into one object and store it in the local storage.

We will pack all the game data into one object and store it.

Time for action – saving the time alongside the score

Carry out the following steps:

1. First, open the `index.html` file from our CSS3 card matching game.

2. Replace the HTML markup with the last score, with the following HTML (it shows both scores and the date time in the game over popup):

```
<p>
  <small>Last Score: <span class='last-score'>0</span><br>
    Saved on: <span class='saved-time'></span>
  </small>
</p>
```

3. The HTML markup is now ready. We will move on to the game logic. Open the `html5games.matchgame.js` file in a text editor.

4. We will modify the `gameover` function. Add the following highlighted code to the `gameover` function. It gets the current date and time when the game ends and packs a formatted date and time with elapsed time together in the local storage:

```
function gameover() {
    // stop the timer
```

```
clearInterval(matchingGame.timer);

// display the elapsed time in the game over popup
$(".score").html($("#elapsed-time"));

// load the saved last score and save time from local storage
var lastScore = localStorage.getItem("last-score");

// check if there is no saved record
lastScoreObj = JSON.parse(lastScore);
if (lastScoreObj === null) {
    // create an empty record if there is no saved record
    lastScoreObj = {"savedTime": "no record", "score": 0};
}
var lastElapsedTime = lastScoreObj.score;

// convert the elapsed seconds into minute:second format
// calculate the minutes and seconds from elapsed time
var minute = Math.floor(lastElapsedTime / 60);
var second = lastElapsedTime % 60;

// add padding 0 if minute and second is less than 10
if (minute < 10) minute = "0" + minute;
if (second < 10) second = "0" + second;

// display the last elapsed time in game over popup
$(".last-score").html(minute+":"+second);

// display the saved time of last score
var savedTime = lastScoreObj.savedTime;
$(".saved-time").html(savedTime);

// get the current datetime
var currentTime = new Date();

// convert date time to string
var now = currentTime.toLocaleString();

//construct the object of datetime and game score
var obj = { "savedTime": now, "score":
    matchingGame.elapsedTime};

// save the score into local storage
localStorage.setItem("last-score", JSON.stringify(obj));
```

```
    // show the game over popup
    $("#popup").removeClass("hide");
}
```

5. We will save the files and open the game in a web browser.

6. When we finish the game for the first time, we will get a screen similar to the following screenshot, which will show our game score and state that there are no previous records:

7. Now try reloading the page and play the game again. When we finish the game for the second time, the game over dialog will show our saved record. The following screenshot shows how it should look:

What just happened?

We just used a `Date` object in JavaScript to get the current date and time when the game is over. In addition, we packed the game over date and time and the game elapsed time in one object and saved it in the local storage. The saved object is encoded in a JSON string. It will also load the last saved date and time and the game elapsed time from the storage and parse it back to the JavaScript object from a string.

Getting the current date and time in JavaScript

The Date object in JavaScript is used to work with the date and time. When we create an instance from the Date object, by default it stores the current date and time. We can get the string representation by using the toLocaleString method.

In addition to the string representation, we can manipulate each component in the date object. The following table lists some useful functions in the Date object to get the date and time:

Function	Description
getFullYear	Returns the year in four digits
getMonth	Returns the month in an integer, starting from 0 (Jan is 0 and Dec is 11)
getDate	Returns the day of the month, starting from 1
getDay	Returns the day of the week, starting from 0 (Sunday is 0 and Saturday is 6)
getHours	Returns the hour, starting from 0 to 23
getMinutes	Returns the minutes
getSeconds	Returns the seconds
getMilliseconds	Returns the milliseconds in 3 digits
getTime	Returns the number of milliseconds since 1 January, 1970, 00:00

 The Mozilla Developer Network provides a detailed reference on using the Date object at: https://developer.mozilla.org/en/JavaScript/Reference/Global_Objects/Date.

Using the native JSON to encode an object into a string

We used JSON to represent the game level data in *Chapter 4, Building the Untangle Game with Canvas and the Drawing API*.

JSON is an object notation format that is friendly for machines to parse and generate. In this example, we packed the final elapsed time and the date and time into an object. Then, we encoded the object into JSON. Modern web browsers come with native JSON support. We can easily encode any JavaScript object into JSON by using the stringify function as follows:

```
JSON.stringify(anyObject);
```

Normally, we only use the first parameter for the `stringify` function. This is the object that we are going to encode as a string. The following code snippet demonstrates the result of an encoded JavaScript object:

```
var jsObj = {};
jsObj.testArray = [1,2,3,4,5];
jsObj.name = 'CSS3 Matching Game';
jsObj.date = '8 May, 2011';
JSON.stringify(jsObj);
// result: {"testArray":[1,2,3,4,5],"name":"CSS3 Matching
  Game","date":"8 May, 2011"}
```

 The `stringify` method can parse objects with data structure into a string well. However, it cannot convert anything from an object into a string. For instance, it will return an error if we try to pass a DOM element into it. It will return the string representing the date if we pass a `Date` object. Alternatively, it will drop all method definitions of the parsing object.

Loading a stored object from a JSON string

The complete form of **JSON** is **JavaScript Object Notation**. From the name, we know that it uses the syntax from JavaScript to represent an object. Therefore, it is very easy to parse a JSON formatted string back to a JavaScript object.

The following code snippet shows how we can use the parse function in the JSON object:

```
JSON.parse(jsonFormattedString);
```

We can open the console in **Web Inspector** to test the JSON JavaScript functions. The following screenshot shows the result of running the code snippets we just discussed when encoding an object and parsing them:

```
●○○                    Web Inspector — about:blank
> var jsObj = {};
  undefined
> jsObj.testArray = [1,2,3,4,5];
  [1, 2, 3, 4, 5]
> jsObj.name = 'CSS3 Matching Game';
  CSS3 Matching Game
> jsObj.date = '8 May, 2011';
  8 May, 2011
> JSON.stringify(jsObj);
  {"testArray":[1,2,3,4,5],"name":"CSS3 Matching Game","date":"8 May,
  2011"}
> var jsonString = JSON.stringify(jsObj);
  undefined
> jsonString
  {"testArray":[1,2,3,4,5],"name":"CSS3 Matching Game","date":"8 May,
  2011"}
> JSON.parse(jsonString);
  ▼ Object
      date: "8 May, 2011"
      name: "CSS3 Matching Game"
    ▼ testArray: Array
        0: 1
        1: 2
        2: 3
        3: 4
        4: 5
> |

  □  >≡  ○
```

Inspecting the local storage in a console window

After we have saved something in the local storage, we may want to know what exactly is saved, before we write the loading part. We can inspect what we have saved by using the storage panel in the **Web Inspector**. It lists all the saved key-value pairs under the same domain. The following screenshot shows that we have the **last-score** key saved with value **{"savedTime":"23/2/2011 19:27:02","score":23}**.

The value is the result of the JSON.stringify function we used to encode the object into JSON. You may also try saving an object directly in the local storage:

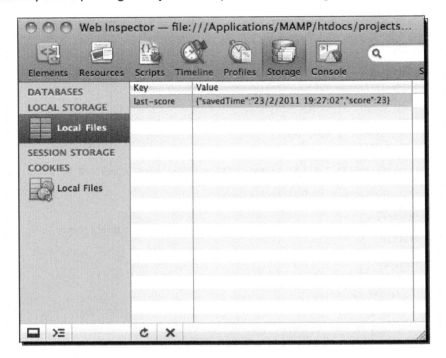

 Besides localStorage, there are other storage approaches that were not discussed. **IndexedDB** is another option. Check the following URL to see more details on this: https://developer.mozilla.org/en/IndexedDB.

Notifying players when they break a new record with a nice ribbon effect

Imagine that we want to encourage players by informing them that they broke a new record compared to the last score. We want to show a ribbon with New Record text on it. Thanks to the new CSS3 properties, we can create a ribbon effect completely in CSS.

Time for action – creating a ribbon in CSS3

We will create a new record ribbon and display it when a player breaks their last score. So, carry out the following steps:

1. First, open `index.html` where we will add the ribbon HTML markup.

2. Add the following highlighted HTML right after `popup-box` and before `popup-box-content`:

```html
<div id="popup-box">
  <div class="ribbon hide">
    <div class="ribbon-body">
      <span>New Record</span>
    </div>
    <div class="triangle"></div>
  </div>
  <div id="popup-box-content">
  ...
```

3. Next, we need to focus on the style sheet. The entire ribbon effect is done in CSS. Open the `matchgame.css` file in a text editor.

4. In the `popup-box` styling, we need to add a relative position to it. We do this as follows:

```css
#popup-box {
  position: relative;
}
```

5. Then, we need to add the following styles that create the ribbon effect in the CSS file:

```css
.ribbon.hide {
  display: none;
}
.ribbon {
  float: left;
  position: absolute;
  left: -7px;
  top: 165px;
  z-index: 0;

  font-size: .5em;
  text-transform: uppercase;
  text-align: right;
}
```

```
.ribbon-body {
  height: 14px;
  background: #ca3d33;
  padding: 6px;
  z-index: 100;
  box-shadow: 2px 2px 0 rgba(150,120,70,.4);
  border-radius: 0 5px 5px 0;

  color: #fff;
  text-shadow: 0px 1px 1px rgba(0,0,0,.3);
}

.triangle {
  position: relative;
  height: 0px;
  width: 0;
  left: -5px;
  top: -32px;
  border-style: solid;
  border-width: 6px;
  border-color: transparent #882011 transparent transparent;
  z-index: -1;
}
```

6. Lastly, we need to modify the game over logic a little bit. Open the `html5games.matchgame.js` file and locate the `gameover` function.

7. Add the following code to the `gameover` function, which compares the current score with the last score to determine the new record:

```
if (lastElapsedTime === 0 || matchingGame.elapsedTime <
lastElapsedTime) {
    $(".ribbon").removeClass("hide");
}
```

8. We will test the game in a web browser. Try finishing a game slowly and then finish another game fast. When you break the last score, the game over popup shows a nice **NEW RECORD** ribbon, as shown in the following screenshot:

What just happened?

We just created a ribbon effect in a pure CSS3 style with some help from JavaScript to show and hide it. The ribbon is composed of a little triangle overlaid by a rectangle, as shown in the following screenshot:

Now, how can we create a triangle in CSS? We can create a triangle by setting both the width and height to 0 and drawing only one border. The size of the triangle is then decided by the border width. The following is the code for the triangle CSS we used in our new record ribbon:

```
.triangle {
    position: relative;
    height: 0px;
    width: 0;
    left: -5px;
    top: -32px;
    border-style: solid;
    border-width: 6px;
    border-color: transparent #882011 transparent transparent;
    z-index: -1;
}
```

The following PVM Garage website provides a detailed explanation on pure CSS3 ribbon usage:

http://www.pvmgarage.com/2010/01/how-to-create-depth-and-nice-3d-ribbons-only-using-css3/

Have a go hero – saving and comparing only to the fastest time

Each time the game finishes, it compares the last score with the current score. Then, it saves the current score. How about changing the code to save the highest score and show the new record ribbon when breaking the highest score?

Saving the entire game progress

We have enhanced our CSS3 card matching game by adding a game over screen and storing the last game record. Imagine now that a player is mid-game and accidentally closes the web browser. Once the player opens the game again, the game starts from the beginning and the game that the player was playing is lost. With the local storage, we can encode the entire game's data into JSON and store it. In this way, players can resume their game later.

We are going to pack the game data into one object and save it into the local storage every second.

Time for action – saving all essential game data in the local storage

We will continue work with our CSS3 card matching game:

1. Open the `matchgame.js` JavaScript file.

2. Add the following code at the top of the JavaScript file after declaring the `matchingGame` variable. This code creates an object named `savingObject` to save the array of the deck, the removed cards and the current elapsed time:

```
matchingGame.savingObject = {};

matchingGame.savingObject.deck = [];

// array to store which card is removed by their index.
matchingGame.savingObject.removedCards = [];

// store the counting elapsed time.
matchingGame.savingObject.currentElapsedTime = 0;
```

3. In the jQuery `ready` function, add the following highlighted code. It clones the order of the deck to the `savingObject`. In addition, it assigns an index to each card in the DOM data attribute:

```
$(document).ready(function(){
    // existing code goes here.
```

```
    // shuffling the deck
    matchingGame.deck.sort(shuffle);

    // copying the deck into saving object.
    matchingGame.savingObject.deck = matchingGame.deck.slice();

    // clone 12 copies of the card DOM
    for(var i=0;i<11;i++){
        $(".card:first-child").clone().appendTo("#cards");
    }

    // existing code goes here.

// embed the pattern data into the DOM element.
$(this).attr("data-pattern",pattern);

// save the index into the DOM element,
//so we know which is the next card.
$(this).attr("data-card-index",index);
. . .
```

4. We have a `countTimer` function that executes every second. We add the following highlighted code in the `countTimer` function. It saves the current elapsed time in `savingObject` and also saves the object in the local storage:

```
function countTimer() {
    matchingGame.elapsedTime++;

    // save the current elapsed time in savingObject.
    matchingGame.savingObject.currentElapsedTime =
      matchingGame.elapsedTime;
    . . .
    // save the game progress
    saveSavingObject();
}
```

5. The game removes cards when the player finds a matching pair. We replace the original `$(".card-removed").remove();` code with the following highlighted code in the `removeTookCards` function. It remembers which cards are removed in `savingObject`:

```
function removeTookCards() {
    // add each removed card into the array
    // which stores the removed cards
    $(".card-removed").each(function(){
```

```
matchingGame.savingObject.removedCards.push(
    $(this).data("card-index"));
    $(this).remove();
});

// check whether all cards are removed and show game over
if ($(".card").length === 0) {
    gameover();
}
}
```

6. We have to remove the saved game data in the local storage when the game is over. Add the following code at the end of the gameover function:

```
function gameover() {
    // existing code goes here.

    //at last, we clear the saved savingObject
    localStorage.removeItem("savingObject");
}
```

7. And last, we use a function to save savingObject in the local storage:

```
function saveSavingObject() {
    // save the encoded saving object in local storage
    localStorage["savingObject"] = JSON.stringify(
    matchingGame.savingObject);
}
```

8. We have modified the code a lot and it is now time to test the game in a web browser. After the game runs, try clearing several matching cards. Then, open the storage panel in the **Web Inspector**. The local storage should contain an entry similar to the one shown in the following screenshot:

Key	Value
savingObject	["deck":["cardBJ","cardAJ","cardAQ","cardBQ","cardBK","cardBJ","cardAK","cardBK","cardAQ","cardAK","cardAJ","cardBQ"],"removedCards":[2,5,4,7],"currentElapsedTime":47]

It is a record with a key savingObject and a value with a long string in a JSON format. The JSON string contains the shuffled deck, removed cards, and the current elapsed time

What just happened?

We have just entered all essential game data into an object named `savingObject`.
This `savingObject` contains all the information that we need to recreate the game later.
It includes the order of cards, removed cards, and the current elapsed time. We will
implement the game resuming logic in the next section.

Lastly, we saved `savingObject` in `localStorage` each second. The object is encoded
in JSON using the `stringify` function we used earlier in this chapter.

Removing a record from the local storage

We need to remove the saved record when the game is over. Otherwise, the new game will
not start. The local storage provides a `removeItem` function to remove a specific record.
Here is how we use the function to remove the record with the given key:

```
localStorage.removeItem(key);
```

 If you want to remove all stored records, then you can use the
`localStorage.clear()` function.

Cloning an array in JavaScript

We cloned the shuffled deck in `savingObject`, so that we could use the order of the deck
to recreate the cards when we resumed the game. However, we cannot copy an array by
assigning the array to another variable. The following code fails to copy array a to array b:

```
var a = [1,2,3,4,5];
var b = a;
a.pop();
// result:
// a: [1,2,3,4]
// b: [1,2,3,4]
```

The `slice` function provides an easy way to clone an array with only primitive types of
elements, for example, an array of integers or an array of strings. We can clone an array with
the `slice` function as long as it does not contain another array or object as an element.
The following code successfully clones array a to b:

```
var a = [1,2,3,4,5];
var b = a.slice();
a.pop();
// result:
// a: [1,2,3,4]
// b: [1,2,3,4,5]
```

The `slice` function is normally used to create a new array by selecting a range of elements from an existing array. When using the `slice` function without any arguments, it clones the entire array. The Mozilla Developer Network provides details on the `slice` function at: `https://developer.mozilla.org/en/JavaScript/Reference/Global_Objects/Array/slice`.

Resuming the game progress

We have saved the game progress, but we have not yet written the logic to resume the game. So, let's move on to the resuming part.

Time for action – resuming a game from the local storage

Carry out the following steps:

1. Open the `matchgame.js` JavaScript file.

2. In the jQuery document `ready` function, we used the saved order of the deck in the previous game instead of shuffling a new deck. Add the following highlighted code in the jQuery `ready` function:

```
$(document).ready(function(){
  // reset the elapsed time to 0.
  matchingGame.elapsedTime = 0;

  // start the timer
  matchingGame.timer = setInterval(countTimer, 1000);

// shuffling the deck
  matchingGame.deck.sort(shuffle);

  // re-create the saved deck
  var savedObject = savedSavingObject();
  if (savedObject !== undefined) {
    matchingGame.deck = savedObject.deck;
  }

  // copying the deck into saving object.
  matchingGame.savingObject.deck = matchingGame.deck.slice();
});
```

3. Still in the jQuery document `ready` function, we append the following highlighted code to the end of the function. It removes any card that was marked as removed in the saved data. We also restore the saved elapsed time from the saved value:

```
$(document).ready(function(){
// existing card creation code goes here.

    // removed cards that were removed in savedObject.
    if (savedObject !== undefined) {
      matchingGame.savingObject.removedCards =
        savedObject.removedCards;
      // find those cards and remove them.
      for(var i in matchingGame.savingObject.removedCards) {
        $(".card[data-card-index="+matchingGame.savingObject.
          removedCards[i]+"]").remove();
      }
    }

    // reset the elapsed time to 0.
    matchingGame.elapsedTime = 0;

    // restore the saved elapsed time
    if (savedObject !== undefined) {
      matchingGame.elapsedTime = savedObject.currentElapsedTime;
      matchingGame.savingObject.currentElapsedTime = savedObject.
        currentElapsedTime;
    }
});
```

4. Finally, we create the following function to retrieve `savingObject` from the local storage:

```
// Returns the saved savingObject from the local storage.
function savedSavingObject() {
    // returns the saved saving object from local storage
    var savingObject = localStorage["savingObject"];
    if (savingObject !== undefined) {
       savingObject = JSON.parse(savingObject);
    }
    return savingObject;
}
```

5. Save all the files and open the game in a web browser. Try playing the game by removing several matching cards. Then, close the browser window and open the game again. The game should resume from the state where we closed the window, as shown in the following screenshot:

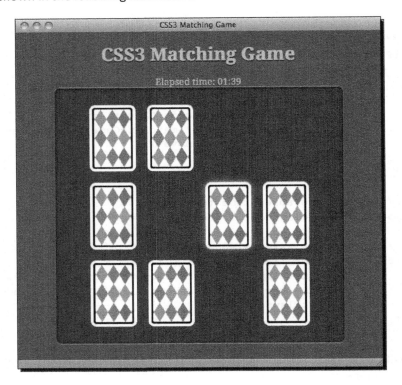

What just happened?

We just finished the loading part of the game by parsing the saved JSON string of the entire game status.

Then, we restored the elapsed time and the order of the deck from the loaded object, `savingObject`. Restoring these two properties is simply a case of variable assigning. The tricky part is recreating removing the card. In the game saving section, we assigned an index to each card's DOM using a **custom data attribute** `data-card-index`. We stored the index of each removed card when saving the game, so we can know which cards are removed when loading the game. Then, we can remove these cards when the game sets up. The following code removes the cards in the jQuery game `ready` function:

```
if (savedObject !== undefined) {
    matchingGame.savingObject.removedCards = savedObject.removedCards;
```

```
    // find those cards and remove them.
    for(var i in matchingGame.savingObject.removedCards) {
        $(".card[data-card-index="+matchingGame.savingObject.
        removedCards[i]+"]").remove();
    }
}
```

> **Tracking the storage changes with the storage event**
>
> Sometimes, we may want to listen to the changes in `localStorage`. We can do that by listening to the `storage` event. It is fired when anything is changed in `localStorage`. The following link from **Dive into HTML5** provides a detailed discussion on how we can use the event: `http://diveintohtml5.org/storage.html#storage-event`.

Pop quiz – using local storage

Q1. Consider whether each of the following statements is true or not:

1. We can save and restore object data directly in the local storage.

2. We can save the data of an object in the local storage by encoding it into a string.

3. We can use `localStorage["hello"] = "world"` to save the value "world" with key "hello" in the local storage.

Caching the game for offline access

We can enable an offline cache by using the AppCache Manifest document. After the page first loads from the Internet, its related files are cached in the device and the user can load the page and play the game even if the device is in offline mode, such as airplane mode.

Time for action – adding the AppCache Manifest

Perform the following set of steps to take the game offline:

1. In the `index.html` file, we add a `manifest` attribute:

```
<html lang="en" manifest="game.appcache">
```

2. Then we create a file named `game.appcache` with the following content:

```
CACHE MANIFEST
# 2015-03-01:v3

CACHE:
```

```
index.html
css/matchgame.css
images/bg.jpg
images/deck.png
images/popup_bg.jpg
images/table.jpg
js/jquery-1.11.2.min.js
js/html5games.matchgame.js

# Resources that require the user to be online.
NETWORK:
*
```

3. In order to test the caching, we need to host the game online. Upload the project folder to a web server, then open the game and inspect the console, we should see messages about the browser downloading or using the AppCache resources, as shown in the following screenshot:

```
Creating Application Cache with manifest http://dev.mz-lab.com/HTML%20Games%20Book/1260_07_Code/2nd_edition/07-offline-appcache/game.appcache
Application Cache Checking event
Application Cache Downloading event
Application Cache Progress event (0 of 8) http://dev.mz-lab.com/HTML5%20Games%20Book/1260_07_Code/2nd_edition/07-offline-appcache/js/jquery-1.11.2.min.js
Application Cache Progress event (1 of 8) http://dev.mz-lab.com/HTML5%20Games%20Book/1260_07_Code/2nd_edition/07-offline-appcache/js/html5games.matchgame.js
Application Cache Progress event (2 of 8) http://dev.mz-lab.com/HTML5%20Games%20Book/1260_07_Code/2nd_edition/07-offline-appcache/images/deck.png
Application Cache Progress event (3 of 8) http://dev.mz-lab.com/HTML5%20Games%20Book/1260_07_Code/2nd_edition/07-offline-appcache/images/popup_bg.jpg
Application Cache Progress event (4 of 8) http://dev.mz-lab.com/HTML5%20Games%20Book/1260_07_Code/2nd_edition/07-offline-appcache/css/matchgame.css
Application Cache Progress event (5 of 8) http://dev.mz-lab.com/HTML5%20Games%20Book/1260_07_Code/2nd_edition/07-offline-appcache/images/table.jpg
Application Cache Progress event (6 of 8) http://dev.mz-lab.com/HTML5%20Games%20Book/1260_07_Code/2nd_edition/07-offline-appcache/images/bg.jpg
Application Cache Progress event (7 of 8) http://dev.mz-lab.com/HTML5%20Games%20Book/1260_07_Code/2nd_edition/07-offline-appcache/index.html
```

What just happened?

We just added an AppCache Manifest file to our `index.html` file. Now once the game is loaded, it works in offline and airplane mode.

The AppCache file

The AppCache file is a plain text file. It starts with CACHE MANIFEST. There are two sections: cache and network. We specify them by using a line with CACHE: and NETWORK: in the AppCache file. An optional fallback section can be provided for fallback assets for files that are not cached.

In the cache section, we specify the file we want to cache, line by line. We need to specify each file explicitly. In the network section, we specify the file that should access the network if it is not listed in the cache section. If we don't specify files, the browser won't fetch non-cached files even if there is an Internet connection. Most of the time, a wildcard (*) fits and works perfectly.

Any line that begins with # is a comment. We usually use one line of comment to specify the version of the cache file. The reason is that once the browser cached the assets, it won't update the cached files until the manifest file itself is changed. So the comment line can force the browser to update the cached resources.

 HTML5Rocks has the following article that provides more details on using the AppCache file, including handling the cached events with JavaScript. Check it out at: `http://www.html5rocks.com/en/tutorials/appcache/beginner/`.

Summary

You learned a lot in this chapter about using the local storage to save the game data in a web browser. Specifically, we saved and retrieved basic data in the key-value pair local storage. We encoded an object into the JSON formatted string and parsed the string back to a JavaScript object. We saved the entire game progress, so the game can resume even if left mid-way. We also take the game offline by using AppCache. Visually, we created a nice 3D ribbon as a new record badge in pure CSS3 styling.

Now that you have learned about improving our previous games by using the local storage, you are ready to move on to the next chapter where you'll learn about an advanced feature named **WebSockets** that we can use to connect players together in a real-time interaction.

8
Building a Multiplayer Draw-and-Guess Game with WebSockets

We built several local single-player games in the previous chapters. In this chapter, we will build a multiplayer game with the help of WebSockets. WebSockets enable us to create event-based server-client architecture. The messages are passed between all connected browsers instantly. We will combine the Canvas drawing, JSON data packing, and several techniques learned in the previous chapters to build the draw-and-guess game.

In this chapter, we will learn the following topics:

◆ Trying an existing multiuser sketchpad that shows drawings from different connected users through WebSockets

◆ Installing a WebSocket server that is implemented by node.js

◆ Connecting the server from a browser

◆ Creating an instant chat room with the WebSocket API

◆ Creating a multiuser drawing pad in the Canvas

◆ Building a draw-and-guess game by integrating the chat room and drawing with game logic

The following screenshot shows the draw-and-guess game that we will create in this chapter:

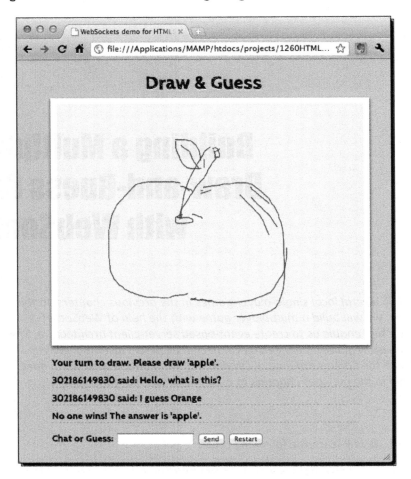

So, let's get on with it.

Installing a WebSocket server

The HTML5 WebSocket provides a client-side API to connect a browser to a backend server. This server has to support the WebSockets protocol in order to keep the connection persistent.

Installing the Node.js WebSocket server

In this section, we will download and install a server named Node.js on which we can install a WebSockets module.

Time for action – installing Node.js

1. Go to the URL, `http://nodejs.org`, which contains the source code of the Node.js server.

2. Click on the **Install** button on the page. This downloads the installation package based on your operating system.

3. Follow the installer's instructions to install the Node.js package. After the installation, we can check whether Node.js is installed by checking its version with the following command:

   ```
   $ node --version
   ```

4. The preceding command should print a version number of the node.js. In my case, it is version 0.12.0:

   ```
   v0.12.0
   ```

5. We also need to check whether the `npm` package manager is installed with the following command:

   ```
   $ npm --version
   ```

6. The preceding command should print a version number of npm, Node.js packages manager. In my case, it is version 2.5.1.

What just happened?

We just downloaded and installed the `Node.js` server. We will build server logic on top of this environment. The WebSocket server does not necessarily run on Node.js. There are different server-side implementations of the WebSockets protocol. We chose Node.js because it uses JavaScript, and we are familiar with it after building four HTML5 games in the previous chapters.

There is a fork from Node.js named io.js (`http://iojs.org`). At the time of writing this book, io.js is still very new. It's worth checking the latest status and their differences on both platforms if you plan on using Node in future projects.

 In some Linux distributions, the binary is renamed from `node` to `nodejs`. You can create a symbolic link of `nodejs` into `node` by using the following command. You may need `sudo` to run the command:

```
ln -s "$(which nodejs)" /usr/bin/node
```

Creating a WebSocket server to send connection count

We just installed the `node.js` server. Now, we will build something with WebSockets. Imagine now that we want a server that accepts connections from browsers and then sends the connection count to all users.

Time for action – running a WebSocket server

1. Create a project folder for our code. Inside it, create a new directory named `server`.

2. Use a terminal or the shell command prompt to change the directory into our newly created folder.

3. Type the following command that will install a WebSocket server:

   ```
   npm install --save ws
   ```

4. Create a new file named `server.js` under the `server` directory with the following content:

   ```
   var port = 8000;

   // Server code
   var WebSocketServer = require('ws').Server;
   var server = new WebSocketServer({ port: port });

   server.on('connection', function(socket) {
     console.log("A connection established");
   });

   console.log("WebSocket server is running.");
   console.log("Listening to port " + port + ".");
   ```

5. Open the terminal and change to the server directory.

6. Type the following command to execute the server:

   ```
   node server.js
   ```

7. You should get the following result if this works:

   ```
   $ node server.js
   WebSocket server is running.
   Listening to port 8000.
   ```

What just happened?

We just created a simple server logic that initialized the WebSockets library and listened to the connection event.

Initializing the WebSocket server

In Node.JS, different functions are packed into modules. When we need a functionality in a specific module, we use require to load it. We load the WebSockets module and then initialize the server using the following code in the server logic:

```
var WebSocketServer = require('ws').Server;
var server = new WebSocketServer({ port: port });
```

Since the ws module is managed by npm, it's installed inside a folder called node_modules. When we require a library with only the name, the Node.js runtime looks for that module in the node_modules folder.

We used 8000 as the server's port number, with which a client connects to this server. We may choose a different port number, but we have to ensure that the chosen port number is not overlapped by other common server services.

Listening to the connection event on the server side

The node.js server is event based. This means that most of the logic is executed when a certain event is fired. The following code that we used in the example listens to the connection event and handles it:

```
server.on('connection', function(socket) {
  console.log("A connection established");
});
```

The connection event comes with a socket argument. We will need to store this socket later because we use this object to interact with the connecting client.

Creating a client that connects to a WebSocket server and getting the total connections count

We built the server in the last example, and now, we will build a client that connects to our WebSocket server and receives messages from the server. The message will contain the total connection count from the server.

Time for action – showing the connection count in a WebSocket application

Carry out the following steps:

1. Create a new directory named `client`.

2. Create an HTML file named `index.html` in the `client` folder.

3. Now, add a few markups in our HTML file. To do this, put the following code in the `index.html` file:

```
<!DOCTYPE html>
<html lang="en">
<head>
  <meta charset="utf-8">
  <title>WebSockets demo for HTML5 Games Development: A
    Beginner's Guide</title>
</head>
<body>
  <!-- game elements goes here later -->
  <script src="js/jquery-2.1.3.min.js"></script>
  <script src="js/html5games.websocket.js"></script>
</body>
</html>
```

4. Create a directory named `js` and put the jQuery JavaScript file inside it.

5. Create a new file named `html5games.websockets.js` as follows:

```
var websocketGame = {
}
// init script when the DOM is ready.
$(function(){
  // check if existence of WebSockets in browser
  if (window["WebSocket"]) {

    // create connection
    websocketGame.socket = new WebSocket("ws://127.0.0.1:8000");

    // on open event
    websocketGame.socket.onopen = function(e) {
      console.log('WebSocket connection established.');
    };

    // on close event
    websocketGame.socket.onclose = function(e) {
```

```
        console.log('WebSocket connection closed.');
    };
  }
});
```

6. After these steps, we should have the following folder structure created in our project directory:

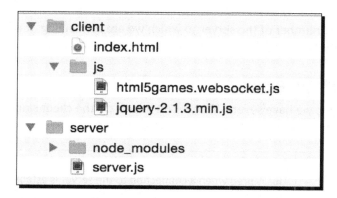

7. We will now test the code. First, you need to run the node server with our `server.js` code using `node server.js` in the **server** directory in the terminal.

8. Next, open the `index.html` file in the client directory, in a web browser twice so that we have two client instances running side by side.

9. Inspect the server terminal. There should be log messages similar to the following indicating the connection information and the total connection count:

```
$ node server.js
WebSocket server is running.
Listening to port 8000.
A connection established.
A connection established.
```

10. In the two web browsers, open the console in **Developer Tools**. You should also see the **WebSocket connection established** message in the console.

What just happened?

We just built a client that established a WebSockets connection to the server that we built in the last section. The client would then print any messages that are received from the server to the console panel in the **Inspector** of **Developer Tools**.

Establishing a WebSocket connection

In any browser that supports WebSockets, we can establish a connection by creating a new WebSocket instance with the following code:

```
var socket = new WebSocket(url);
```

The `url` argument is a string with the WebSockets URL. In our example, we are running our server locally. Therefore, the URL we have used is `ws://127.0.0.1:8000`, where 8000 represents the port number of the server to which we are connecting. It is 8000 because the server was listening to port 8000 when we built the server-side logic.

WebSocket client events

Similar to the server, we have several WebSocket events on the client side. The following table lists the events that we will use to deal with WebSockets:

Event name	Description
onopen	This is fired when a connection to the server is established
onmessage	This is fired when any message from the server is received
onclose	This is fired when the server closes the connection
onerror	This is fired when there is any error in the connection

Sending a message to all connected browsers

Once the server gets a new `connection` event, we send the updated count of the connection to all clients. Sending a message to all clients is easy. We just need to call the `sendAll` function in the `server` instance with a `string` argument as the message.

The following code snippet sends a server message to all connected browsers:

```
var message = "a message from server";
server.sendAll(message);
```

Time for action – sending total count to all users

Perform the following steps to create our foundation logic for the game:

1. In the server folder, we create a new file named `game.js`. We will store the room and game logic in this file.

2. We define a `User` class that stores the socket connection object and creates a random ID.

```
function User(socket) {
  this.socket = socket;
  // assign a random number to User.
  // Long enough to make duplication chance less.
  this.id = "1" + Math.floor( Math.random() * 1000000000);
}
```

3. We also define a `Room` class. We store a collection of user instances in this class.

```
function Room() {
  this.users = [];
}
```

4. We define the two instance methods in the `Room` class that manages the adding and removing of users.

```
Room.prototype.addUser = function(user){
  this.users.push(user);
  var room = this;

  // handle user closing
  user.socket.onclose = function(){
    console.log('A connection left.');
    room.removeUser(user);
  }
};
Room.prototype.removeUser = function(user) {
  // loop to find the user
  for (var i=this.users.length; i >= 0; i--) {
    if (this.users[i] === user) {
      this.users.splice(i, 1);
    }
  }
};
```

5. Then, we define another method that is in charge of sending messages to all the connected users in the room:

```
Room.prototype.sendAll = function(message) {
  for (var i=0, len=this.users.length; i<len; i++) {
    this.users[i].socket.send(message);
  }
};
```

6. Before moving on, we need to export our newly defined User and Room classes to let other files use them:

```
module.exports.User = User;
module.exports.Room = Room;
```

7. In the server.js file, we replace the connection handler with the following code, which sends the user count to all the connected users:

```
var User = require('./game').User;
var Room = require('./game').Room;
var room1 = new Room();
server.on('connection', function(socket) {
  var user = new User(socket);
  room1.addUser(user);
  console.log("A connection established");
  var message = "Welcome " + user.id
      + " joining the party. Total connection: "
      + room1.users.length;
  room1.sendAll(message);
});
```

8. We then move to the client. In the html5games.websocket.js file inside the **clients | js** folder, we add a handler to print out the messages received from the server.

```
// on message event
websocketGame.socket.onmessage = function(e) {
  console.log(e.data);
};
```

9. Finally, we test the code. Launch the server by executing node server.js in the server directory. Then, open the index.html file, and we should see something similar to the following screenshot on the console:

What just happened?

We defined two classes, User and Room, in a game.js file, which we use to manage all the connected sockets.

Defining class and instant instance methods

In JavaScript, **object-oriented programming** is done by using functions and prototypes. When we create a room instance by calling `new Room()`, the browser clones all properties and methods in `Room.prototype` to the instance.

Handling a newly connected user

For each connected user, we need to interact with them via an events handler. We add the user object into an array for easy management. We need to handle the `onclose` event when a user disconnects. To do this, we remove that user from the array.

Exporting modules

After defining our classes in the `game.js` file, we exported them. By exporting them to the module, we can import them in the other file by using the `require` method, as follows:

```
var User = require('./game').User;
var Room = require('./game').Room;
```

Sending messages to the client

WebSockets have the ability to send messages from the server to a user. Traditionally, the client requests the server and then the server responds. In a socket server, all users are connected, so messages can be triggered and sent in both directions. Here, we loop through all the users to send a broadcast message:

```
Room.prototype.send = function(message) {
  for (var i=0, len=this.users.length; i<len; i++) {
    this.users[i].socket.send(message);
  }
};
```

Then we listen to the server message on the client, by using the `onmessage` event handler.

```
// on message event
websocketGame.socket.onmessage = function(e) {
  console.log(e.data);
};
```

Building a chatting application with WebSockets

We now know how many browsers are connected. Suppose we want to build a chat room where users can type a message in their respective browsers and send the message to all the connected users instantly.

Sending a message to the server

We will let the user input a message and then send the message to the `node.js` server. The server will then forward the message to all the connected browsers. Once a browser receives the message, it displays it in the chat area. In this case, the users are connected to the instant chat room once they load the web page.

Time for action – sending a message to the server through WebSockets

1. First, code the server logic.

2. Open `servergame.js`. Add the following function to the file that handles user messages:

```
Room.prototype.handleOnUserMessage = function(user) {
  var room = this;
  user.socket.on("message", function(message){
    console.log("Receive message from " + user.id + ": " +
message);
  });
};
```

3. Add the following code inside the `Room.prototype.addUser` method that calls our newly created function:

```
this.handleOnUserMessage(user);
```

4. Now, move on to the `client` folder.

5. Open the `index.html` file and add the following markup in the `body` section. This provides inputs for the user to type and send messages to the server:

```
<input type="text" id="chat-input" autocomplete="off">
<input type="button" value="Send" id="send">
```

6. Then, add the following code to the `html5games.websocket.js` JavaScript file. This sends the message to the server when the user clicks on the `send` button or presses the *Enter* key:

```
$("#send").click(sendMessage);

$("#chat-input").keypress(function(event) {
  if (event.keyCode === 13) {
    sendMessage();
  }
});
```

```
function sendMessage() {
    var message = $("#chat-input").val();
    websocketGame.socket.send(message);
    $("#chat-input").val("");
}
```

7. Before testing our code, check the server terminal and see whether the node server is still running. Press *Ctrl + C* to terminate it and run it again by using the `node server.js` command.

8. Open `index.html` in a web browser. You should see an input text field with a **Send** button, as shown in the following screenshot:

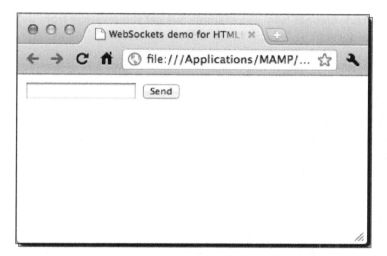

9. Try to type something in the input text field and then click on the **Send** button or press *Enter*. The input text will be cleared.

10. Now, switch to the server terminal, and you will see the server printing the text that we just sent. You can also put the browser and server terminal side by side to see how the message is sent instantly from the client to the server. The following screenshot shows the server terminal with messages from two connected browsers:

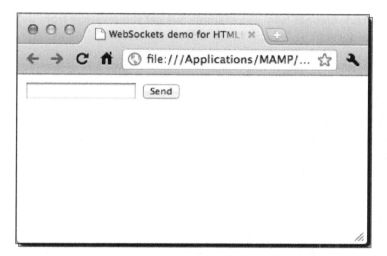

What just happened?

We just extended our connection example by adding an input text field for the users to type some text there and send it out. The text is sent as a message to the WebSocket server. The server will then print the received message in the terminal.

Sending a message from the client to the server

In order to send a message from the client to the server, we call the following `send` method in the `WebSocket` instance:

```
websocketGame.socket.send(message);
```

In the following code snippet from our example, we get the message from the input text field and send it to the server:

```
var message = $("#chat-input").val();
websocketGame.socket.send(message);
```

Receiving a message on the server side

On the server side, we need to handle the message we just sent from the client. We have an event named `message` in the connection instance in the WebSocket `node.js` library. We can listen to the connection message event to receive a message from each client connection.

The following code snippet shows how we use the message event listener to print the message on the server terminal:

```
socket.on("message", function(message){
  console.log("Receive message: " + message);
});
```

Sending every received message on the server side to create a chat room

In the last example, the server could receive messages sent from browsers. However, the server does nothing except print the received messages in the terminal. Therefore, we will add some logic to the server to send the messages out.

Time for action – sending messages to all connected browsers

Carry out the following steps:

1. Open the `game.js` file in the **server** folder for the server-side logic.

2. Add the following highlighted code to the message event listener handler:

```
user.socket.on("message", function(message){
  console.log("Receive message from " + user.id + ": " + message);
  // send to all users in room.
  var msg = "User " + user.id + " said: " + message;
  room.sendAll(msg);
});
```

3. That is it for the server side. Move on to the `client` folder and open the `index.html` file.

4. We want to display the chat messages in the chat history area. To do this, add the following code to the HTML file:

```
<ul id="chat-history"></ul>
```

5. Next, we need the client-side JavaScript to handle the received message from the server. We used it to print it out into the console panel, replace the `console.log` code with the following highlighted code in the `onmessage` event handler:

```
socket.onmessage = function(e) {
  $("#chat-history").append("<li>"+e.data+"</li>");
};
```

6. Let's test our code. Terminate any running node server by pressing *Ctrl + C*. Then, run the server again.

7. Open the `index.html` file twice and put them side by side. Type something in the text field and press *Enter*. The message will appear on both the opened browsers. If you open many instances of the HTML file, the message would appear on all the browsers. The following screenshot shows two browsers displaying the chat history side by side:

What just happened?

This is an extension of our previous examples. We discussed how a server sends the connection count to all the connected clients. We also discussed how the client sends a message to the server. In this example, we combine these two techniques to let the server send the received messages to all the connected users.

Comparing WebSockets with polling approaches

If you have ever built a web page's chat room by using a server-side language and a database, then you may wonder what the difference is between the WebSocket implementation and the traditional one.

The traditional chat room method is often implemented by using a **polling** approach. The client asks the server for an update periodically. The server responds to the client with either no update or the updated data. However, the traditional approach has several problems. The client does not get new data updated from the server until the next time it asks the server. This means that the data update is periodically delayed with time and the response is not instant enough. If we want to improve this issue by shortening the polling duration, then more bandwidth is utilized because clients need to keep sending requests to the server.

The following graph shows requests between the client and the server. It shows that many useless requests are sent, but the server responds to the client without any new data:

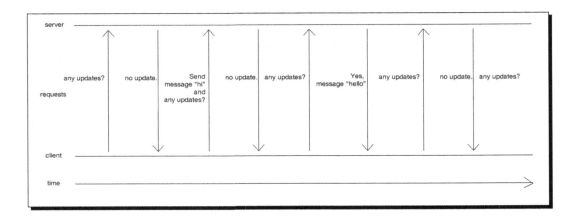

There is a better polling approach named **long polling**: the client sends a request to the server and waits for the response. Instead of the traditional polling approach where the server responds with "no update", the server does not respond at all until there is something that needs to be pushed to the server. In this approach, the server can push something to clients whenever there is an update. Once a client receives a response from the server, it creates another request and waits for the next server notification. The following graph shows the long polling approach where clients ask for updates and the server responds only when there is an update:

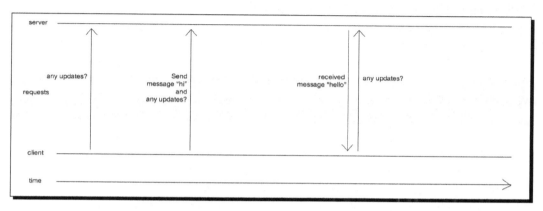

In the WebSockets approach, the number of requests are way less than the polling approach. This is because the connection between the client and server is persistent. Once the connection is established, a request from either the client side or the server side is sent only when there is any update. For instance, a client sends a message to the server when it wants to update something to the server. The server also sends messages to clients only when it needs to notify the clients of a data update. No other useless requests are sent during the connection. Therefore, less bandwidth is utilized. The following graph shows the WebSockets approach:

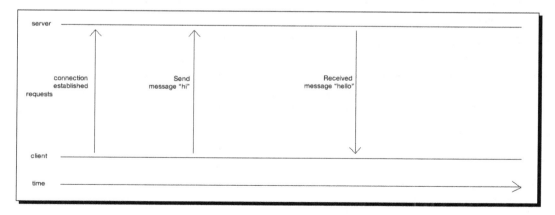

Making a shared drawing whiteboard with Canvas and WebSockets

Suppose we want a shared sketchpad. Anyone can draw something on the sketchpad and all others can view it. We learned how messages are communicated between clients and servers. We will go further and send drawing data.

Building a local drawing sketchpad

Before we deal with data sending and server handling, let's focus on making a drawing whiteboard. We will use the Canvas to build a local drawing sketchpad.

Time for action – making a local drawing whiteboard with the Canvas

Carry out the following steps:

1. We will focus only on the client side in this section. Open the index.html file and add the following canvas markup:

    ```
    <canvas id='drawing-pad' width='500' height='400'>
    </canvas>
    ```

2. We will draw something in the Canvas and we will need the mouse position relative to the Canvas for this. We did this in *Chapter 4, Building the Untangle Game with Canvas and the Drawing API*. Add the following style to the Canvas:

    ```
    <style>
      canvas{position:relative;}
    </style>
    ```

3. Then, open the html5games.websocket.js JavaScript file to add the drawing logic.

4. Replace the websocketGame global object with the following variable at the top of the JavaScript file:

    ```
    var websocketGame = {
        // indicates if it is drawing now.
        isDrawing : false,

        // the starting point of next line drawing.
        startX : 0,
        startY : 0,
    }
    ```

```
// canvas context
var canvas = document.getElementById('drawing-pad');
var ctx = canvas.getContext('2d');
```

5. In the jQuery `ready` function, add the following mouse event handler code. The code handles the mouse's down, move, and up events:

```
// the logic of drawing in the Canvas
$("#drawing-pad").mousedown(function(e) {
  // get the mouse x and y relative to the canvas top-left point.
  var mouseX = e.originalEvent.layerX || e.offsetX || 0;
  var mouseY = e.originalEvent.layerY || e.offsetY || 0;

  websocketGame.startX = mouseX;
  websocketGame.startY = mouseY;

  websocketGame.isDrawing = true;
});

$("#drawing-pad").mousemove(function(e) {
  // draw lines when is drawing
  if (websocketGame.isDrawing) {
    // get the mouse x and y
    // relative to the canvas top-left point.
    var mouseX = e.originalEvent.layerX || e.offsetX || 0;
    var mouseY = e.originalEvent.layerY || e.offsetY || 0;

    if (!(mouseX === websocketGame.startX &&
      mouseY === websocketGame.startY)) {
      drawLine(ctx, websocketGame.startX,
        websocketGame.startY,mouseX,mouseY,1);

      websocketGame.startX = mouseX;
      websocketGame.startY = mouseY;
    }
  }
});

$("#drawing-pad").mouseup(function(e) {
  websocketGame.isDrawing = false;
});
```

6. At last, we have the following function to draw a line in the Canvas with the given starting and ending points:

```
function drawLine(ctx, x1, y1, x2, y2, thickness) {
    ctx.beginPath();
    ctx.moveTo(x1,y1);
    ctx.lineTo(x2,y2);
    ctx.lineWidth = thickness;
    ctx.strokeStyle = "#444";
    ctx.stroke();
}
```

7. Save all files and open the `index.html` file. You should see an empty space where you can draw something by using the mouse. The drawings are not sent to the server yet, so others cannot view your drawings:

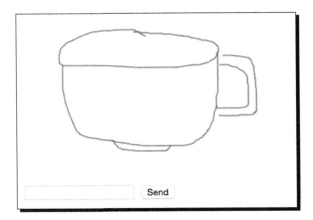

What just happened?

We just created a local drawing pad. This is like a whiteboard where the player can draw in the Canvas by dragging the mouse. However, the drawing data is not sent to the server yet; all drawings are only displayed locally.

The `drawing line` function is the same that we used in *Chapter 4, Building the Untangle Game with Canvas and the Drawing API*. We also used the same code to get the mouse position relative to the `canvas` element. However, the logic of the mouse events is different from *Chapter 4, Building the Untangle Game with Canvas and the Drawing API*.

Drawing in the Canvas

When we draw something on the computer, it often means that we click on the Canvas and drag the mouse (or pen). The line is drawn until the mouse button is up. Then, the user clicks on another place and drags again to draw lines.

In our example, we have a Boolean flag named `isDrawing` to indicate whether the user is drawing. The `isDrawing` flag is `false` by default. When the mouse button is at a point, we turn the flag to `true`. When the mouse is moving, we draw a line between the moved point and the last point when the mouse button was. Then, we set the `isDrawing` flag to `false` when the mouse button is up. This is how the drawing logic works.

Have a go hero – drawing with colors

Can we modify the drawing sketchpad by adding color support? How about adding five buttons with red, blue, green, black, and white colors? The player can choose the color when drawing. Alternatively, we can also provide different brush width options to the user.

Sending the drawing to all the connected browsers

We will go further by sending our drawing data to the server and let the server send the drawing to all the connected browsers.

Time for action – sending the drawing through WebSockets

Carry out the following steps:

1. First, we need to modify the server logic. Open the `game.js` file and add two constants at the beginning of the file, as follows:

```
// Constants
var LINE_SEGMENT = 0;
var CHAT_MESSAGE = 1;
```

2. In the `Room.prototype.addUser` method, add the following code at the beginning of the method:

```
this.users.push(user);
var room = this;
// tell others that someone joins the room
var data = {
  dataType: CHAT_MESSAGE,
  sender: "Server",
  message: "Welcome " + user.id
      + " joining the party. Total connection: " + this.users.
length
};
room.sendAll(JSON.stringify(data));
```

3. We use JSON-formatted string for communicating both drawing actions and chat messages. Add the following code to the user sockets on the message event handler:

```
user.socket.on("message", function(message){
    console.log("Receive message from " + user.id + ": " + message);

    // construct the message
    var data = JSON.parse(message);
    if (data.dataType === CHAT_MESSAGE) {
        // add the sender information into the message data object.
        data.sender = user.id;
    }

    // send to all clients in room.
    room.sendAll(JSON.stringify(data));
});
```

4. In `server.js`, there is no need to send the welcome message to the room since this is now handled by the `Room.addUser` method. Remove the following code from the `server.js` file:

```
room1.sendAll(message);
```

5. On the client side, we need the logic to respond to the server with the same data object definition. Open the `html5games.websocket.js` JavaScript file in the **js** directory under **client**.

6. Add the following constants to the `websocketGame` global variable. The same constants with the same values are also defined in the server-side logic.

```
// Contants
LINE_SEGMENT : 0,
CHAT_MESSAGE : 1,
```

7. When handling the message event on the client-side, convert the JSON-formatted string back to the data object. If the data is a chat message, then we display it as the chat history, otherwise we draw it in the Canvas as a line segment. Replace the `onmessage` event handler with the following code:

```
websocketGame.socket.onmessage = function(e) {
    // check if the received data is chat or line segment
    console.log("onmessage event:",e.data);
    var data = JSON.parse(e.data);
    if (data.dataType === websocketGame.CHAT_MESSAGE) {
        $("#chat-history").append("<li>" + data.sender
            + " said: "+data.message+"</li>");
    }
    else if (data.dataType === websocketGame.LINE_SEGMENT) {
```

```
        drawLine(ctx, data.startX, data.startY,
          data.endX, data.endY, 1);
    }

};
```

8. When the mouse is moving, we not only draw the line in the Canvas but also send the line data to the server. Add the following highlighted code to the `mousemove` event handler:

```
$("#drawing-pad").mousemove(function(e) {
    // draw lines when is drawing
    if (websocketGame.isDrawing) {
        // get the mouse x and y
        // relative to the canvas top-left point.
        var mouseX = e.originalEvent.layerX || e.offsetX || 0;
        var mouseY = e.originalEvent.layerY || e.offsetX || 0;

        if (!(mouseX === websocketGame.startX &&
          mouseY === websocketGame.startY)) {
            drawLine(ctx, websocketGame.startX, websocketGame.
              startY,mouseX,mouseY,1);

            // send the line segment to server
            var data = {};
            data.dataType = websocketGame.LINE_SEGMENT;
            data.startX = websocketGame.startX;
            data.startY = websocketGame.startY;
            data.endX = mouseX;
            data.endY = mouseY;
            websocketGame.socket.send(JSON.stringify(data));

            websocketGame.startX = mouseX;
            websocketGame.startY = mouseY;
        }

    }
});
```

9. Lastly, we need to modify the send message logic. We now pack the message in an object and format it as JSON when sending it to the server. Change the `sendMessage` function to the following code:

```
function sendMessage() {
    var message = $("#chat-input").val();

    // pack the message into an object.
```

```
var data = {};
data.dataType = websocketGame.CHAT_MESSAGE;
data.message = message;

websocketGame.socket.send(JSON.stringify(data));
$("#chat-input").val("");
}
```

10. Save all the files and relaunch the server.

11. Open the `index.html` file in two browser instances.

12. First, try the chat room feature by typing some messages and sending them. Then, try drawing something in the Canvas. Both browsers should display the same drawing, as shown in the following screenshot:

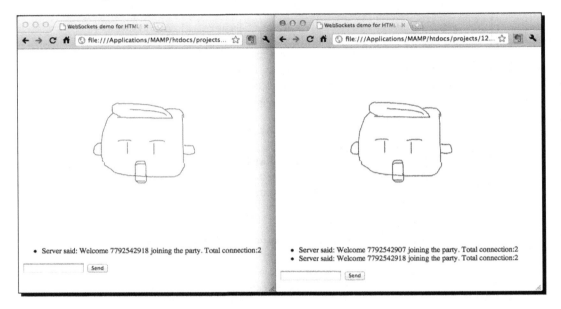

What just happened?

We just built a multiuser sketchpad. This is similar to the sketchpad we tried at the beginning of this chapter. We extended what you learned when building a chat room by sending a complex data object as a message.

Defining a data object to communicate between the client and the server

In order to communicate correctly between the server and clients when there is a lot of data packed into one message, we have to define a data object that both the client and server understand.

There are several properties in the data object. The following table lists the properties and why we need them:

Property name	Why we need this property
dataType	This is an important property that helps us to understand the entire data. The data is either a chat message or drawing line segment data.
sender	If the data is a chat message, the client needs to know who sent the message.
message	When the data type is a chat message, we surely need to include the message content itself into the data object.
startX	When the data type is a drawing line segment, we include the *x/y*
startY	coordinates of the starting point of the line.
endX	When the data type is a drawing line segment, we include the *x/y*
endY	coordinates of the ending point of the line.

In addition, we have the following constants defined on both the client side and the server side; these constants are for the dataType property:

```
// Contants
LINE_SEGMENT : 0,
CHAT_MESSAGE : 1,
```

With these constants, we can compare datatypes with the following readable code, instead of using the meaningless Integer:

```
if (data.dataType === websocketGame.CHAT_MESSAGE) {…}
```

Packing the drawing lines data into JSON for sending

We used the JSON.stringify function in the last chapter when we stored a JavaScript object into a JSON-formatted string in the local storage. Now, we need to send the data in string format between the server and the client. We use the same method to pack the drawing lines data into an object and send it as a JSON string.

The following code snippet shows how we pack the line segment data on the client side and send it to the server with a JSON-formatted string:

```
// send the line segment to server
var data = {};
data.dataType = websocketGame.LINE_SEGMENT;
data.startX = startX;
data.startY = startY;
data.endX = mouseX;
data.endY = mouseY;
websocketGame.socket.send(JSON.stringify(data));
```

Recreating the drawing lines after receiving them from other clients

The JSON parsing often comes as a pair of `stringify`. When we receive a message from the server, we have to parse it to the JavaScript object. The following code on the client side parses the data and either updates the chat history or draws a line based on the data:

```
var data = JSON.parse(e.data);
if (data.dataType === websocketGame.CHAT_MESSAGE) {
  $("#chat-history").append("<li>"+data.sender+" said:
    "+data.message+"</li>");
}
else if (data.dataType === websocketGame.LINE_SEGMENT) {
  drawLine(ctx, data.startX, data.startY, data.endX, data.endY, 1);
}
```

Building a multiplayer draw-and-guess game

We built an instant chat room earlier in this chapter. Moreover, we just built a multiuser sketchpad. How about combining these two techniques and building a draw-and-guess game? A draw-and-guess game is a game in which one player is given a word to draw. All other players do not know the word and guess the word according to the drawing. The one who draws and who correctly guesses the word earn points.

Time for action – building the draw-and-guess game

We will implement the game flow of the draw-and-guess game as follows:

1. First, we will add the game logic on the client side.

2. Open the `index.html` file in the client directory. Add the following restart button right after the *send* button:

```
<input type="button" value="Restart" id="restart">
```

3. Open the `html5games.websocket.js` JavaScript.

4. We need a few more constants to determine different states during the game play. Add the following highlighted code to the top of the file:

```
// Constants
LINE_SEGMENT : 0,
CHAT_MESSAGE : 1,
GAME_LOGIC : 2,

// Constant for game logic state
WAITING_TO_START : 0,
GAME_START : 1,
GAME_OVER : 2,
GAME_RESTART : 3,
```

5. In addition, we want a flag to indicate this player is in charge of drawing. Add the following Boolean global variable to the code:

```
isTurnToDraw : false,
```

6. When the client receives a message from the server, it parses it and checks whether it is a chat message or a line drawing. We have another type of message now named GAME_LOGIC for handling the game logic. The game logic message contains different data for different game states. Add the following code to the `onmessage` event handler:

```
else if (data.dataType === websocketGame.GAME_LOGIC) {
  if (data.gameState === websocketGame.GAME_OVER) {
    websocketGame.isTurnToDraw = false;
    $("#chat-history").append("<li>" + data.winner
        +" wins! The answer is '"+data.answer+"'.</li>");
    $("#restart").show();
  }
  if (data.gameState === websocketGame.GAME_START) {
    // clear the Canvas.
    canvas.width = canvas.width;

    // hide the restart button.
    $("#restart").hide();

    // clear the chat history
```

```
    $("#chat-history").html("");

    if (data.isPlayerTurn) {
      websocketGame.isTurnToDraw = true;
      $("#chat-history").append("<li>Your turn to draw.
        Please draw '" + data.answer + "'.</li>");
    }
    else {
      $("#chat-history").append("<li>Game Started. Get Ready.
        You have one minute to guess.</li>");
    }
  }
}
```

7. There is one last step in the client-side logic. We want to restart the game by sending a restart signal to the server. At the same time, we clear the drawing and chat history. To do this, add the following code inside the `html5games.websocket.js` file.

```
// restart button
$("#restart").hide();
$("#restart").click(function(){
  canvas.width = canvas.width;
  $("#chat-history").html("");
  $("#chat-history").append("<li>Restarting Game.</li>");

  // pack the restart message into an object.
  var data = {};
  data.dataType = websocketGame.GAME_LOGIC;
  data.gameState = websocketGame.GAME_RESTART;
  websocketGame.socket.send(JSON.stringify(data));

  $("#restart").hide();
});
```

8. It is now time to move on to the server side. We need more states to control the game flow. Replace the constants at the beginning of the `game.js` file with the following code.

```
// Constants
var LINE_SEGMENT = 0;
var CHAT_MESSAGE = 1;
var GAME_LOGIC = 2;
// Constant for game logic state
var WAITING_TO_START = 0;
var GAME_START = 1;
var GAME_OVER = 2;
var GAME_RESTART = 3;
```

9. In the previous example, the server side was just in charge of sending any incoming message to all connected browsers. This is not enough for a multiplayer game. The server will act as the game master that controls the game flow and determination of the winning condition. We extend the `Room` class with `GameRoom` that can handle the game flow.

10. Now, add the following code to the end of the `game.js` file. This is the constructor function of a new class called `GameRoom`, which initializes game logic.

```
function GameRoom() {
  // the current turn of player index.
  this.playerTurn = 0;

  this.wordsList = ['apple','idea','wisdom','angry'];
  this.currentAnswer = undefined;

  this.currentGameState = WAITING_TO_START;

  // send the game state to all players.
  var gameLogicData = {
    dataType: GAME_LOGIC,
    gameState: WAITING_TO_START
  };

  this.sendAll(JSON.stringify(gameLogicData));

}
```

11. Then, we extend the existing `Room` functionality into the `GameRoom` prototype so that `GameRoom` will have access to the `Room` class' prototype function by default.

```
// inherit Room
GameRoom.prototype = new Room();
```

12. Define the following `addUser` function in the `GameRoom` class. Append the code after our existing `GameRoom` code. This keeps the original room's `addUser` function and adds extra logic that waits until enough players join to start the game:

```
GameRoom.prototype.addUser = function(user) {
  // a.k.a. super(user) in traditional OOP language.
  Room.prototype.addUser.call(this, user);

  // start the game if there are 2 or more connections
  if (this.currentGameState === WAITING_TO_START && this.users.
length >= 2) {
    this.startGame();
  }
};
```

13. Unlike the previous example in which the server only passes user messages to all of the connected clients, now the server needs to determine whether the messages from the user are part of the game flow. Append the following code after the existing GameRoom logic; It overrides the original room's handleOnUserMessage function into new logic that handles chat messages, line segments, and the control of the game flow:

```
GameRoom.prototype.handleOnUserMessage = function(user) {
  var room = this;
  // handle on message
  user.socket.on('message', function(message){
    console.log("[GameRoom] Receive message from "
        + user.id + ": " + message);

    var data = JSON.parse(message);
    if (data.dataType === CHAT_MESSAGE) {
      // add the sender information into the message data object.
      data.sender = user.id;
    }
    room.sendAll(JSON.stringify(data));

    // check if the message is guessing right or wrong
    if (data.dataType === CHAT_MESSAGE) {
      console.log("Current state: " + room.currentGameState);

      if (room.currentGameState === GAME_START) {
        console.log("Got message: " + data.message
            + " (Answer: " + room.currentAnswer + ")");
      }

      if (room.currentGameState === GAME_START &&
        data.message === room.currentAnswer) {
        var gameLogicData = {
          dataType: GAME_LOGIC,
          gameState: GAME_OVER,
          winner: user.id,
          answer: room.currentAnswer
        };

        room.sendAll(JSON.stringify(gameLogicData));

        room.currentGameState = WAITING_TO_START;

        // clear the game over timeout
        clearTimeout(room.gameOverTimeout);
```

```
      }
    }


    if (data.dataType === GAME_LOGIC &&
      data.gameState === GAME_RESTART) {
      room.startGame();
    }
  });
};
```

14. Let's continue with the GameRoom logic. Add the following new function to the game.js file. This creates a new game inside the room by picking a player as a drawer and the others as guessers; then, it randomly picks a word for the drawer to draw:

```
GameRoom.prototype.startGame = function() {
  var room = this;

  // pick a player to draw
  this.playerTurn = (this.playerTurn+1) % this.users.length;

  console.log("Start game with player " + this.playerTurn
      + "'s turn.");

  // pick an answer
  var answerIndex = Math.floor(Math.random() *
    this.wordsList.length);
  this.currentAnswer = this.wordsList[answerIndex];

  // game start for all players
  var gameLogicDataForAllPlayers = {
    dataType: GAME_LOGIC,
    gameState: GAME_START,
    isPlayerTurn: false
  };

  this.sendAll(JSON.stringify(gameLogicDataForAllPlayers));

  // game start with answer to the player in turn.
  var gameLogicDataForDrawer = {
    dataType: GAME_LOGIC,
    gameState: GAME_START,
    answer: this.currentAnswer,
    isPlayerTurn: true
```

```
};

// the user who draws in this turn.
var user = this.users[this.playerTurn];
user.socket.send(JSON.stringify(gameLogicDataForDrawer));


// game over the game after 1 minute.
gameOverTimeout = setTimeout(function(){
  var gameLogicData = {
    dataType: GAME_LOGIC,
    gameState: GAME_OVER,
    winner: "No one",
    answer: room.currentAnswer
  };

  room.sendAll(JSON.stringify(gameLogicData));

  room.currentGameState = WAITING_TO_START;
},60*1000);

  room.currentGameState = GAME_START;
};
```

15. At last, we export the `GameRoom` class so that other files, such as `server.js`, can access the `GameRoom` class:

```
module.exports.GameRoom = GameRoom;
```

16. In `server.js`, we must call our new `GameRoom` constructor instead of the generic `Room` constructor. Replace the original related code to `Room` with the following `GameRoom` code:

```
var GameRoom = require('./game').GameRoom;
var room1 = new GameRoom();
```

17. We will save all the files and relaunch the server. Then, we will launch the `index.html` file in two browser instances. One browser will get a message from the server informing the player to draw something. The other browser, on the other hand, will inform the player to guess what the other player is drawing within one minute.

18. The player who is told to draw something can draw in the Canvas. The drawings are sent to all the other connected players. The players who are told to guess cannot draw anything in the Canvas. Instead, players type what they guess in the text field and send it to the server. If the guess is correct, then the game ends. Otherwise, the game continues until the one-minute countdown finishes.

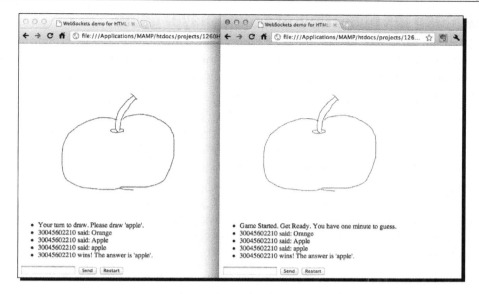

What just happened?

We just created a multiplayer draw-and-guess game in WebSockets and Canvas. The main difference between the game and the multiuser sketchpad is that the server now controls the game flow instead of letting all the users draw.

Inheriting the Room class

In JavaScript, we can inherit a defined class with a new class. We define GameRoom that inherits the Room class. The GameRoom class will have the Room logic that it inherits plus the extra logic that is specifically designed for the game flow. Inheritance is done by creating an instance of the class into the prototype, as follows:

```
GameRoom.prototype = new Room();
```

Now, GameRoom has the prototype methods from Room. We can then define more logic in GameRoom such as the startGame method. We can also override the existing logic by defining a new prototype method in the GameRoom class with the same name; for example, we override the handleOnUserMessage method to send the game starting and winning logic.

Sometimes, we want to extend an existing logic instead of replacing the old one with a new one. In such a case, we need to execute the logic that we have overridden by the method with the same name. We can use the following code to execute the method that's in the original prototype; we used this approach in the addUser method to keep the original logic:

```
// a.k.a. super(user) in traditional OOP language.
Room.prototype.addUser.call(this, user);
```

Controlling the game flow of a multiplayer game

Controlling the game flow of a multiplayer game is much more difficult than a single game. We can simply use a few variables to control the game flow of a single game, but we have to use message passing to inform each player of specific updated game flow.

First, we require the following highlighted GAME_LOGIC constant for dataType. We use this data to send and receive a message that is related to the game logic control:

```
// Constants
var LINE_SEGMENT = 0;
var CHAT_MESSAGE = 1;
var GAME_LOGIC = 2;
```

There are several states in the game flow. Before the game starts, the connected players are waiting for the game to start. Once there are enough connections for the multiplayer game, the server sends a game logic message to all the players to inform them of the start of the game.

When the game is over, the server sends a game over state to all the players. Then, the game finishes and the game logic halts until any player clicks on the restart button. Once the restart button is clicked, the client sends a game restart state to the server instructing the server to prepare a new game. Then, the game starts again.

We declare the four game states as the following constants in both the client and server so that they understand them:

```
// Constant for game logic state
var WAITING_TO_START = 0;
var GAME_START = 1;
var GAME_OVER = 2;
var GAME_RESTART = 3;
```

The following code on the server side holds an index to indicate which player's turn is now:

```
var playerTurn = 0;
```

The data which is sent to the player (whose turn it is) is different from the data that is sent to other players. The other players receive the following data with only a game start signal:

```
var gameLogicDataForAllPlayers = {
  dataType: GAME_LOGIC,
  gameState: GAME_START,
  isPlayerTurn: false
};
```

On the other hand, the player (whose turn is to draw) receives the following data with the word information:

```
var gameLogicDataForDrawer = {
  dataType: GAME_LOGIC,
  gameState: GAME_START,
  answer: this.currentAnswer,
  isPlayerTurn: true
};
```

Room and Game Room

By the end of this example, we have created two types of rooms: a normal room and a game room. Specifically, a normal room has the most basic features: managing users and chatting within the room. The game room, which is built on top of the normal room, adds another large block of logic to manage a draw-and-guess game flow. The game flow includes waiting for the game to start, starting the game, determining game over, and triggering time out. All these game flow controls are encapsulated into the GameRoom class.

In the future, we can easily expand the multiplayer game by adding different types of game into it. For example, we can create a 2-player tic-tac-toe game by creating a TicTacToeGameRoom class that shares similar waiting and restarting game logic in GameRoom. However, the TicTacToeGameRoom class will handle other game flows such as passing the game board data and handling a tied game. Since all game logic is encapsulated inside the specific game room, different types of multiplayer game won't affect each other.

Improving the game

We have just created a multiplayer game that is playable. However, there is still a lot to improve. In the following sections, we list two possible improvements of the game.

Improving the styles

The game looks very plain now. We can improve its visual outlook by adding CSS styles and decorative images to it. In the code bundle, you will find an example with extra CSS styles applied to make the game look better. You may try different styling effects also.

Storing drawn lines on each game

In the game, the drawer draws lines and other players guess the drawing. Now, imagine that two players are playing and the third player joins them. As there is no storage for the drawn lines anywhere, the third player cannot see what the drawer has drawn. This means that the third player has to wait until the game ends to play.

Have a go hero

How can we let a player who has joined late continue the game without losing the drawn lines? How can we reconstruct the drawing for a newly connected player? How about storing all drawing data of the current game on the server?

Improving the answer checking mechanism

The answer checking on the server side compares the message with the `currentAnswer` variable to determine whether a player guessed correctly. The answer is treated as incorrect if the case does not match. It looks strange when the answer is "apples" and the player is told that their answer is wrong when they guess "apple".

Have a go hero

How can we improve the answer checking mechanism? How about improving the answer checking logic to treat the answer as correct when using a different case or even similar words? The current game is quite plain in style. Please add your decoration to the game to make it more appealing to the players.

Summary

We learned a lot in this chapter about connecting browsers to WebSockets. The messages and events from one browser are sent to all connected browsers in almost real time.

Specifically, we learned how WebSockets provide real-time events by drawing on an existing multiplayer sketchpad. It shows drawings from other users who are connected. We chose Node.js as the server-side WebSocket server. By using this server, we can easily build an event-based server to handle WebSocket requests from browsers. We discussed the relationship between the server and a client, which compares WebSockets with other approaches such as long-polling. We built an instant chat room application. We learned how to implement a server script to send all incoming messages to other connected browsers. We also learned how to display a received message from the server on the client side. Next, we built a multiuser drawing board and finally a draw-and-guess game by integrating the chatting along with the drawing pad.

Now that you have learned how to build a multiplayer game, we are ready to build physics games with the help of the physics engine in the next chapter.

Building a Physics Car Game with Box2D and Canvas

9

2D Physics Engines is a hot topic in game development. With the help of a physics engine, we can easily create a playable game by just defining an environment and a simple rule. Taking existing games as examples, players in the Angry Birds game fly birds to destroy the enemy's castle. In Cut the Rope, candy drops into the monster's mouth to progress to the next level.

In this chapter, we will learn the following topics:

- Installing the Box2D JavaScript library
- Creating a static ground body in the physics world
- Drawing the physics world on the Canvas
- Creating a dynamic box in the physics world
- Advancing the world time
- Adding wheels to the game
- Creating the physics car
- Adding force to the car with a keyboard input
- Checking a collision in the Box2D world
- Adding level support to our car game
- Replacing the Box2D outline drawing with graphics
- Adding a final touch to make the game fun to play

The following screenshot shows what we will get by the end of this chapter; it is a car game in which a player moves the car towards the destination point:

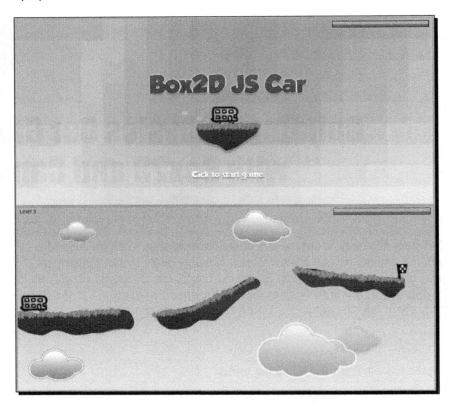

You can also play the game at `http://makzan.net/html5-games/car-game/` to get a glimpse of the final result.

So, let's get on with it.

Installing the Box2D JavaScript library

Now, suppose that we want to create a car game. We apply force to the car to make it move forward. The car moves on a ramp and then flies through the air. Afterwards, the car falls on the destination ramp and the game finishes. Every collision in every part of the physics world counts on this movement. If we have to make this game from scratch, then we have to calculate at least the velocity and angle of each part. Luckily, the physics library helps us to handle all these physical problems. All we have to do is to create the physics model and present it in the canvas. The engine we use is Box2D.

Box2D is a 2D physics simulation engine. The original Box2D was written in C by Erin Catto. It was later ported to Flash ActionScript. Later on, its 2.1a version was ported to JavaScript. You can find the JavaScript version of Box2D 2.1a in their Google Code project at `https://code.google.com/p/box2dweb/`.

> At the time of writing this book, Google Code announced that they would close down in 2016. I have forked the library into a URL (`https://github.com/makzan/Box2DWeb-Fork`) in case the original repository is not accessible.

Time for action – installing the Box2D physics library

We will set up the Box2D library. We must carry out the following steps to prepare our project:

1. First, let's set up our game project. Create a folder with the following file structure. The HTML file contains an HTML template with empty content and includes all the scripts and style files. You may find the full document's source in the code bundle. Please also download the Box2D source file into the `js` folder.

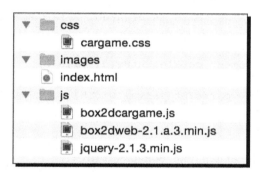

2. In the HTML body, we must define a canvas, as follows:

```
<canvas id="game" width="1300" height="600"></canvas>
```

3. We must then alias several Box2D classes that we will use in our game; this makes it easier to refer them in the code:

```
// Box2D alias
var b2Vec2 = Box2D.Common.Math.b2Vec2
  , b2BodyDef = Box2D.Dynamics.b2BodyDef
  , b2Body = Box2D.Dynamics.b2Body
  , b2FixtureDef = Box2D.Dynamics.b2FixtureDef
  , b2World = Box2D.Dynamics.b2World
```

```
    , b2PolygonShape = Box2D.Collision.Shapes.b2PolygonShape
    , b2CircleShape = Box2D.Collision.Shapes.b2CircleShape
    , b2DebugDraw = Box2D.Dynamics.b2DebugDraw
    , b2RevoluteJointDef = Box2D.Dynamics.Joints.
        b2RevoluteJointDef;
```

4. Now, we will create an empty world to test our Box2D library installation. Open the box2dcargame.js JavaScript file and put the following code in the file to create the world:

```
var carGame = {
}

var canvas;
var ctx;
var canvasWidth;
var canvasHeight;

function initGame() {

    carGame.world = createWorld();

    console.log("The world is created. ",carGame.world);

    // get the reference of the context
    canvas = document.getElementById('game');
    ctx = canvas.getContext('2d');
    canvasWidth = parseInt(canvas.width);
    canvasHeight = parseInt(canvas.height);
};

// Create and return the Box2D world.
function createWorld() {
    // Define the gravity
    var gravity = new b2Vec2(0, 10);

    // set to allow sleeping object
    var allowSleep = true;

    // finally create the world with
    // gravity and sleep object parameter.
    var world = new b2World(gravity, allowSleep);
    return world;
}
```

```
// After all the definition, we init the game.
initGame();
```

5. Open the `index.html` file in a web browser. We should see a grey canvas with
   nothing there.

We have not presented the physics world to the canvas yet. This is why we only see a blank
canvas on the page. However, we have printed the newly created world in the console log.
The following screenshot shows the console tracing the world object with many properties
beginning with m_. These are the physical states of the world:

```
The world is created.   ▼ ea                                    box2dcargame.js:46
                          m_allowSleep: false
                          m_bodyCount: 1
                        ▶ m_bodyList: v
                          m_contactCount: 0
                          m_contactList: null
                        ▶ m_contactManager: T
                        ▶ m_contactSolver: ia
                          m_controllerCount: 0
                          m_controllerList: null
                          m_debugDraw: null
                          m_destructionListener: null
                        ▶ m_gravity: r
                        ▶ m_groundBody: v
                          m_inv_dt0: 0
                        ▶ m_island: da
                          m_jointCount: 0
                          m_jointList: null
                        ▶ s_stack: Array[0]
                        ▶ __proto__: ea
```

What just happened?

We have just installed the Box2D JavaScript library and created an empty world to test the
installation.

Using b2World to create a new world

The `b2World` class is a core class in the Box2D environment. All our physics bodies,
including the ground and car, are created in this world. The following code shows us how
to create a world:

```
var world = new b2World(gravity, doSleep);
```

The `b2World` class takes two arguments to initialize, which are listed in the following table with their description:

Argument	Type	Discussion
gravity	b2Vec2	This represents the gravity of the world
doSleep	Bool	This defines whether the world ignores slept objects or not

Setting the gravity of the world

We have to define the gravity of the world. The gravity is defined by `b2Vec2`. The `b2Vec2` class is a vector of *x* and *y* axes. Therefore, the following code defines gravity with 10 units downwards:

```
var gravity = new b2Vec2(0, 10);
```

Setting Box2D to ignore the sleeping object

A sleeping body is a dynamic body that skips simulation until it wakes up. The physics library calculates the mathematical data and collision of all the bodies in the world. The performance will slow down when there are too many bodies in the world to get calculated in every frame. When a sleeping body collides with another object, it will wake up and then turn back to sleeping mode again until the next collision.

Creating a static ground body in the physics world

The world is empty now. If we are going to place objects there, the objects will fall and finally leave our sight. Now, suppose we want to create a static ground body in the world so that objects can stand on it. We can do this in Box2D.

Time for action – creating a ground in the world

Carry out the following steps to create a static ground:

1. Open the `box2dcargame.js` JavaScript file.

2. Define the following `pxPerMeter` variable in the file; this is the unit setting in the Box2D world:

```
var pxPerMeter = 30; // 30 pixels = 1 meter
```

3. Add the following function to the end of the JavaScript file; this creates a fixed body as the playground:

```
function createGround() {
  var bodyDef = new b2BodyDef;
```

```
var fixDef = new b2FixtureDef;

bodyDef.type = b2Body.b2_staticBody;
bodyDef.position.x = 250/pxPerMeter;
bodyDef.position.y = 370 /pxPerMeter;

fixDef.shape = new b2PolygonShape();
fixDef.shape.SetAsBox(250/pxPerMeter, 25/pxPerMeter);
fixDef.restitution = 0.4;

// create the body from the definition.
var body = carGame.world.CreateBody(bodyDef);
body.CreateFixture(fixDef);

return body;
}
```

4. Call the `createGround` function in the `initGame` function after we have created the world as follows:

```
createGround();
```

5. As we are still defining the logic and have not yet presented the physics world visually, we will see nothing if we open the browser. However, it is worth getting into the habit of trying it and inspecting the console window for an error message if there is any.

What just happened?

We have created a ground body with the shape and body definitions. This is a common process that we will use a lot to create different kinds of physical bodies in the world. So, let's get into the details of how we made it.

Pixel per meter

The size and position unit in Box2D is calculated in meters. We use pixels in screen. Therefore, we define a variable that converts a unit between meters and screen pixels. We set the value to 30, which indicates that 30 pixels equal to 1 meter. You can explore different values for your physics world.

We should not use 1 pixel to 1 meter, otherwise our object would become very large in the Box2D scale. Imagine we have a car with 100 px width, it will become 100 meters long, which is not realistic at all. By defining 30 px/meter, or any reasonable value, an object with width 100 px on screen will be about 3.33 meters long in simulation, which Box2D can handle well. For more details, please refer to the Box2D manual section 1.7 at http://www.box2d.org/manual.html.

Creating a shape with a fixture

A fixture contains the physics properties and its shape. The physics properties define density, friction, and restitution, where restitution is basically the bounciness of the object. A shape defines the geometrical data. The shape can be a circle, rectangle, or a polygon. The following code that we used in the preceding example defines a box shape definition. The SetAsBox function takes two arguments: half width and half height. It is a half value, so the final area of the shape is four times the value:

```
fixDef.shape = new b2PolygonShape();
fixDef.shape.SetAsBox(250/pxPerMeter, 25/pxPerMeter);
fixDef.restitution = 0.4;
```

Creating a body

After defining the fixture, we can then create a body definition with the given shape definition. Then, we set the initial position of the body and finally ask the world instance to create a body from our body definition. The following code shows how we create a body in the world with the given shape definition:

```
bodyDef.type = b2Body.b2_staticBody;
bodyDef.position.x = 250/pxPerMeter;
bodyDef.position.y = 370 /pxPerMeter;

// create the body from the definition.
var body = carGame.world.CreateBody(bodyDef);
body.CreateFixture(fixDef);
```

A body can be either a static body or a dynamic body. Static bodies are immovable and will not have collisions with other static bodies. Therefore, these bodies can be used as the ground or walls to become the level environment. On the other hand, a dynamic body will move following a collision with other bodies (static or dynamic) and due to gravity. We will create a dynamic box body later.

Setting the bouncing effect with the restitution property

The restitution value is between 0 and 1. In our case, the box is falling on the ground. When the restitution value is 0 on both the ground and the box, the box does not bounce at all. When either the box or the ground has a restitution value of 1, the collision is perfectly elastic.

When two bodies collide, the restitution value of that collision is the maximum value between both restitution values of both the bodies. Therefore, if a box with a restitution value of 0.4 drops on the ground with a restitution value of 0.6, this collision will use 0.6 to calculate the bouncing velocity.

Drawing the physics world in the canvas

We have created the ground, but it is only in the mathematics model. We do not see anything in the canvas because we have not drawn anything on it yet. In order to show what the physics looks like, we have to draw something according to the physics world.

Time for action – drawing the physics world into the Canvas

Carry out the following steps to draw the useful debug view:

1. First, open the `box2dcargame.js` JavaScript file:

    ```
    var shouldDrawDebug = false;
    ```

2. Add a function that draws the debugging lines:

    ```
    function showDebugDraw() {
      shouldDrawDebug = true;

      //setup debug draw
      var debugDraw = new b2DebugDraw();
      debugDraw.SetSprite(document.getElementById('game').
    getContext('2d'));
      debugDraw.SetDrawScale(pxPerMeter);
      debugDraw.SetFillAlpha(0.3);
      debugDraw.SetLineThickness(1.0);
      debugDraw.SetFlags(b2DebugDraw.e_shapeBit |
        b2DebugDraw.e_jointBit);

      carGame.world.SetDebugDraw(debugDraw);

      carGame.world.DrawDebugData();
    }
    ```

3. Add a `showDebugDraw` function call at the end of the `initGame` method:

    ```
    showDebugDraw();
    ```

4. Now, reopen the game in a browser, and we should see the outline of the ground body in the canvas, as shown in the following screenshot:

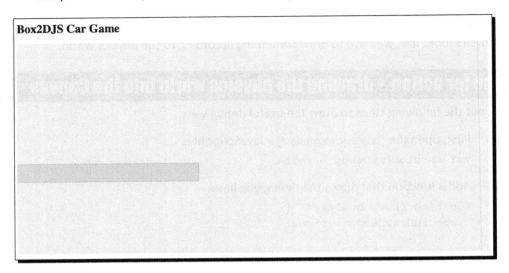

What just happened?

We have just defined a method that asks the Box2D engine to draw the physics bodies in a canvas. This is useful for debugging before we successfully add our own graphics. We can set what to display via the `SetFlags` method.

The flags are bitwise variable. This means that each bit in the flag controls one drawing type. We combine the flag by using the bitwise operator or (|). For example, we show the shape and joint with the following code.

```
debugDraw.SetFlags(b2DebugDraw.e_shapeBit | b2DebugDraw.e_jointBit);
```

There are different types of debug drawings besides the shape and joint:

Bit flag	Discussion
e_aabbBit	This draws all the bounding boxes
e_centerOfMassBit	This draws the center of the mass
e_controllerBit	This draws all the dynamics controllers
e_jointBit	This draws all the joint connections
e_pairBit	This draws the broad-phrase collision pairs
e_shapeBit	This draws all the shapes

Creating a dynamic box in the physics world

Imagine now that we drop a box into the world. The box falls from the air and finally hits the ground. The box bounces up a little and finally lands on the ground. This is different from what we created in the last section. In the last section, we created a static ground, which was immovable and could not be affected by gravity. Now, we will create a dynamic box.

Time for action – putting a dynamic box in the world

Carry out the following steps to create our first dynamic body:

1. Open our JavaScript file and add the following box creation code to the page loaded event handler. Place the code after the `createGround` function:

```
// temporary function
function createBox() {
    var bodyDef = new b2BodyDef;
    var fixDef = new b2FixtureDef;

    bodyDef.type = b2Body.b2_dynamicBody;
    bodyDef.position.x = 50/pxPerMeter;
    bodyDef.position.y = 210/pxPerMeter;

    fixDef.shape = new b2PolygonShape();
    fixDef.shape.SetAsBox(20/pxPerMeter, 20/pxPerMeter);

    var body = carGame.world.CreateBody(bodyDef);
    body.CreateFixture(fixDef);

    return body;
}
```

2. We need to call our newly created `createBox` function. Place the following code after we call the `createGround` function inside `initGame`.

3. Now, we will test the physics world in a browser. You should see that a box is created at the given initial position. However, the box is not falling down; this is because we still have to do something to make it fall:

What just happened?

We just created a dynamic body in the world. In contrast to the ground body that is immovable, this box is affected by the gravity and the velocity changes during a collision. When a body contains a shape with any mass or density, it is a dynamic body. Otherwise, it is static. Therefore, we define a density to our box. Box2D will make it dynamic and calculate the mass according to the density and size of the body automatically.

Advancing the world time

The box is dynamic but it does not fall down. Are we doing anything wrong here? The answer is no. We have set up the box correctly, but we forget to advance the time in the physics world.

In the Box2D physics world, all calculations are done in a systematic iteration. The world calculates the physical transformation of all things according to the current step. When we move the step to the next level, the world calculates again as the new state.

Time for action – setting up the world step loop

We will make the world time advance by carrying out the following steps:

1. In order to advance the world step, we have to call the step function in the world instance periodically. We used setTimeout to keep calling the step function. Put the following function in our JavaScript logic file:

```
function updateWorld() {
  // Move the physics world 1 step forward.
  carGame.world.Step(1/60, 10, 10);

  // display the build-in debug drawing.
  if (shouldDrawDebug) {
    carGame.world.DrawDebugData();
  }
}
```

2. Next, we will set up an interval in the `initGame` method:

   ```
   setInterval(updateWorld, 1/60);
   ```

3. We will again simulate the world in a browser. The box is created at the initialized position and falls on the ground correctly. The following screenshot shows the sequence of a box dropping on the ground:

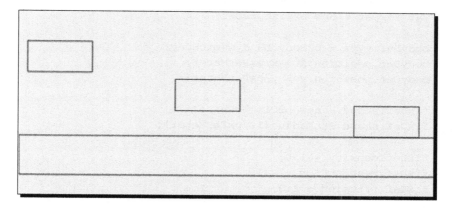

What just happened?

We have advanced the time of the world. Now, the physics library simulates the world in a frequency of 60 times per second. In the game loop, we call the `Step` function to the Box2D world. The `Step` function simulates the physics world one step forward. During the step, the physics engine calculates everything that happens in the world, including forces and gravity.

Adding wheels to the game

Now, we have a box in the game. Imagine now we create two circular bodies as the wheels. Then, we will have the basic components of a car—the body and the wheels.

Time for action – putting two circles in the world

We will add two circles to the world by carrying out the following steps:

1. Open the `html5games.box2dcargame.js` JavaScript file to add the wheel bodies.

2. Add the following code after the box creation code. This calls the `createWheel` function which we will write to create a circular shaped body:

```
// create two wheels in the world
createWheel(25, 230);
createWheel(75, 230);
```

3. Now let's work on the `createWheel` function. We design this function to create a circle-shaped body in the given world at the given *x* and *y* coordinates in the world. To do this, put the following function in our JavaScript logic file:

```
function createWheel(x, y) {
  var bodyDef = new b2BodyDef;
  var fixDef = new b2FixtureDef;

  bodyDef.type = b2Body.b2_dynamicBody;
  bodyDef.position.x = x/pxPerMeter;
  bodyDef.position.y = y/pxPerMeter;

  fixDef.shape = new b2CircleShape();
  fixDef.shape.SetRadius(10/pxPerMeter);

  fixDef.density = 1.0;
  fixDef.restitution = 0.1;
  fixDef.friction = 4.3;

  var body = carGame.world.CreateBody(bodyDef);
  body.CreateFixture(fixDef);

  return body;
}
```

4. We will now reload the physics world in a web browser. This time, we should see a result similar to the one shown in the following screenshot, with a box and two wheels falling down from air:

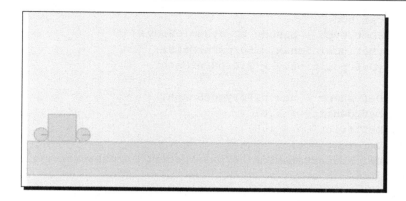

What just happened?

When simulating the physics world, both the box and wheels drop and collide with each other and the ground.

Creating a circular body is similar to creating a box body. The only difference is that we use a `CircleDef` class instead of the box shape definition. In the circle definition, we define the circle size by using the `radius` property instead of the `extents` property.

Creating a physical car

We have prepared the car box body and two wheel bodies. We are just one step away from making a car. Imagine that now we have a glue stick to glue the wheels to the car body. Then, the car and wheels will not separate anymore, and we will have a car. We can use **joint** to achieve this. In this section, we will use `joint` to stick the wheels and the car body together.

Time for action – connecting the box and two circles with a revolute joint

Carry out the following steps to create a car with the box and wheels:

1. We are still working only on the logic part. Open our JavaScript logic file in a text editor.

2. Create a function named `createCarAt`, which takes the coordinates as arguments. Then, move the body and the wheel creation code in this function. Afterwards, add the following highlighted joint creation code. At last, return the car body:

```
function createCarAt(x, y) {
  var bodyDef = new b2BodyDef;
  var fixDef = new b2FixtureDef;
```

```
    // car body
    bodyDef.type = b2Body.b2_dynamicBody;
    bodyDef.position.x = 50/pxPerMeter;
    bodyDef.position.y = 210/pxPerMeter;

    fixDef.shape = new b2PolygonShape();
    fixDef.density = 1.0;
    fixDef.friction = 1.5;
    fixDef.restitution = .4;
    fixDef.shape.SetAsBox(40/pxPerMeter, 20/pxPerMeter);

    carBody = carGame.world.CreateBody(bodyDef);

    carBody.CreateFixture(fixDef);

    // creating the wheels
    var wheelBody1 = createWheel(x-25, y+20);
    var wheelBody2 = createWheel(x+25, y+20);

    // create a joint to connect left wheel with the car body
    var jointDef = new b2RevoluteJointDef();
    jointDef.Initialize(carBody, wheelBody1, new b2Vec2( (x-25)/
pxPerMeter ,  (y+20)/pxPerMeter ));
    carGame.world.CreateJoint(jointDef);

    // create a joint to connect right wheel with the car body
    var jointDef = new b2RevoluteJointDef();
    jointDef.Initialize(carBody, wheelBody2, new b2Vec2( (x+25)/
pxPerMeter ,  (y+20)/pxPerMeter ));
    carGame.world.CreateJoint(jointDef);

    return carBody;

}
```

3. In the `initGame` function, we created two wheels. Remove these lines of code that calls the `createWheel` function in the `initGame` function.

4. Then, all we need to do is create a car with the initial position. Add the following code to the `initGame` function after calling the `createGround` function:

```
carGame.car = createCarAt(50, 210);
```

5. It is time to save the file and run the physics world in a browser. At this time, the wheels and the car body are not separate pieces. They glue together as a car and drop on the ground correctly, as shown in the following screenshot:

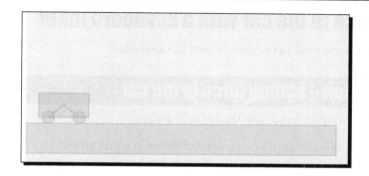

What just happened?

A joint is useful to add constraint between two bodies (or between a body and the world). There are many kinds of joints and what we used in this example is called the **revolute joint**.

Using a revolute joint to create an anchor point between two bodies

The revolute joint sticks two bodies together with a common anchor point. The two bodies are then glued together and are only allowed to rotate based on the common anchor point. The left-hand side of the following screenshot shows that the two bodies are connected with an anchor. In our code example, we set the anchor point to be exactly the center point of the wheel. The right-hand side of the following screenshot shows how we set the joint. The wheel rotates because the rotation origin is at the center. This setup makes the car and wheels look real:

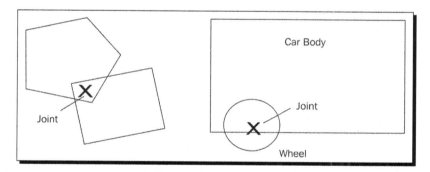

There are other types of joints that are useful in different ways. Joints are useful to create a game environment, and as there are several types of joints, each joint type is worth a try, and you should think about how to use them. The following link consists of the Box2D manual that explains each type of joint and how we can use them on different environment setups: `http://www.box2d.org/manual.html#_Toc258082974`.

Adding force to the car with a keyboard input

We have the car ready now. Let's move it with our keyboard.

Time for action – adding force to the car

Carry out the following steps to take the keyboard input:

1. Open the `box2dcargame.js` JavaScript file in a text editor.

2. In the page loaded event handler, we add the following `keydown` event handler at the beginning of the code. This listens to the right arrow key and the left arrow key to apply force in different directions:

```
$(document).keydown(function(e){
  switch(e.keyCode) {
    case 39: // right arrow key to apply force towards right
      var force = new b2Vec2(100, 0);
      carGame.car.ApplyForce(force, carGame.car.
        GetWorldCenter());
      return false;
      break;
    case 37: // left arrow key to apply force towards left
      var force = new b2Vec2(-100, 0);
      carGame.car.ApplyForce(force, carGame.car.
        GetWorldCenter());
      return false;
      break;
  }
});
```

3. We have added forces to bodies. We need to clear forces in each step, otherwise the force accumulates:

```
function updateWorld() {
  // existing code goes here.
  // Clear previous applied force.
  carGame.world.ClearForces();
}
```

4. Save the files and run our game in the browser. When you press the *arrow* keys, the car starts moving. If you keep pressing the key, the world will keep adding force to the car and make it speed away:

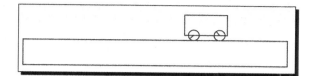

What just happened?

We just created an interaction with our car body. We can move the car left and right by pressing the arrow keys. It seems like the game is getting interesting now.

Applying force to a body

We can apply force to any body by calling the `ApplyForce` function in that body. The following code shows the usage of the function:

```
body.ApplyForce(force, point);
```

This function takes two arguments, which are listed in the following table:

Argument	Type	Discussion
force	b2Vec2	This is the force vector to apply to the body
point	b2Vec2	This is the point where the force is applied

Clearing Force

After we apply the force to bodies, the force would constantly apply to that body until we clear it. In most cases, we clear the force after each step.

Understanding the difference between ApplyForce and ApplyImpulse

Besides the `ApplyForce` function, we can also move any body by using the `ApplyImpulse` function. Both functions move the body, but they move them using a different approach. If we want to change the instance velocity of a body, then we use `ApplyImpulse` once on the body to change its velocity to meet our target value. On the other hand, we need to constantly apply force to a body to increase the speed.

For example, if we want to increase the velocity of the car, similar to like stepping on the pedal, we need to apply force to the car. If we are creating a ball game in which we need to kick-start the ball, we may use the `ApplyImpulse` function to add an instance impulse to the ball's body.

Can you think about a different situation where we will need to apply force or impulse to the body?

Adding ramps to our game environment

Now, we can move the car. However, the environment is not interesting enough to play. Imagine now there are some ramps for the car to jump, and there is a gap between two platforms over which a player has to fly the car. It will become more interesting to play with different ramp setups.

Time for action – creating the world with ramps

Carry out the following steps to create a ramp in the physics world:

1. We open the game logic JavaScript file.

2. In the `createGround` function, we update the function to take four arguments. The changed code is highlighted as follows:

```
function createGround(x, y, width, height, rotation) {
    var bodyDef = new b2BodyDef;
    var fixDef = new b2FixtureDef;

    bodyDef.type = b2Body.b2_staticBody;
    bodyDef.position.x = x /pxPerMeter;
    bodyDef.position.y = y /pxPerMeter;
    bodyDef.angle = rotation * Math.PI / 180;

    fixDef.shape = new b2PolygonShape();
    fixDef.shape.SetAsBox(width/pxPerMeter, height/pxPerMeter);
    fixDef.restitution = 0.4;
    fixDef.friction = 3.5;

    // create the body from the definition.
    var body = carGame.world.CreateBody(bodyDef);
    body.CreateFixture(fixDef);

    return body;
}
```

3. Now, we have a function to create the ground body. We will now replace the ground creation code in the page loaded handler function with the following code:

```
// create the ground
createGround(250, 270, 250, 25, 0);
// create a ramp
createGround(500, 250, 65, 15, -10);
createGround(600, 225, 80, 15, -20);
createGround(1100, 250, 100, 15, 0);
```

4. Save the file and preview the game in a browser. We should now see a ramp and a destination platform, as shown in the following screenshot. Try to control the car by making it jump over the ramp to reach the destination without falling down. Refresh the page to restart the game if you fail:

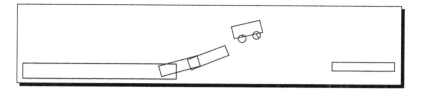

What just happened?

We just wrapped the ground box creating code with a function so that we can easily create a combination of ground bodies. These ground bodies composite the level environment of the game.

In addition, this is the first time we are rotating a body. We set the rotation of the body by using the `rotation` property which takes a value in radians. By setting the rotation of a box, we can have a ramp with a varying slope setup in our game.

Have a go hero

We have set up a ramp now, and we can play with the car within the environment. How about using different kinds of joints to set up the playground? For example, how about a pulley joint to act as a lift? On the other hand, how about including a dynamic board with a joint at the center?

Checking collisions in the Box2D world

The Box2D physics library calculates all collisions automatically. Imagine now that we set up a ground body as the destination. Players win when they successfully move the car to hit the destination. As Box2D already calculates all collisions, all we have to do is get the detected collision list and determine whether our car has hit the destination ground.

Time for action – checking a collision between the car and the destination body

Carry out the following steps to handle collision:

1. Again, we start from our game logic. Open the `box2dcargame.js` JavaScript file in a text editor.

2. We set up a destination ground in the ground creation code and assign it to our `gamewinWall` reference inside the `carGame` global object instance as follows:

```
carGame.gamewinWall = createGround(1200, 215, 15, 25, 0);
```

3. Next, we move on to the `step` function. In each step, we get the complete contact list from the world and check whether any two colliding objects are the car and the destination ground:

```
function checkCollision() {
  // loop all contact list
  // to check if the car hits the winning wall.
  for (var cn = carGame.world.GetContactList(); cn != null;
    cn = cn.GetNext()) {
    var body1 = cn.GetFixtureA().GetBody();
    var body2 = cn.GetFixtureB().GetBody();
    if ((body1 === carGame.car && body2 === carGame.
      gamewinWall) || (body2 === carGame.car &&
        body1 === carGame.gamewinWall))
    {
      if (cn.IsTouching()) {
        console.log("Level Passed!");
      }
    }
  }
}
```

4. When we call our game loop function, `updateWorld`, we call our newly-created collision checking function.

```
checkCollision();
```

5. We will now save the code and open the game in a browser again. This time, we have to open the console window to track whether we get the **Level Passed!** output when the car hits the wall. Try to finish the game, and we should see the output in the console once the car hits the destination:

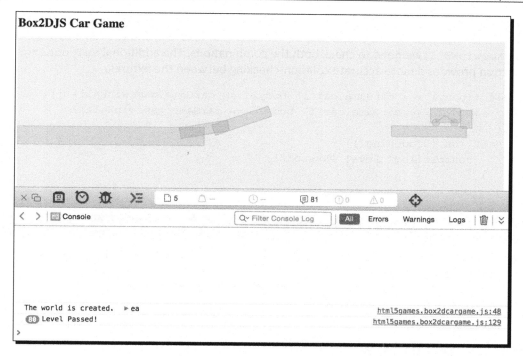

What just happened?

We just created the game winning logic by checking the collision contacts. The player wins when the car successfully reaches the destination ground object.

Getting the collision contact list

In each step, Box2D calculates all collisions and puts them into a **contact list** in the `world` instance. We can get the contact list by using the `carGame.world.GetContactList()` function. The returned contact list is a **link list**. We can travel through the entire link list by using the following `for` loop:

```
for (var cn = carGame.world.GetContactList(); cn != null; cn =
cn.GetNext()) {
    // We have fixture 1 and fixture 2 of each contact node.
    var body1 = cn.GetFixtureA().GetBody();
    var body2 = cn.GetFixtureB().GetBody();
}
```

When we get the collided shapes, we check whether the body of that shape is a car or the destination body. As the car shape may be in fixture 1 or fixture 2, and the same applies to `gamewinWall`, we need to check both the combinations. The additional `isTouching` function provides a more accurate collision-checking between the fixtures.

```
if ((body1 === carGame.car && body2 === carGame.gamewinWall) ||
    (body2 === carGame.car && body1 === carGame.gamewinWall))
{
  if (cn.IsTouching()) {
    console.log("Level Passed!");
  }
}
```

Have a go hero

We created a game over dialog in *Chapter 7, Saving the Game's Progress*. How about using that technique here to create a dialog showing the player passed the level when they hit the winning wall? This will also be useful as a level transition later when we add different level setups to the game.

Restarting the game

You may have already tried refreshing the page several times in the last example to make the car successfully jump to the destination. Imagine now if we could press a key to reinitialize the world. Then, we can follow the trial-and-error method until success.

Time for action – restarting the game while pressing the R key

We will assign the *R* key as the restart key for our game. Now, let's perform the following set of steps:

1. Again, we only need to change the JavaScript file. Open the `box2dcargame.js` JavaScript file in a text editor.

2. We need a function to remove all the bodies:

```
function removeAllBodies() {
  // loop all body list to destroy them
  for (var body = carGame.world.GetBodyList(); body != null;
    body = body.GetNext()) {
    carGame.world.DestroyBody(body);
  }
}
```

3. We move the create world, ramp, and the car code into a function named `restartGame`. They were originally in the page loaded handler function:

```
function restartGame() {
  removeAllBodies();

  // create the ground
  createGround(250, 270, 250, 25, 0);

  // create a ramp
  createGround(500, 250, 65, 15, -10);
  createGround(600, 225, 80, 15, -20);
  createGround(1100, 250, 100, 15, 0);

  // create a destination ground
  carGame.gamewinWall = createGround(1200, 215, 15, 25, 0);

  // create a car
  carGame.car = createCarAt(50, 210);
}
```

4. Then, in the `initGame` function, we call the `restartGame` function to initialize the game as follows:

```
restartGame();
```

5. Finally, we add the following highlighted code to the `keydown` handler to restart the game when the *R* key is pressed:

```
$(document).keydown(function(e){
  switch(e.keyCode) {
    case 39: // right arrow key to apply force towards right
      var force = new b2Vec2(300, 0);
      carGame.car.ApplyForce(force, carGame.car.
        GetWorldCenter());
      break;
    case 37: // left arrow key to apply force towards left
      var force = new b2Vec2(-300, 0);
      carGame.car.ApplyForce(force, carGame.car.
        GetWorldCenter());
      break;
    case 82: // r key to restart the game
      restartGame();
      break;
  }
});
```

6. How about restarting the game when the player passes the level? To do this, add the following highlighted code inside the logic where we checked the collision between the car and the winning flag:

```
console.log("Level Passed!");
restartGame();
```

7. It is time to test the game in a browser. Try playing the game and press the *R* key to restart the game.

What just happened?

We refactored our code to create a `restartGame` function. The world is destroyed and initialized again each time we call this function. We can destroy the existing world and create a new empty one by creating a new world instance of our world variable as follows:

```
carGame.world = createWorld();
```

Have a go hero

Now the only way to restart the game is by pressing the restart key. How about creating a ground at the bottom of the world that checks for any falling cars? When the car drops and hits the bottom ground, we know that the player has failed and then they can restart the game.

Adding a level support to our car game

Imagine now that we can level up to the next environment setup after finishing each game. We will need several environment setups for each level.

Time for action – loading the game with levels data

We will refactor our code to support the loading of static ground bodies from a levels data structure. Let's work on it by carrying out the following steps:

1. Open the `box2dcargame.js` JavaScript file in a text editor.

2. We will need each ground setup on each level. Put the following code at the top of the JavaScript file. It is an array of levels. Each level is another array of objects with the position, dimension, and rotation of the static ground body:

```
var carGame = {
   currentLevel: 0
}
carGame.levels = new Array();
carGame.levels[0] = [{"type":"car","x":50,"y":210,"fuel":20},
```

```
{"type":"box","x":250, "y":270, "width":250,
  "height":25, "rotation":0},
{"type":"box","x":500,"y":250,"width":65,"height":15,
  "rotation":-10},
{"type":"box","x":600,"y":225,"width":80,"height":15,
  "rotation":-20},
{"type":"box","x":950,"y":225,"width":80,"height":15,
  "rotation":20},
{"type":"box","x":1100,"y":250,"width":100,"height":15,
  "rotation":0},
{"type":"win","x":1200,"y":215,"width":15,"height":25,
  "rotation":0}];

carGame.levels[1] = [{"type":"car","x":50,"y":210,"fuel":20},
{"type":"box","x":100, "y":270, "width":190,
  "height":15, "rotation":20},
{"type":"box","x":380, "y":320, "width":100, "height":15,
  "rotation":-10},
{"type":"box","x":666,"y":285,"width":80,"height":15,
  "rotation":-32},
{"type":"box","x":950,"y":295,"width":80,"height":15,
  "rotation":20},
{"type":"box","x":1100,"y":310,"width":100,"height":15,
  "rotation":0},
{"type":"win","x":1200,"y":275,"width":15,"height":25,
  "rotation":0}];

carGame.levels[2] = [{"type":"car","x":50,"y":210,"fuel":20},
{"type":"box","x":100, "y":270, "width":190,
  "height":15, "rotation":20},
{"type":"box","x":380, "y":320, "width":100,
  "height":15, "rotation":-10},
{"type":"box","x":686,"y":285,"width":80,"height":15,
  "rotation":-32},
{"type":"box","x":250,"y":495,"width":80,"height":15,
  "rotation":40},
{"type":"box","x":500,"y":540,"width":200,"height":15,
  "rotation":0},
{"type":"win","x":220,"y":425,"width":15,"height":25,
  "rotation":23}];
```

3. Replace the `restartGame` function with the following code. This changes the function to accept a `level` argument. Then, create the ground or car by the level data:

```
function restartGame(level) {
    carGame.currentLevel = level;

    // destroy existing bodies.
    removeAllBodies();// create the world

    // create a ground in our newly created world
    // load the ground info from level data
    for(var i=0;i<carGame.levels[level].length;i++) {
        var obj = carGame.levels[level][i];

        // create car
        if (obj.type === "car") {
            carGame.car = createCarAt(obj.x, obj.y);
            continue;
        }

        var groundBody = createGround(obj.x, obj.y,
          obj.width, obj.height, obj.rotation);

        if (obj.type === "win") {
            carGame.gamewinWall = groundBody;
        }
    }
}
```

4. In the page loaded handler function, change the `restartGame` function called by providing `currentLevel` as follows:

```
restartGame(carGame.currentLevel);
```

5. We also need to provide the `currentLevel` value in the restart key handler:

```
case 82: // r key to restart the game
    restartGame(carGame.currentLevel);
    break;
```

6. Lastly, change the following highlighted code in the game's win logic. We move a level up in the game when the car hits the destination:

```
if ((body1 === carGame.car && body2 === carGame.gamewinWall) ||
    (body2 === carGame.car && body1 === carGame.gamewinWall))
{
  if (cn.IsTouching()) {
```

```
        console.log("Level Passed!");
        restartGame(carGame.currentLevel+1);
    }
}
```

7. We will now run the game in the web browser. Finish the level and the game should restart at the next level:

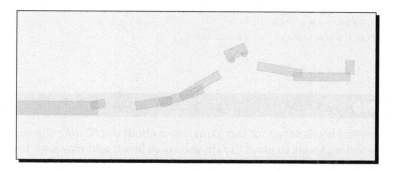

What just happened?

We just created a data structure to store the levels. Then, we created the game with the given level number and constructed the world with the level data.

Each level data is an array of objects. Each object contains properties of each ground body in the world. This includes basic properties such as position, size, and rotation. There is also a property named `type`. It defines whether the body is a normal box body, car data, or the destination winning ground:

```
carGame.levels[0] = [{"type":"car","x":50,"y":210,"fuel":20},
{"type":"box","x":250, "y":270, "width":250, "height":25,
"rotation":0},
{"type":"box","x":500,"y":250,"width":65,"height":15,"rotation":-10},
{"type":"box","x":600,"y":225,"width":80,"height":15,"rotation":-20},
{"type":"box","x":950,"y":225,"width":80,"height":15,"rotation":20},
{"type":"box","x":1100,"y":250,"width":100,"height":15,"rotation":0},
{"type":"win","x":1200,"y":215,"width":15,"height":25,"rotation":0}];
```

When creating the world, we use the following code to loop through all objects in the level array. We then create the car and ground bodies and reference the game winning ground according to the type:

```
for(var i=0;i<carGame.levels[level].length;i++) {
  var obj = carGame.levels[level][i];

  // create car
```

```
if (obj.type === "car") {
  carGame.car = createCarAt(obj.x,obj.y);
  continue;
}

var groundBody = createGround(obj.x, obj.y, obj.width,
  obj.height, obj.rotation);

if (obj.type === "win") {
  carGame.gamewinWall = groundBody;
}
}
```

Have a go hero

Now, we have several levels setup for our game. How about duplicating the level data to create more interesting levels to play? Create your own levels and play with them. It is just like how a kid builds blocks and plays with them.

Replacing the Box2D outline drawing with graphics

We have created a game that is at least playable with several levels. However, they are just some outline boxes. We cannot even distinguish between the destination body and other ground bodies in the game. Imagine now that the destination is a racing flag and there is a car graphic to represent it. This will make the game's purpose clearer.

Time for action – adding a flag graphic and a car graphic to the game

Carry out the following steps to draw two graphics on our physics objects:

1. We will first download the graphics we need for this example. To download the graphics, go to `http://mak.la/book-assets`.

2. Put the image files for this chapter in the `images` folder.

3. Now, it is time to edit the `index.html` file. Add the following HTML markup to the `body` section:

```
<div id="asset">
  <img id="flag" src='images/flag.png'>
  <img id="bus" src="images/bus.png">
  <img id="wheel" src="images/wheel.png">
</div>
```

4. We want to hide the asset DIV that contains our `img` tags. Open the `cargame.css` file and add the following CSS rule to keep the asset DIV out of our sight:

```
#asset {
  position: absolute;
  top: -9999px;
}
```

5. We will now move on to the logic part. Open the `box2dcargame.js` JavaScript file.

6. In the `restartGame` function, add the highlighted code to assign the reference of the `flag` image to the winning destination flag:

```
if (obj.type === "win") {
  carGame.gamewinWall = groundBody;
  groundBody.SetUserData( document.getElementById('flag') );
}
```

7. Next, assign the reference of the `bus` image tag to the user data in the car shape. Add the following highlighted code to the car box definition creation:

```
function createCarAt(x, y) {
  var bodyDef = new b2BodyDef;
  var fixDef = new b2FixtureDef;

  // car body
  bodyDef.type = b2Body.b2_dynamicBody;
  bodyDef.userData = document.getElementById('bus');

  // existing code goes here.
}
```

> We used to get the reference of an element by the jQuery `$(selector)` method. The jQuery selector returns an array of the element objects with additional jQuery data wrapped. If we want to get the original document element reference, then we can either use the `document.getElementById` method or `$(selector).get(0)`. As `$(selector)` returns an array, `get(0)` gives the first original document element in the list

8. Then, we need to handle the wheels. We assign the `wheel` image tag to the wheel body's `userData` property. Add the following highlighted code to the `createWheel` function

```
function createWheel(x, y) {
  var bodyDef = new b2BodyDef;
  var fixDef = new b2FixtureDef;
```

```
    bodyDef.type = b2Body.b2_dynamicBody;
    bodyDef.userData = document.getElementById('wheel');

    // existing code goes here
}
```

9. We have to draw the images in the canvas. Create a new drawWorld function in the box2dcargame.js file with the following code.

```
// drawing functions
function drawWorld(world, context) {
  for (var body = carGame.world.GetBodyList(); body != null;
    body = body.GetNext()) {
    if (body.GetUserData() !== null && body.GetUserData() !==
      undefined) {
      // the user data contains the reference to the image
      var img = body.GetUserData();

      // the x and y of the image. We have to subtract the half
width/height
      var x = body.GetPosition().x;
      var y = body.GetPosition().y;
      var topleftX = - $(img).width()/2;
      var topleftY = - $(img).height()/2;

      context.save();
      context.translate(x * pxPerMeter,y * pxPerMeter);
      context.rotate(body.GetAngle());
      context.drawImage(img, topleftX, topleftY);
      context.restore();
    }
  }
}
```

10. Finally, call the drawWorld function in the updateWorld function:

```
function updateWorld() {
  ctx.clearRect(0, 0, canvasWidth, canvasHeight);

  // existing code goes here.

  // render graphics
  drawWorld(carGame.world, ctx);
}
```

11. Save all files and run the game in a web browser. We should see a yellow bus graphic, two wheels, and a flag as the destination. Play the game now and the game should move on to the next level when the bus hits the flag:

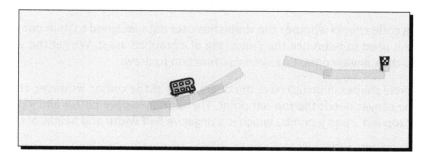

What just happened?

We are now presenting our game with minimal graphics. At least, players easily know what they are controlling and where they should go.

The Box2D library uses a canvas to render the physics world. Therefore, all techniques that we learned about a canvas can be applied here. In *Chapter 5, Building a Canvas Game's Masterclass*, we learned the use of the `drawImage` function to display an image in the canvas. We used this technique to draw the flag graphic in the canvas of the physics world.

Using userData in shape and body

How do we know which physics body needs to be displayed as the flag image? There is a property named `userData` in every Box2D shape and body. This property is used to store any custom data related to that shape or body. For example, we may store the filename of the graphic file or just directly store the reference to the image tag.

We have a list of image tags referencing the graphic assets that we need in the game. However, we do not want to display the image tags—they are just for the purpose of loading and referencing. We hide the asset image tags by setting their position out of the HTML bound with the following CSS style. We do not use `display:none` because we cannot get the width and height of the element that is not displayed at all. We need the width and height to position graphics correctly in the physics world:

```
#asset {
    position: absolute;
    top: -9999px;
}
```

Drawing graphics in every frame according to the state of its physics body

The drawing from Box2D is just for development use before we replace it with our graphics.

The following code checks whether the shape has user data assigned to it. In our example, the user data is used to reference the `image` tag of a graphics asset. We get the `image` tag and pass it to the Canvas context `drawImage` function to draw.

All box and circle shapes in Box2D have the origin point at the center. However, the image drawing in the canvas needs the top-left point. Therefore, we have both *x* and *y* coordinates and offset of top-left *x* and *y* points, which is a negative half width and height of the image:

```
if (body.GetUserData() !== null && body.GetUserData() !== undefined) {
    // the user data contains the reference to the image
    var img = body.GetUserData();

    // the x and y of the image.
    // We have to subtract the half width/height
    var x = body.GetPosition().x;
    var y = body.GetPosition().y;
    var topleftX = - $(img).width()/2;
    var topleftY = - $(img).height()/2;

    context.save();
    context.translate(x,y);
    context.rotate(s.GetBody().GetRotation());
    context.drawImage(img, topleftX, topleftY);
    context.restore();
}
```

Rotating and translating an image in the canvas

We used the `drawImage` function to draw an image directly with the coordinates. However, the situation is different here. We need to rotate the drawn image. This is done by rotating the context before drawing and then restoring the rotation afterwards. We can do this by saving the context state, translating it, rotating it, and then calling the `restore` function. The following code shows how we draw an image at a given position and rotation. The `topleftX` and `topleftY` are the offset distances from the image's center origin to the top-left point:

```
context.save();
context.translate(x,y);
context.rotate(s.GetBody().GetRotation());
context.drawImage(img, topleftX, topleftY);
context.restore();
```

 We do not need to make the physics body area exactly the same as its graphics. For example, if we have a round circular chicken, we can represent it in the physics world by just a ball body. Using a simple physics body can improve the performance a lot.

Have a go hero

We have learned using CSS3 transitions to animate a scoreboard. How about applying it to this car game? Moreover, how about adding some engine sounds to the car? Just try applying what we have learned throughout this book to give players a complete game experience.

Adding a final touch to make the game fun to play

Imagine now that we want to publish the game. The game logic is basically there, but it looks quite ugly with the black and white environment. In this section, we will add some final touches to the game so that it is much more attractive. We will also apply some constraints to limit the time of `ApplyForce`. This constraint makes the game more fun because it requires a player to think before he applies too much force to the car.

Time for action – decorating the game and adding a fuel limitation

Carry out the following steps to turn our debug draw into a rich graphical game:

1. First, we need some background images for the starting screen, game winning screen, and environment backgrounds for each level. These graphics can be found from the code bundle named `box2d_final_game`. The following screenshot shows the graphics that we need in this section:

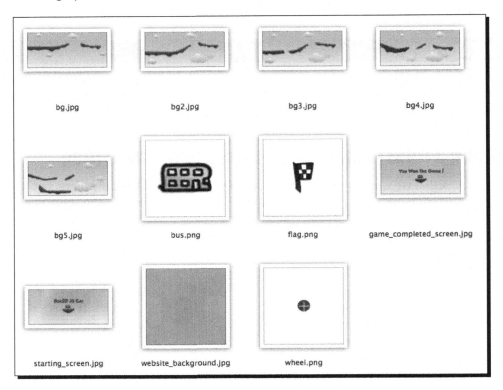

2. Open the `index.html` file and replace the canvas element with the following markup. This creates two more game components named `current level` and `fuel remaining`, and it groups the game components into a `game-container` DIV:

```
<section id="game-container">
    <canvas id="game" width='1300' height='600'
    class="startscreen"></canvas>

    <div id="fuel" class="progressbar">
```

```
        <div class="fuel-value" style="width: 100%;"></div>
    </div>

    <div id="level"></div>
</section>
```

3. Next, we will copy the `cargame.css` file from the code bundle. This contains several class-style definitions for the game. The game should look similar to the one shown in the following screenshot after we have applied the new stylesheet:

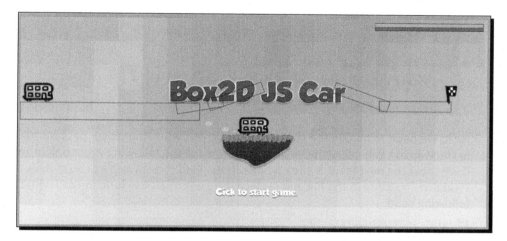

4. Now, we will move on to the JavaScript part. Open the `html5games.box2dcargame.js` file.

5. Update the `carGame` object declaration with the following additional variable:

```
var carGame = {
    // game state constant
    STATE_STARTING_SCREEN : 1,
    STATE_PLAYING : 2,
    STATE_GAMEOVER_SCREEN : 3,

    state : 0,

    fuel: 0,
    fuelMax: 0,

    currentLevel: 0
}
```

6. Now, we have the starting screen. Instead of starting the game once, the page is loaded. We'll display the starting screen and wait for the player to click on the game canvas. Add the following logic to the `initGame` function:

```
// set the game state as "starting screen"
carGame.state = carGame.STATE_STARTING_SCREEN;

// start the game when clicking anywhere in starting screen
$('#game').click(function(){
    if (carGame.state === carGame.STATE_STARTING_SCREEN) {
        // change the state to playing.
        carGame.state = carGame.STATE_PLAYING;

        // start new game
        restartGame(carGame.currentLevel);
    }
});
```

7. Next, we need to handle the game-winning screen when the player passes all levels. In the winning flag-collision-checking logic, we use the following logic to determine if we show the next level or the ending screen. Find the `console.log("Level Passed!");` code in the file and replace the `restartGame` function call with the following code:

```
if (cn.IsTouching()) {
    console.log("Level Passed!");

    if (carGame.currentLevel < carGame.levels.length - 1) {
        restartGame(carGame.currentLevel+1);
    } else {
        // show game over screen
        $('#game').removeClass().addClass('gamebg_won');

        // clear the physics world
        carGame.world = createWorld();
    }
}
```

8. Then, we will handle the game playing background. We prepared each game background for each level setting. We will switch the background in the `restartGame` function, which corresponds to reconstructing the world:

```
$("#level").html("Level " + (level+1));

// change the background image to fit the level
$('#game').removeClass().addClass('gamebg-level'+level);
```

9. With the game graphics now, we do not need the physics object outline drawing any more. We can turn off the debug drawing by setting the `shouldDrawDebug` object to `false`:

```
var shouldDrawDebug = false;
```

10. Finally, let's add some constraints. Remember that in our level data, we include a mystery fuel data for the car. This is an indicator of how much fuel the car contains. We will use this fuel to limit the player's input. The fuel reduces each time a force is applied to the car. The player cannot apply any additional force once the fuel runs out. This limitation makes the game more fun to play.

11. Update the arrow keys' `keydown` function with the following logic. The new code is highlighted here:

```
switch(e.keyCode) {
    case 39: // right arrow key to apply force towards right
        if (carGame.fuel > 0) {
            var force = new b2Vec2(300, 0);
            carGame.car.ApplyForce(force, carGame.car.
                GetWorldCenter());
            carGame.fuel -= 1;
            $(".fuel-value").width(carGame.fuel/carGame.fuelMax * 100
                +'%');
        }
        return false;
        break;
    case 37: // left arrow key to apply force towards left
        if (carGame.fuel > 0) {
            var force = new b2Vec2(-300, 0);
            carGame.car.ApplyForce(force, carGame.car.
                GetWorldCenter());
            carGame.fuel -= 1;
            $(".fuel-value").width(carGame.fuel/carGame.fuelMax * 100
                +'%');
        }
        return false;
        break;
    case 82: // r key to restart the game
        restartGame(carGame.currentLevel);
        break;
}
```

12. In addition, in the car-creating logic in the restart game function, we initialize the fuel as follows:

```
// create car
if (obj.type === "car") {
```

```
carGame.car = createCarAt(obj.x,obj.y);
carGame.fuel = obj.fuel;
carGame.fuelMax = obj.fuel;
$(".fuel-value").width('100%');
continue;
}
```

13. Now, run the game in a browser. We should get five graphic levels. The following screenshot shows how the last four levels look:

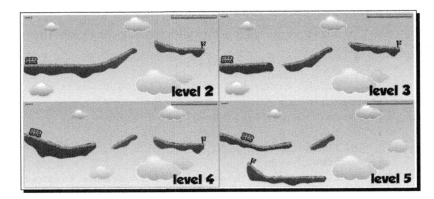

14. After passing all the levels, we will get the following winning screen:

What just happened?

We just decorated our game with more graphics. We also drew each level environment, a background image. The following screenshot illustrates how the visual ground represents the logical physics boxes. Unlike the car and the winning flag, the ground graphics are not associated with the physics ground. This is just a background image with the graphics in their respective positions. We can use this approach because those logical boxes will never move:

We can then prepare several CSS styles for each level with the level number in the class name, such as `.gamebg-level1` and `.gamebg-level2`. With each class linked with each level background, we can change the background when switching a level using the following code:

```
$('#game').removeClass().addClassddClass('gamebg-level'+level);
```

Adding fuel to add a constraint when applying force

Now, we limit the player's input by providing limited fuel to use. The fuel decreases when players apply force to the car. We used the following `keydown` logic to decrease the fuel and prevent additional force when the car is running out of fuel:

```
case 39:
  if (carGame.fuel > 0) {
    var force = new b2Vec2(300, 0);
    carGame.car.ApplyForce(force, carGame.car.GetCenterPosition());
    carGame.fuel -= 1;
    $(".fuel-value").width(carGame.fuel/carGame.fuelMax * 100 +'%');
  }
```

Presenting the remaining fuel in a CSS3 progress bar

In our game, we present the remaining fuel as a progress bar. The progress bar is actually a DIV inside another DIV. The following markup shows the structure of the progress bar. The outer DIV defines the maximum value and the inner DIV shows the actual value:

```
<div id="fuel" class="progressbar">
   <div class="fuel-value" style="width: 100%;"></div>
</div>
```

The following screenshot illustrates the structure of the progress bar:

With this structure, we can show specific progress by setting the width as a percentage value. We use the following code to update the progress bar according to the percentage of the fuel:

```
$(".fuel-value").width(carGame.fuel/carGame.fuelMax * 100 +'%');
```

This is the basic logic to set up a progress bar and control it with the width style.

Adding touch support for tablets

We added touch support in *Chapter 6, Adding Sound Effects to Your Games*. In this game, we will add touch support to make it playable on tablets.

Time for action – adding touch support

Carry out the following steps to make our game work in a tablet with touch inputs:

1. In `index.html` file, we add the following touch controls before the end of the `#game-container`:

    ```
    <div id="left-button" class="touch-control"></div>
    <div id="right-button" class="touch-control"></div>
    <div id="restart-button" class="touch-control">Restart</div>
    ```

2. We can also add a `<meta>` tag inside the `<head>` tag to control the viewport to fit the game into the iPad's 1024 px width.

    ```
    <meta name="viewport" content="width=device-width, initial-
    scale=0.78, minimum-scale=0.78, maximum-scale=0.78">
    ```

3. For these controls, we add some basic styles to position them. To do this, append the following code to the `cargame.css` file:

    ```
    .touch-control {
      position: absolute;
    }
    #left-button {
      top: 0;
      left: 0;
      width: 50%;
    ```

```
  height: 100%;
}
#right-button {
  top: 0;
  right: 0;
  width: 50%;
  height: 100%;
}
#restart-button {
  top: 0;
  left: 50%;
  left: calc( 50% - 50px );
  width: 100px;
  height: 50px;
  text-align: center;
  line-height: 50px;
}
```

4. Now, we move to the box2dcargame.js file, and we add a function named handleTouchInputs():

```
function handleTouchInputs() {
  // Touch support
  if (!window.Touch) {
    $('.touch-control').hide();
  } else {
    $('#right-button').bind('touchstart', function(){
      if (carGame.state === carGame.STATE_STARTING_SCREEN) {
        // change the state to playing.
        carGame.state = carGame.STATE_PLAYING;

        // start new game
        restartGame(carGame.currentLevel);
      } else {
        carGame.isRightButtonActive = true;
      }
    });
    $('#left-button').bind('touchstart', function(){
      if (carGame.state === carGame.STATE_STARTING_SCREEN) {
        // change the state to playing.
        carGame.state = carGame.STATE_PLAYING;

        // start new game
        restartGame(carGame.currentLevel);
      } else {
```

```
            carGame.isLeftButtonActive = true;
        }
    });
    $('#right-button').bind('touchend', function() {
        carGame.isRightButtonActive = false;
    });
    $('#left-button').bind('touchend', function() {
        carGame.isLeftButtonActive = false;
    });
    $('#restart-button').bind('touchstart', function(){
        restartGame(carGame.currentLevel);
    })
  }
}
```

5. We call our `handleTouchInputs` function within the `initGame` function:

```
handleTouchInputs();
```

6. We apply the force continuously until the touch up event. We can slightly adjust the value to fit the tablet. To do this, add the following code at the end of the existing `updateWorld` function:

```
// apply force based on the touch event
if (carGame.isRightButtonActive) {
  if (carGame.fuel > 0) {
    var force = new b2Vec2(50, 0);
    carGame.car.ApplyForce(force, carGame.car.
      GetWorldCenter());
    carGame.fuel -= 0.1;
    $(".fuel-value").width(carGame.fuel/carGame.fuelMax * 100
      +'%');
  }
} else if (carGame.isLeftButtonActive) {
  if (carGame.fuel > 0) {
    var force = new b2Vec2(-50, 0);
    carGame.car.ApplyForce(force, carGame.car.
      GetWorldCenter());
    carGame.fuel -= 0.1;
    $(".fuel-value").width(carGame.fuel/carGame.fuelMax * 100
      +'%');
  }
}
```

7. Save all the files and run the game in a tablet, say an iPad or an Android, and we should be able to control the car by pressing the left and right sides of the game. We can also restart the level by pressing the restart button.

What just happened?

We just added touch support to our game to make it playable on a tablet. We created two touch areas for the left and right force. We also created a restart button that's only viewable on touch devices:

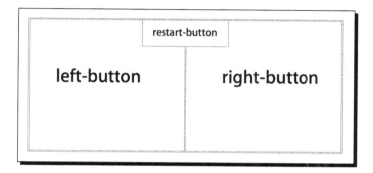

We listen to the `touchstart` and `touchend` event on these buttons. The `touchstart` event is not like the `keydown` event that keeps firing the events. We need a Boolean to know whether the touch has started and keep a track until it ends. During touch pressing, we apply the forces in the `updateWorld` method. The frequency is different, so we adjusted the value of force and fuel consumption to make it work better in tablets.

Controlling the viewport scale

When designing mobile web pages, we often use viewport to tell the browser to use the device width as the web page's view port width:

```
<meta name="viewport" content="width=device-width, initial-scale=1">
```

In games, especially games that require tapping frequently, we may want to fix the zooming feature by setting the same value to the minimum scale and the maximum scale. Moreover, we can control the scale value to zoom the game to fit the tablet devices.

```
<meta name="viewport" content="width=device-width, initial-scale=0.78,
minimum-scale=0.78, maximum-scale=0.78">
```

Touch-specific buttons

There is no keyboard on tablet and mobile devices. We have to create on-screen inputs for these devices. We created three on-screen buttons in this game example: left, right and restart buttons. We hid these buttons in the desktop by checking the availability of `window.Touch`:

```
if (!window.Touch) {
  $('.touch-control').hide();
}
```

Summary

You learned a lot in this chapter about using the Box2D physics engine to create a car adventure game in canvas.

Specifically, we set up the game with the JavaScript physics engine. Then, we created static and dynamic bodies in the physics world. We set up the car by using joints to constrain bodies and wheels. We controlled the car with keyboard inputs by adding force to it. At last, we determined game-over and level-up by adding collisions in the physics world. We have now learned how to use the Box2D physics library to create a canvas-based physics game.

In the next chapter, we are going to discuss different distribution channels and put our game into a native Mac application.

10
Deploying HTML5 Games

We have created several HTML5 games throughout the book. In this chapter, we discuss several approaches through which we can deploy our games to let others play them.

In this chapter, you will learn the following topics:

- ◆ Deploying the game to a web page.
- ◆ Deploying the game as a mobile web app.
- ◆ Wrapping the game into an OS X app.
- ◆ Deploying the game to the App Store.

There are different channels to deploy HTML5 games. We can put the game online in a normal web page or deploy it as a mobile web app. Otherwise, we can deploy the game on the Chrome Web Store. For native app stores, we have different app store options according to the types of the games. We choose desktop or mobile app stores to deploy our games. For desktop games, we can deploy the game to the Mac App Store or Windows Store. For games for mobile devices, we can deploy them to the iOS app store and Android app stores.

The most direct approach to deploy HTML5 games to app stores is by using Web View components from the target platform to host the HTML file and the related assets.

Preparing the deploying materials

When deploying the game, we usually need to prepare for the store listing. This means we need to make the app icon, several screenshots, and game description. Some stores may optionally accept a short game play video.

Putting the game on the Web

The requirement of the server depends on the technology we used in the game. For games that only involved client-side HTML, CSS, and JavaScript, we can use any web hosting, including the static website hosting service. Often, these static hosting services allow you to easily upload the website in a ZIP file or via cloud storage such as Dropbox.

Amazon S3 is also an affordable choice for hosting a static website. For example, my HTML5 games are hosted on S3 with **Amazon CloudFront** as the Content Delivery Network (CDN) to boost the caching and loading performance. You can check out a site for HTML5 games at `http://makzan.net/html5-games-list/`.

Another popular and free way to host static websites is via the GitHub page. GitHub is a service that hosts the Git repository, and it provides every repository with a static website hosting feature. You can learn more about it in their guide at `https://help.github.com/categories/github-pages-basics/`.

 Some services mentioned in this chapter require you to use Git version control to push the code to their server. Git is a code version control system. You may learn about it via the online resource at `http://git-scm.com/book/`.

Hosting the node.js server

For games that require a server, such as the multiplayer game, we need to host the game server. Take our draw-and-guess game as an example; we need a hosting that supports the running of the Node.js server. To get a list of hosting that supports running Node.js, go to: `https://github.com/joyent/node/wiki/Node-Hosting`.

Some of them, such as Heroku, are free during low usage and charge you after your application gets popular and needs to use more server resources. This pricing model is good for us to test the game with the public without paying a high price for a server renting fee.

Deploying as a mobile web app in the home screen

We can make the game able to be installed on mobile devices' home screens by configuring several `meta` tags.

Time for action – adding a meta tag for a mobile web app

We will take an audio game as an example to begin with. Let's perform the following steps:

1. Open the `index.html` file in the code editor.

2. Add the following code within the head section.

```
<meta name="apple-mobile-web-app-capable" content="yes">
<meta name="apple-mobile-web-app-status-bar-style"
  content="black">
<link rel="apple-touch-icon" href="game-icon.png">
<link rel="apple-touch-startup-image" href="launch-screen.png">
```

3. Test the game on an iOS device or a simulator. To do this, try tapping on the **Share** button and then select **Add to Home Screen**. You should see the icon and the name of the game. Continue to add the game to the home screen.

4. Then, open the game from the home screen. It will open in fullscreen mode.

5. Double-click on the home button to enable the app-switching screen. You will be able to see that the app has its own place, similar to a natively installed application.

> If you are developing on Mac, you may use the iOS simulator that comes with the free Xcode development IDE from Apple. Simply drag the HTML file into the simulator, and you can test your game in mobile Safari.

What just happened?

We have added several `meta` tags that are recognized by mobile operating systems, specifically iOS. The idea of a mobile web app was introduced with the debut of the first iPhone in 2007. We tell the system that our web browser is capable of being displayed like an app. Then, the system makes the web page very similar to an app to the user's perspective.

The default icon size is 60 x 60. We can also provide pixel-perfect icons by specifying each dimension for the iPhone and iPad:

```
<link rel="apple-touch-icon" href="default-icon-60x60.png">
<link rel="apple-touch-icon" sizes="76x76" href="icon-ipad.png">
<link rel="apple-touch-icon" sizes="120x120" href="icon-iphone-retina.
png">
<link rel="apple-touch-icon" sizes="152x152" href="icon-ipad-retina.
png">
```

Building an HTML5 game into a Mac OS X app

In this section, I will show you how we can wrap an HTML5 game with a Web View and build it into a native application. This section includes code with other programming languages in a different development environment.

Time for action—putting the HTML5 games into a Mac app

Follow the steps in Mac Xcode. We need a Mac and the Apple Xcode to create a Mac OS X app. Download Xcode from the Mac App Store if you haven't got it.

 Even if you don't have a Mac, you can still have a look at how we wrap the Web View with an application. The concept is more important than the steps in this section.

1. Launch Xcode and create a new project. Select **Cocoa Application** under **OS X**:

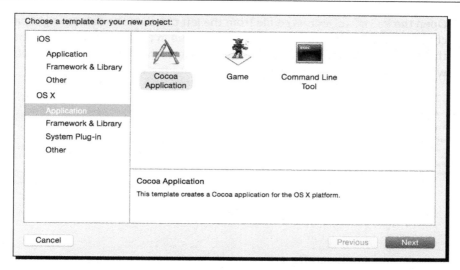

2. In the Options View, give the name of the game as **Product Name**. **Organization Name** can be your name or a company's name. Use a reversed domain as **Organization Identifier**. Choose **Objective-C** for this code example. We keep the default value for the other options.

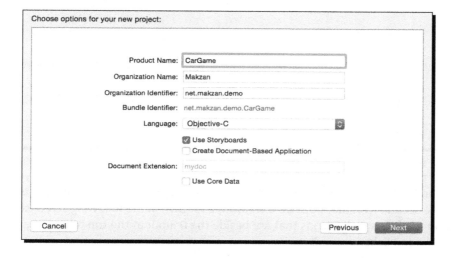

3. Open the `Main.storyboard` file from the left panel. In the bottom-right panel, choose the third tab (which is highlighted in blue in the following screenshot). Drag the **Web View** component into the Window View. The Web View should become full width and height when you drag and drop it into the view:

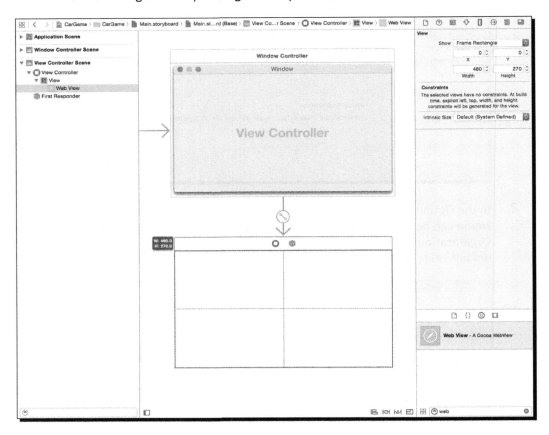

4. At the bottom of the window, there are several icons that configure how you can handle the resizing of the app window. Keep the **Web View** selected and then select the second icon that pops up a window, as shown in the following screenshot. Click on the four spacing icons that are beside the **0** input at the top to turn them into solid red lines:

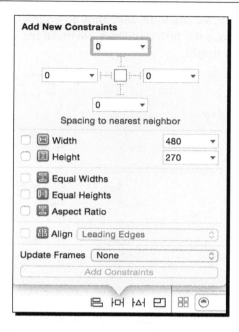

5. After selecting the four spacings at the top, click on the **Add Constraints** button. This tells the Web View to maintain **0** spacing between all the four edges when the window resizes.

6. Then, we set the window size to fit our game. To do this, select the window. On the top-right panel, choose the fifth tab. Then, we make the window's size exactly 1,300 px width and 600 px height:

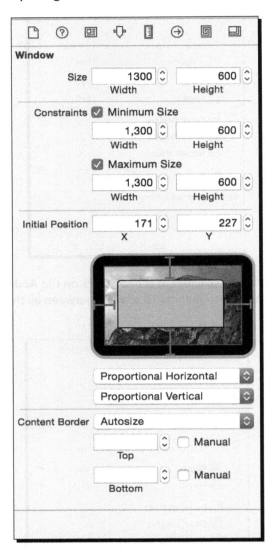

7. Then, we enable the **Show Assistant Editor** option in the **View** menu. Keep the `Main.storyboard` option on the left and open the `ViewController.h` file in the right panel.

8. On the left panel, identify the **Web View** component. Right-click on the component and drag it to the interface section in the `ViewController.h` file. This allows us to name the component for future reference. Name the Web View component as `gameWebView`:

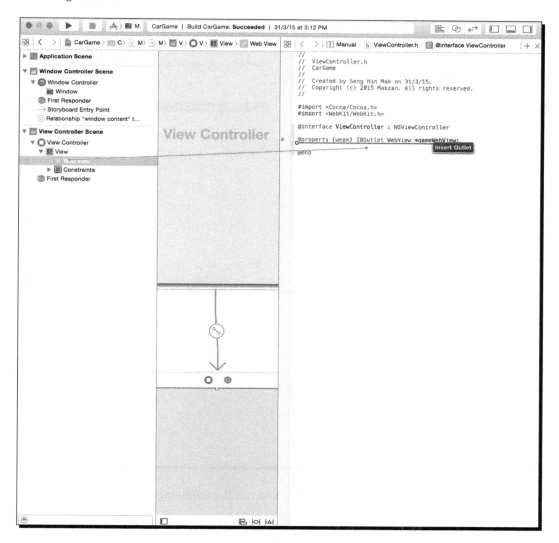

9. We have now configured the view. Let's move on to the code. We used the Web View component that is part of the WebKit framework. We need to include it in the project. To do this, select the **CarGame** project on the left panel. In the **Linked Framework and Libraries** section under the **General** tab, click on the plus icon to add the WebKit framework:

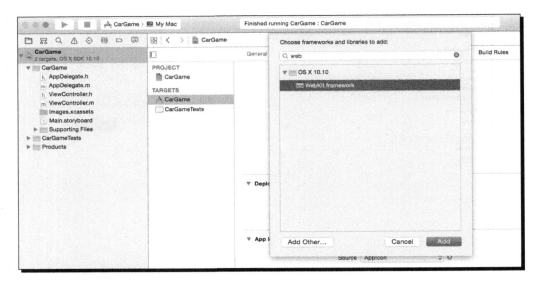

10. Now, we should see `WebKit.framework` in the **Linked Frameworks and Libraries** section:

11. Click on the `ViewController.m` file and put the following code inside the `viewDidLoad` function:

```
NSURL *url = [NSURL URLWithString:@"http://makzan.net/html5-games/
car-game/"];
NSURLRequest *request = [NSURLRequest requestWithURL:url];
[[self.gameWebView mainFrame] loadRequest:request];
```

12. Now, your `ViewController.m` file should look like the following screenshot:

```objc
#import "ViewController.h"

@implementation ViewController

- (void)viewDidLoad {
    [super viewDidLoad];

    // Do any additional setup after loading the view.

    NSURL *url = [NSURL URLWithString:@"http://makzan.net/html5-games/car-game/"];
    NSURLRequest *request = [NSURLRequest requestWithURL:url];
    [[self.gameWebView mainFrame] loadRequest:request];
}

- (void)setRepresentedObject:(id)representedObject {
    [super setRepresentedObject:representedObject];

    // Update the view, if already loaded.
}

@end
```

13. Finally, click on the **Play** button on the top left of the Xcode that is shown in the following screenshot:

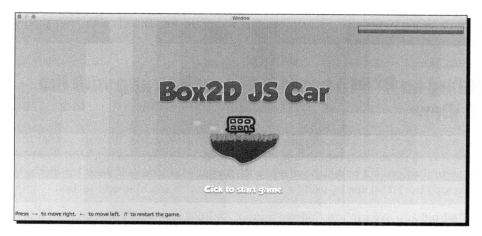

After you click on the Play button, the application will build and open a window with our car game running, as shown in the following screenshot:

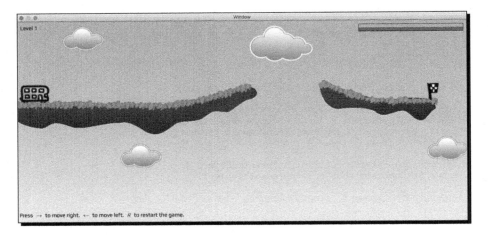

What just happened?

We just wrapped our game with a native application by using the Web View component. We used Xcode and Objective-C to demonstrate the behind-the-scenes scenario of wrapping the Web View. You can actually apply the same techniques in other languages and platforms, for example, using Swift in iOS or even building Windows applications with their Web View components in the Windows platform.

Building an HTML5 game into a mobile app with the Web View

We had a glimpse of how wrapping the game in a Web View works. It's very similar to wrapping a Web View into a mobile app. For example, in iOS, we use the Xcode and create an iPhone or iPad project to which we add a Web View in the default view. Inside the Web View, we load the HTML file by using a similar technique in the Mac app section.

For an Android app, we can use Android Studio. Android uses a different programming language; it uses Java, but the concept is the same. We create a Web View component in the main view and load our HTML5 game via a URL.

Please note that we need a certificate to deploy an iOS app into app store. To obtain the certificate, we need to join the Apple Developer Program that requires an annual fee. For the Mac app, we can distribute the game on our own or deploy it to the Mac App Store with a Mac developer certificate.

Building with the PhoneGap build

There is another option to build Android and iPhone apps from web apps—by using the PhoneGap build service. The service allows you to upload a ZIP file of the web game. Then, it uses Web View to display the HTML, similar to our previous Web View examples.

The difference is that PhoneGap provides several hardware resources via its JavaScript API. Since our game hasn't used any PhoneGap API, it gives pretty much the same result as wrapping the Web View ourselves and building using the PhoneGap.

If you don't have any native programming experience, PhoneGap or a similar cloud building service is a good choice. If you are comfortable with native development environment, I prefer wrapping the Web View myself. This provides more flexibility for future development in case we need to mix native and Web View to make it a hybrid application.

Besides a PhoneGap build, there are other services that try to put HTML5 games into the native app platform. CocoonJS (`https://www.ludei.com/cocoonjs/`) is another platform for this purpose. Instead of just wrapping the Web View inside a native application, CocoonJS tries to convert the canvas drawing API into the operating system's OpenGL command to gain further performance.

App store's reviewing process

There are different review processes per deploying channel. For example, Apple often takes 1 to 4 weeks to review the app before allowing it on their app stores. On the other hand, Google often takes hours to review apps on the Play Store. If you are new to the store, it often takes an extra week to get familiar with its configuration tool. So, be ready 4 weeks in advance if you need to push the game on the app stores to a deadline, such as a client project.

 We didn't go through the process of uploading our game to app stores because their configuration and store listing may change over time. The important thing is to have all the material and target builds ready. With all the material ready, uploading and configuring for each store shouldn't be a burden.

Summary

In this chapter, you learned about publishing the game to different platforms. Specifically, we discussed static website hosting services to deploy our HTML5 games. We listed servers that run node.js. We updated our code to work well with the home screen web app. We tried to put our HTML5 game into Web View in Xcode. We also discussed the building of mobile apps and their review process.

We discussed different aspects of making HTML5 games with CSS3 and JavaScript in nine chapters. We learned how to build a traditional Ping Pong game in DOM and built a card-matching game in CSS3 and an Untangle puzzle game with Canvas. Then, we explored how to add sounds to the game and created a mini piano musical game around it. Next, we discussed saving and loading game statuses by using the local storage. We also built a draw-and-guess real-time multiplayer game with WebSockets. Then, we created a car game with a physics engine in this chapter. Finally, we discussed how we can deploy our HTML5 games to different platforms.

Throughout the book, we built different types of games, and you learned some essential techniques that you need to make HTML5 games. The next step is to go on and deploy your own games. To help develop your own games, there are some resources that can be helpful. The following list gives some useful links for HTML5 game development:

- General HTML5:
    - HTML5 Game Development (http://www.html5gamedevelopment.com/)
    - HTML5 Rocks (http://www.html5rocks.com/)

- HTML5 game engines
    - ImpactJS (`http://impactjs.com/`)
    - CreateJS (`http://createjs.com/`)
    - Phaser (`http://phaser.io/`)
- Game sprites and textures

    - Lost Garden (`http://lunar.lostgarden.com/labels/free%20 game%20graphics.html`)
    - HasGraphics sprites, textures, and tilesets (`http://hasgraphics.com/ category/sprites/`)
    - Subtle Patterns (`http://subtlepatterns.com`)

Pop Quiz Answers

Chapter 2, Getting Started with DOM-based Game Development

Preparing the HTML documents for a DOM-based game

Pop quiz

Q1	4

Setting up the Ping Pong game elements

Pop quiz

Q1	3

Chapter 3, Building a Card-matching Game in CSS3

Storing internal custom data with an HTML5 custom data attribute

Pop quiz

Q1	3

Accessing custom data attribute with jQuery

Pop quiz

Q1	4

Chapter 4, Building the Untangle Game with Canvas and the Drawing API

Drawing a circle in the Canvas

Pop quiz

Q1	2

Using mouse events to interact with objects drawn in the Canvas

Detecting mouse events in circles in the Canvas

Pop quiz

Q1	2
Q2	2

Clearing the Canvas

Pop quiz

Q1	1
Q2	4

Chapter 5, Building a Canvas Game's Masterclass

Drawing text in the Canvas

Pop quiz – drawing text in the Canvas

Q1	3
Q2	2

Drawing images in the Canvas

Pop quiz – styling a Canvas background

Q1	2

Chapter 6, Adding Sound Effects to Your Games

Adding a sound effect to the Play button

Pop quiz – using the audio tag

Q1	2
Q2	Place the fallback content inside the `<audio>` tag

Chapter 7, Saving the Game's Progress

Saving the entire game progress

Pop quiz – using local storage

Q1	false
Q2	true
Q3	true

Index

drawing lines
recreating, after receiving from clients 238
drawing lines data
packing, into JSON 237
dynamic box
creating, in physics world 259, 260

E

EaselJS
URL 3
Ejecta
URL 8
elapsed played time
game over dialog, creating with 185-188
elapsed time
calculating 188
embedded web font
using, inside Canvas 122
entire game progress
saving, in local storage 202-205

F

fallback content 85
features, CSS3
about 4
CSS3 animation 6
CSS3 transform 6
CSS3 transition 5
file format, WebAudio
AAC 153
Ogg 153
WAV 154
files
code, dividing into 90
fill function 87
fillText function, arguments
String 120
X 120
Y 120
flipping cards
code execution, delaying on 72
font
embedding, from Google Fonts directory 77-79
Fontdeck
URL 80

font delivery services
selecting 80
footer 18
force
adding, to car 266, 267
applying, to body 267
clearing 267
function
circle drawing code, inserting into 88-90
circle drawing, wrapping in 88
functions, Date object
getDate 195
getDay 195
getFullYear 195
getHours 195
getMilliseconds 195
getMinutes 195
getMonth 195
getSeconds 195
getTime 195
function type, data function
.data(key) 75
.data(key, value) 75

G

game
caching, for offline access 209, 210
putting, on Web 296
restarting 272-274
web fonts, embedding into 77
game environment
ramps, adding to 268, 269
game flow
controlling, of multiplayer draw-and-guess
game 246
game guide animation
creating 131-136
game logic
adding, to matching game 68-72
game loop 101
game objects
moving, with CSS3 transition 48
game over dialog
creating 185
creating, with elapsed played time 185-188

J

JavaScript
about 1
array, cloning in 205, 206
array, randomizing in 72, 73
basic class definition, defining in 93
current date and time, obtaining in 195
random numbers, generating in 91
JavaScript code
best practice 19
JavaScript Interval
ball, moving with 34-37
DOM object, moving with 33
JavaScript library 16
JavaScript Object Notation. *See* **JSON**
JavaScript timer
creating, with setInterval function 37
joint 263
jQuery
about 16
custom data attribute, accessing with 75, 76
DOM elements, cloning with 66
first child of element, selecting with
child filters 66
Ping Pong game elements, manipulating
with 27
running, inside scope 20
URL 17
using 25
jQuery CSS function 27
jQuery file
selecting 19
jQuery library
installing 16-18
JSON
about 195, 196
drawing lines data, packing into 237
JSON string
stored object, loading into 196

K

keyboard-driven mini piano musical game
creating 169, 170
element, removing in array 172, 173
music dot hits, determining on key down 172

three music lines, hitting by key down 171
keyboard input
used, for adding force to car 266, 267

L

layers 156
left paddle
auto moving 42
left paddle movement
controlling 41
level property
circles 118
relationships 118
level support
adding, to car game 274-277
license, fonts
reference link 79
line drawing API 96
line drawing functions
lineTo 96
lineWidth 96
moveTo 96
stroke 96
line intersection
about 105
detecting, in Canvas 103
determining 106, 107
lines
drawing, in Canvas 94
line segment 106
link list 271
local drawing sketchpad
building, with Canvas 230-232
local storage
about 183
entire game data, saving in 202-205
game progress, resuming from 207-209
inspecting, in console window 197
objects, saving in 192-194
record, removing from 205
size limitations 191
string value, storing 191
local storage object
treating, as associative array 192
local variable 29
long polling 229

S

scenes
  creating, in mini piano musical game 156
scope
  jQuery, running inside 20
selection 25
semantics 18
setInterval function
  JavaScript timer, creating with 37
setItem function
  arguments 190
shapes
  drawing, arc function used 86
shared drawing whiteboard
  creating, with Canvas 230
  creating, with WebSockets 230
  data object, defining for communication
    between client and server 237
slice function
  reference link 206
sort function
  reference link 73
sort function, argument
  compare_function 73
sound
  pausing 152
  playing 151
sound effect
  adding, to Play button 146-149
SoundJS
  URL 181
sound volume
  adjusting, of audio element 152
splice function
  arguments 173
  reference link 173
sprite animation
  about 135, 136
  URL, for tutorial 136
Spritely
  URL 136
sprite sheet
  animating, in Canvas 131
  downloading, of playing cards 59
static ground body
  creating, in physics world 254

stored object
  loading, from JSON string 196
straight lines
  drawing, between circle 94, 95
string
  object, encoding into 195
stroke function 87
style
  path, beginning for 87
  tweening, CSS3 transition used 52
styling guide, W3C
  references 96

T

tablets
  touch support, adding for 108, 109, 290-293
text
  displaying, in HTML 42
  drawing, in Canvas 119
text-based scoreboard
  creating 43, 44
toggling a class style 56
touches
  handling 109
Touch Events 2
touchmove event 110
touch support
  adding, for tablets 108, 109, 290-293
transition property
  arguments 53
Twitch
  URL 8
Typekit
  URL 80

U

untangleGame object, variables
  boldLineThickness 117
  circleRadius 117
  circles 117
  currentLevel 117
  levelProgress 117
  levels 117
  lines 117
  targetCircle 117
  thinLineThickness 117

Untangle puzzle game
  about 82
  completeness progress, displaying 119
  creating, in Canvas 112-117
  current level, displaying 119
  embedded web font, using inside Canvas 122
  graphics, adding 124-126
  leveling data, defining 118
  level-up, determining 118
  progress level text, displaying inside canvas
      element 119-122
  reference link 112
  URL 82
userData property
  using, in body 281
  using, in shape 281

V

vertical center alignment 66

W

W3C, CSS Transforms Modules
  URL 52
Web
  game, putting on 296
WebAudio
  file format 153
web fonts
  about 77
  embedding, into game 77

WebGL 3
WebGL-2D
  URL 3
WebSocket
  about 3
  client events 220
  comparing, with polling approaches 228, 229
  drawing, sending through 233-236
  shared drawing whiteboard, creating with 230
WebSocket application
  connection count, displaying in 218, 219
WebSocket connection
  establishing 220
WebSocket server
  client, creating for connecting to 217
  connection event, listening on server side 217
  creation, for sending connection count 216
  initializing 217
  installing 214
  running 216, 217
Web View
  HTML5 game, building into mobile app 306
world time
  advancing 260, 261

X

X-Type
  about 10
  URL 10

HTML5 Game Development [Video]

ISBN: 978-1-84969-588-6   Duration: 01:58 hours

Build two HTML5 games in two hours with these fast-paced beginner-friendly videos

1. Create two simple yet elegant games in HTML5.

2. Build games that run on both desktops and mobile browsers.

3. Presented in a modular approach, with elegant code and illustrated concepts to help you learn quickly.

Learn HTML5 by Creating Fun Games

ISBN: 978-1-84969-602-9   Paperback: 374 pages

Learn one of the most popular markup languages by creating simple yet fun games

1. Learn the basics of this emerging technology and have fun doing it.

2. Unleash the new and exciting features and APIs of HTML5.

3. Create responsive games that can be played on a browser and on a mobile device.

Please check **www.PacktPub.com** for information on our titles

HTML5 Game Development with GameMaker

ISBN: 978-1-84969-410-0   Paperback: 364 pages

Experience a captivating journey that will take you from creating a full-on shoot 'em up to your first social web browser game

1. Build browser-based games and share them with the world.

2. Master the GameMaker Language with easy to follow examples.

3. Every game comes with original art and audio, including additional assets to build upon each lesson.

HTML5 Game Development with ImpactJS

ISBN: 978-1-84969-456-8   Paperback: 304 pages

A step-by-step guide to developing your own 2D games

1. A practical hands-on approach to teach you how to build your own game from scratch.

2. Learn to incorporate game physics.

3. How to monetize and deploy to the web and mobile platforms.

Please check **www.PacktPub.com** for information on our titles